Organization for Manufacturing

Organizatio

Ivan R. Vernon, Editor

Published by
Society of
Manufacturing Engineers
Dearborn, Michigan
1970

sme

r Manufacturing *With an Afterword by Dr. George Strauss*

Authors

In organizing, developing, and writing this book, the co-authors listed below have generously donated their time, effort, and professional skills in order to contribute to the advancement of manufacturing management.

Donald L. Bowman, Deputy Director
Pre-Retirement Planning Center
Drake University

Dr. Victor C. Doherty III, Chairman
Management Department
School of Business Administration
Wayne State University

Richard I. Huston, Manager
Organization Planning Department
Ford Motor Company

Norman D. Lukens, Senior Associate
Cresap, McCormick and Paget, Inc.

John H. Pond, Manager
Professional Management
   Development
Denver Division, Martin Marietta
   Corporation

Dr. Jack D. Rogers, Director
M.B.A. Programs
School of Business Administration
University of California (Berkeley)

Lee M. Rohde, Manager
Management Practice
IBM Corporation

Don M. Whitesell
Organization Planning Department
Ford Motor Company

Emory W. Zimmers
Manufacturing R&D
Abex Corporation

Manufacturing Management Series

658.402
068

Organization for Manufacturing

Library of Congress Catalog Card Number: 79-110568
International Standard Book Number: 0-87263-018-8

Manufactured in the United States of America

preface

A COMPANY IS MORE THAN BUILDINGS, equipment, and people. A manufacturing firm cannot be created by renting floor space, installing machinery, and hiring personnel. The enterprise has little chance of success unless a suitable organization is established.

How can a company be organized for profitable operations? What are some organizational forms that have proved workable over the years? Is it good practice to change the structure to meet a shift in competitive conditions? What is the function of organizational documentation? What is involved in staffing the organization? In developing its personnel? What types of organizations are available to meet special problems in manufacturing? How will the manufacturing organization of the future differ from the organization of today?— These are a few of the questions considered in *Organization for Manufacturing*.

This book offers answers to the questions that manufacturing managers ask most about the organizing function of management. The authors are men with experience in manufacturing, whose backgrounds qualify them to speak with authority. Hopefully, their experience will challenge your thinking as you begin considering how your own organization can be made to operate more effectively.

A word should be said about how this book came into being. The outline was prepared by the Manufacturing Organization and Personnel Development Subdivision of SME's Manufacturing Management Division. After refining the outline, Subdivision members either accepted writing responsibilities or suggested authors whom they felt were well qualified in the various areas. The members of the Subdivision include the chairman, George P. Wood, Administrator of Minority Relations, Martin Marietta Corporation; Donald L. Bowman, Deputy Director, Pre-Retirement Planning Center, Drake University; Thomas

H. Hazlett, Director, Engineering Extension, University of California (Berkeley Campus); Norman D. Lukens, Senior Associate, Cresap, McCormick & Paget (Chicago Office); John P. Makielski, Manager, Manpower Planning and Organization, Brake & Steering Division, Bendix Corporation; John H. Pond, Manager, Professional and Management Development, Denver Division, Martin Marietta Corporation; Ross G. Renninger, Factory Manager, TMW Division, North American Rockwell Corporation; and Lee M. Rohde, Manager of Management Practice, IBM Corporation. Special acknowledgment is also due George W. Woodsum, Manager of Personnel Development, IBM Corporation, chairman of the Manufacturing Organization and Personnel Development Subdivision when the early planning for this book began. Mr. Woodsum relinquished the Subdivision chairmanship to serve as chairman of the Manufacturing Management Division. The composition of the Divisions and Subdivisions of the Society's Technical Division structure does change from time to time, and this listing is intended only to acknowledge the contribution of the individuals who were concerned with the planning for this book.

THE AUTHORS

The authors, some of whom are members of the Subdivision, are listed on the title page. They are not identified with the individual chapters for which they were primarily responsible. The reason for this is that each author contributed more to this book than his specific chapter. The authors individually and collectively prepared chapter outlines and revised these outlines. After writing their own chapters, they then reviewed the manuscripts for all the other chapters, and provided comments to the writers. It is felt that through this participative process a more integrated text has been created, a book that is more than a collection of various viewpoints.

Nevertheless, it seems desirable to recognize the primary authors of each chapter. Professor Victor C. Doherty III, Chairman of Wayne State University's Management Department, provided the Introduction. Chapter 2, "Principles and Practice," was written by Donald L. Bowman, and Chapter 3, "Types of Organization," was prepared by Professor Jack Rogers. Richard Huston and Don Whitesell wrote Chapter 4, "Specialized Types of Organization," and Norman Lukens furnished Chapter 5, "Organizational Documentation." Chapter 6, "Organizational Staffing and Development," was written by John Pond; Chapter 7, "Communication," by Emory Zimmers; and Chapter 8, "Organizational Change," by Lee M. Rohde. The Afterword was written by Professor George Strauss, of the University of California. Dr. Strauss was provided with only the most tenuous of outlines, and he was invited to think freely, as he has done, about the shape of things to come.

As stated on the title page, each of these authors participated in the preparation of this book without compensation. The Society of Manufacturing Engineers expresses its sincere appreciation to these authors for their contributions to the advancement of manufacturing management.

ADDENDUM FOR INSTRUCTORS

Organization for Manufacturing is intended to be used as a textbook for courses emphasizing the organizational aspects of manufacturing. This book does not take a highly theoretical approach, nor is that its intent. The purpose rather is to consolidate the best of current practice and to inform the student and the working manager of those aspects of organizational theory that are currently relevant. This book is primarily designed for management courses taking an applied approach. If the course is designed to provide aspects of both practice and theory, then this book may still be used by assigning additional readings in the theory of organizations. *Modern Aspects of Manufacturing Management: Selected Readings,* published by SME, contains a number of articles that will be useful in this context. James D. Thompson's book, *Organizations in Action,* is also a good starting point, and the text by Daniel Katz and Robert L. Kahn, *The Social Psychology of Organizations,* likewise contains much of value. Beyond this, readings could be selected from the works of other authors such as Herbert A. Simon, Rensis Likert, Douglas McGregor, and Peter F. Drucker.

June 8, 1970   IVAN R. VERNON
Dearborn, Michigan

contents

Organization for Manufacturing

chapter 1

introduction *

MANUFACTURING MANAGEMENT is considered by a number of business writers to be one of the most significant emerging areas on the American industrial scene. One authority, Peter F. Drucker, described the current challenge to operating management in the following terms:

> . . . managerial, professional, and technical people, . . . they are the real core of the problem and the real opportunity, capital investment in machinery—in physical goods—is not going to mean much. Their work is not physical; it is work of the mind. The only way to increase their productivity is to increase the output and effectiveness of the mind. This can be accomplished only if we succeed both in making each of these men more productive in his own right and then in making his contribution more effective throughout the entire company. . . . Let me say again that I am not talking about the management of highly educated people in special programs such as research. I am talking about highly educated people in the ordinary, everyday, line organization.[1]

A number of statements have been made recently regarding the need to reassess the contributions of line management, to study the sources of the evolving administrative challenge, and to evaluate its effect on the competitive industrial environment. These statements originate not merely from the dreams of academicians or the hopes of advanced business leaders, but from the observations of practicing managers who realize that the primary substance of business is the organization.

The purpose of this chapter is to introduce the reader to the nature, character, and significance of the formal organization in a manufactur-

---

[1] Peter F. Drucker, from Dan H. Fenn, ed., *Management's Mission in a New Society* (New York: McGraw-Hill, 1956).

ing environment. The chapter will explain and review the forms of organization, the definition of organization, the purpose of organization, the evolution of organization, and the implications of organization theories on the study of organization for manufacturing.

FORMS OF ORGANIZATION

Ownership of property or having the rights and privileges of ownership is characteristic of those responsible for the use of property within our society. Pinpointing business ownership responsibility provides the answers to a number of important legal questions such as:

1) *Responsibility for profit and loss.* A manufacturing company has assets such as plant, equipment, working capital, and inventories. Who is entitled to the profits generated by the organization's assets? Who is responsible for losses, and for losses which exceed the company's assets?
2) *Responsibility for contracts.* Business expects individuals and other businesses to contribute to the objectives of the enterprise. Who is financially liable to ensure that contracts, both oral and written, with suppliers, employees, and representatives are fulfilled?
3) *Responsibility for the product.* Manufacturing organizations produce products. Who is responsible for the stated and implied warrantees and guarantees on the company's products? Who ensures that the product meets legal norms and standards?
4) *Responsibility for legal codes and laws.* Business firms exist in a complex society. Who is responsible to ensure that business codes are met, taxes are paid, and regulations such as those concerning air pollution and zoning are complied with? Who is responsible in cases of patent, trademark, and copyright infringement?

In our society the answers to these questions and to a great number of other legal questions is the "organization," the business enterprise. It is the organization that is primarily responsible and hence legally liable for the use of the company's property and other assets.

The administrators, managers, and employees of the organization are not normally held to be liable personally for the actions they take and the decisions they make as members of the organization. The employee acts as a representative or agent for the organization and is legally responsible to use his talents wisely and within the scope of his authority. It is the responsibility of the organization to see that the sum of the actions taken by its representatives or agents conform with the law and constitute responsible business practices.

It is important that those of us who act as agents—administrators, managers, supervisors, workers—understand the significance of the various forms that organizations can take in our society, so that we can better comprehend our basic working environment.

In the United States we have two basic forms of business ownership—personal and corporate. The personal owner, who is called a proprietor, is personally responsible for the affairs of his business. He assigns authority to his representatives and subordinates; he is personally responsible for business losses, contracts, warrantees, and guarantees. It is the owner who is subject to taxes and to regulations as an individual for the affairs of his firm. The organization of business under conditions of proprietorship is really an extension of the owner. Claims against the business are claims against the owner, and profits of the business are profits of the owner.

A more complex form of personal ownership is the partnership. A partnership is made up of two or more individuals, and as a legal form of business organization, has all of the characteristics of a proprietorship except in this instance there are two or more people personally liable for the activities of the business.

The other basic organization form of business ownership is the corporation. An individual or a group who may wish to start a business can petition the state to create a corporation that will both own and operate the business. The corporation is an artificial "person" who owns the business property and is responsible for its use. The investors of capital in a corporation receive in return for their investment stock or shares of the corporation. The stockholders elect a board of directors to represent their interest, select the operating officer or officers of the corporation, and ensure that the corporation and its operating personnel act in a wise and legal manner.

The day-to-day decisions and activities of the corporation rests in the hands of its employees. The stockholders and directors are not personally liable for financial losses beyond that of their original investment.[2] The officers and members of the corporation, acting as representatives, are not personally liable for their corporate actions and decisions so long as they performed within the scope of their assigned authority and in a wise manner. It is the corporate "person" that is legally liable, for it is the owner of the property and has the sole right to its use. Profits earned by the corporation are corporate profits. Employees are entitled to wages and stockholders to dividends which are paid from surplus accumulations in the corporation's net worth.

A more complex form of corporate ownership is the conglomerate. A

---

[2] Stockholders in financial institutions may be liable beyond their actual investment.

conglomerate exists when a corporation owns the stock of one or more additional corporations. The conglomerate as a stockholder has the same limited responsibility and rights as do other stockholders in our society, and therefore has all of the characteristics of the corporation.[3]

The organization form of business ownership is primarily concerned with outlining the relationship between business and society. The internal organization of a business is based on concepts that take note of the legal form but are more operational in character.

DEFINITION OF ORGANIZATION

The business organization is the structure by means of which business activities are accomplished. These activities are designed to carry out business objectives in an efficient manner while operating in a relatively uncertain competitive, social, political, and economic environment.

One of the major responsibilities of business managers is to select, organize, and assign the human and physical resources that are available to the company. The visible evidence that organizing activity has been performed can be observed in published organization charts and manuals and in stated policies, procedures, and rules.

The organization is designed to obtain maximum efficiency in its production systems. In order to accomplish this objective the organization assigns job and department descriptions to pinpoint authority and to limit the scope of activities of its members. Also it assigns its limited resources to each unit to ensure the effective utilization of the company's assets. These efforts to stabilize the production system and to lend a degree of certainty to them create for each unit a quasi-independent domain, which surrounds itself with occupational or work-related beliefs, language, and rituals. Each unit tends to guard its precinct of authority, resources, and contribution to the company. This tendency toward unit identity reinforces the assignment of authority and resources and helps focus the organizational units on the objectives of effective and efficient operations.

The organization is also designed to operate in and respond to the uncertain competitive, social, political, and economic environment. In order to satisfy this objective various specialist positions are designated within the organization. These specialists, in addition to their other duties, are responsible for monitoring the environment and interpreting and evaluating the pressures and opportunities that they perceive. To monitor and appraise the resources available both within and outside the company, many organizations assign boundary-spanning activities

---

[3] But the conglomerate may not be a "trust"—that is, a company holding controlling interest in a number of companies in the same type of business.

to finance, purchasing, and personnel. In order to expand as well as interpret both the company's markets for its product and its social/political environment, many organizations develop public relations and market research departments.

Of course the production systems in the internal organization must maintain their competitive position and potential within their industry, and some organizations provide assistance to their domain-conscious managers by creating departments specializing in organization, engineering, research and development, and personnel development. These and other specialized boundary-spanning activities provide both service and direction to output-centered departments with their authoritative relationships usually prescribed and reinforced by central administrative offices.

At the beginning of this section organization was defined as the realized structure by which business activities are accomplished. Naturally, the organization chart, manuals, policies, and rules are not in themselves the business organization. These administrative instruments are merely the plan of activities. The activities themselves are performed by humans who are influenced in their interpretation and use of the organization plan by occupational norms, apparent competency of others, power, pride, interdepartmental competition, status, budgets, and a host of other human, professional, and situational factors. Organization is how work activities are structured, related, and carried out by managers who derive their formal authority and title from the organization plan.

There are three different types of activities covered by this concept of organization. First, there are those activities which are carried on to achieve effectiveness and efficiency and to ensure that this effectiveness and efficiency is maintained. Second, there are the activities designed to investigate, interpret, and evaluate the threats, pressures, and opportunities that exist in the environment surrounding the organization. Third, there are the activities which are intended to implement changes within the production systems based on environmental information such as technological advancements, changes in environment demand, improvements in management practice, and changes in the practices of government, labor, and suppliers. These activities form a conceptual base for relating the formal, planned organization to actual organizational practice. On this basis the manager can appreciate the organization as his practical working environment.

PURPOSE OF ORGANIZATION

The purpose of the organization is to program, direct, and assess the operational activities of its members. To program or reprogram operational activities, the organization planner must first investigate five basic sources of information:

1) *Supply.* What is the cost, quantity, and quality of resources available to the company? What advantages and disadvantages does the company have in its markets? What changes, if any, might occur in these markets in the relevant future?
2) *Demand.* What is the demand for the company's product? Who are our customers, and why do they buy from us? Who are not our customers, and why don't they buy from us? What changes, if any, might occur in consumer demand for our product?
3) *Competition.* What companies directly compete with us? What competitive advantage does each company have in the market? What other companies and industries could affect our competitive market? What changes, if any, might occur in competition in the near future?
4) *Regulation.* What regulations affect our company, industry, and markets? What changes, if any, might occur in regulations in the future?
5) *Operations.* What is our assessment of the current organizational design? What changes can be made to bring the organization design into harmony with the planned business objectives and strategy?

With the information derived from these sources the planner designs programs for operational activities. The planner's output or product usually takes the form of organization charts, manuals, policies, procedures, and rules.

The planned organization program is the framework within which the various operational activities are supposed to occur. The management of the day-to-day efforts of the organization takes place in situational settings with individuals who are influenced by departmental and personal, social, political, and economic considerations. The purpose of organization as a directive instrument is to contain and focus both work situations and personnel, so that they can make an effective and efficient contribution to the company's planned objectives.

Organization is a necessary basis for assessing personnel contributions. In establishing the organization's program and direction functions, certain criteria were designated as pertinent to the company's output preferences and the cause/effect relationships necessary to achieve them. These criteria form the basis for comparing organization programs with organization performance. A comparative analysis and evaluation based on these criteria provide those responsible for the administration of the organization a basis for action. Such action might consist of the redesign of programs, improvements in the management direction process, and for the reconsideration of the effectiveness of the organization's assessment and control function.

When organization is formally used to program, direct, and assess activities, the company exposes itself to some of the shortcomings of the formal organization. The organization assigns work through departmentation and job description, designates authority by office and title, establishes set rules and procedures, and creates a structural environment centered on the impersonal organization.

A major advantage of work specialization is that the company can employ occupational specialists in each of its task areas. The use of specialists provides unique skills to operations and also provides a communication link with activities and occupational advancements made by similar specialists in other organizations. A major disadvantage of specialization is resistance to changes that threaten occupation and work norms or which threaten the specialist role or zone of influence within the organization.

In delegating specific authority to each position within the organization, the company is able to pinpoint accountability for success and failure in the performance of assigned tasks. Authority allocation provides each employee with knowledge of the rights and privileges of his position, of what is expected of him, and of where and how he fits into the work process. A major drawback of formal authority is that some office or position holders tend to rely on their formal position rather than their ability to command the respect of others. In situations where the competency of an employee is less than what his position demands, the other people in that work setting tend to have lower morale because of their frustrations in dealing with him. They may also demonstrate a loss of respect for the formal organization by establishing an informal organization in order to by-pass him.

Organizations use rules and procedures to regulate the work process and to govern the relationships between interacting employees. These two tools of organization provide the direction necessary to get the work accomplished and provide the certainty necessary to establish criteria for efficiency. A major disadvantage of rules and procedures is that rather than being a means to an end they sometimes become ends in themselves. There are many cases of managers who have failed to mature in their roles, and as a consequence tend to substitute organization rules and procedures for managerial responsibility and discretion. They pride themselves on running "tight ships," but pose a problem in that their "ship" with its disciplined and correct crew never seems to be headed toward any worthwhile objectives.

The organization in establishing specializations, authority, procedures, and rules by position rather than by person has created an environment designed for efficiency. This focus on the depersonalized position promotes objective personnel practices, for personnel actions must be taken and defended on data directly related to the employee's work position. It decreases the likelihood of evaluations based on the arbitrary whim of a supervisor or on personality grounds. Position emphasis also influences how people relate in the organization by requiring each person to represent his specialization and authority in actions with others. A major shortcoming of an impersonal environment is that the man is treated organizationally as a machine. The employee's basic social and ego needs are frequently frustrated by the analytical and impersonal environment surrounding him. He sees his role in the company as that of a robot or a punched card, and tends either to join social groups that are negative in their work attitudes or to mentally retreat from work involvement and settle for "putting his time in."

Organization is the structure of reality; it cannot be avoided. The directing, programing, and assessing purposes and functions of organization are formally designated by those who are responsible for business organization. The formal work system provides both advantages and disadvantages to the business firm, and consequently must be reviewed and evaluated frequently not only to see how effective it is in achieving its goals, but also to determine its capacity to meet the realities of today and tomorrow.

EVOLUTION OF ORGANIZATION AND ORGANIZATION THEORY

The preceding thoughts and concepts are the essential definitions and descriptions necessary for an understanding of the organizational reality as it applies to manufacturing management. The organization issues and problems facing today's manager cannot be solved by definitions or descriptions, but must be met and solved by creative men who direct manufacturing operations. Many if not most of the major issues confronting manufacturing are concerns of several divisions and departments within the company, various companies within the industry, and of industry in general. The solutions to problems resulting from major business issues calls for the integration of many specialists both within and outside of manufacturing operations.

Concern over employee attitude and performance changes, the community's physical environment, product safety and performance standards, and numerous other issues have changed the objectives of many manufacturing managers. It is no longer sufficient for them to ensure least-cost, orderly, and efficient manufacturing processes. While these objectives are necessary for business operation they are not sufficient to meet the current needs of the business socio/political/economic environment. If the manufacturing manager is to retain his proper influence within the business, he must be prepared to work with and make adjustments for organization-centered problems with the same degree of interest and professional development that he has so often demonstrated in meeting the technical demands caused by proper competition and technological advancements.

At the beginning of this chapter Peter F. Drucker's challenge to operating management was cited. This challenge is for an increase in the productivity of line managers through an increase in their mental creativity. This challenge to manufacturing managers in no way denies their outstanding increases in personal productivity over the preceding seventy years. Rather, it calls attention to the fact that the advancements which have made the United States the world's leading manufacturer have been a part of an evolutionary process that is still continuing. The development and refinement of production skills, leadership methodology, and organization are not only manufacturing landmarks but also responses to business' integration of new elements or the reevaluation of existing elements in its structure. Integration has been the principal form of advancement. Integration requires a keen sense of organization, for it is through organization that integration is accomplished in modern society.

If the manager of today is to comprehend the current organization, the use and purpose of organization theories, and the current pressures to reevaluate production and product values, abilities, and capabilities, it is necessary for him to understand the concept of progress through integration. He must realize that this concept is the basic process in the evolutionary development, expansion, and survival of American manufacturing enterprises. Manufacturing specialists of today should focus not so much on their technical abilities in production, but on their personal productivity in assisting both the business organization and the production unit in interpreting, resolving, and adjusting to meet changes. It is these changes in the competitive environment that reflect the current movement in business integration and progress. In order to provide the modern manager with a better understanding of the environment for his company, we will briefly review the evolutionary development of the manufacturing organization.

Capitalization Era—Nineteenth Century

In the nineteenth century the United States was by today's standards an underdeveloped country with well over one-half of its population directly employed in agriculture. Industrial firms tended to be family-owned and family-operated proprietorships and partnerships localized to serve the needs of a city or town. The major industrialists of this era concentrated most of their energies in the field of finance and transportation.

This emphasis on transportation and finance reflected the major integration challenge to business of that day. The geographical growth and development of the country had encouraged many Americans to leave the population centers of the East and relocate over a vast area with new, small widely separated urban centers. In order for the nation to integrate its dispersed resources and markets, new transportation and communication networks had to be established. These networks required large capital investments, and once developed required additional sums of money to support the expansion of trade between population centers. The results of these activities were the building of railroads, the development and growth of banks, the development of stock exchanges for corporate securities and shares, and the birth of business legislation aimed at bringing order to interstate commerce and industry development.

The impact of the development of transportation and finance systems on the small localized firm was significant. The availability of transportation and financing offered the more alert manufacturer the opportunity to integrate these resources into his firm. With these resources he could expand his manufacturing capacity and compete in markets beyond his immediate locality. The manufacturer who was slow to integrate found that he could not refuse to change and still survive, for his local market, where he had enjoyed monopoly power, was now being invaded by growing, expansion-minded manufacturers from other urban centers.

As this integration movement continued to grow in the later part of the nineteenth century, an organization theory centered in business economics and finance was developed for those people who dealt with or were a part of this more complex business environment. The major problems of integration were the acquisition and use of capital and the development of supplies of raw materials and markets for the finished goods. The owner-manufacturer, who most often was the only manager in the business, concentrated his energies on these major problems. He relied on skilled workers, who usually supplied their own tools, to organize and direct the production activities of the firm. The owner retained basic control over production by using business economics and finance concepts to establish raw material and labor cost norms for his company. The organization chart of a typical company of this day changed, as indicated in Fig. 1-1, to accommodate the integration requirements for this stage in the evolutionary process.

Of the several organizational changes shown perhaps the employment of an accountant at a managerial level was the most significant, for this is the first time that a professional manager was employed in manufacturing companies on a fairly broad scale. The significant role played by today's finance directors, controllers, and budget directors

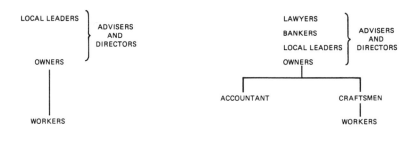

Fig. 1-1. Organization chart for a nineteenth-century company.

was first seen at this early stage in the evolution of the modern manufacturing organization. Another change which was important in terms of its impact on organization was the authority and responsibility given to hired craftsmen over the training and direction of new workers. Using workers to lead other workers rather than employing supervisors for this purpose led to the distinction which exists today between "white" and "blue" collar workers. The last of the major adjustments was the introduction and employment of professional advisers and directors, whose offices were outside of the company. In this more complex form, the local leaders had less voice in communicating to the company its social responsibilities. This was the first major step in the process of electing boards of directors that today are composed almost entirely of high-level professional people whose occupations are linked with business.

Production Era—Early Twentieth Century

By the turn of the century many manufacturing companies had expanded their businesses to such an extent that they were encountering serious market competition from other manufacturers and were taking steps to meet this new challenge. Market competition normally meant price competition and therefore owners and managers started to focus their attention on production costs.

Manufacturers soon found that in order to maintain control over costs some rational organization, that is, the rational control of the organization's efforts, was necessary. Owners and managers who recognized this need began employing highly educated professionals, primarily engineers, who had experience in such industries as mining and transportation, and had been attracted to manufacturing by its recent success and growth. These technical-professionals began introducing their knowledge and experience to manufacturing, and because of the technical character of their approach to management, their contribution became known as scientific management.

One of the initial phases of the scientific management movement was the introduction of organization concepts related to management-owner control over production and the production facility. These concepts had been developed and refined by military institutions and the Catholic church over many centuries, and were in common use in transportation and mining companies. One of the effects of integrating these concepts into manufacturing organizations was the vertical integration of the production function with that of management. Another effect was the establishment of the formal organization with its specified work, hierarchy of authority, rules and procedures, and its impersonal criteria for behavior. Companies that successfully integrated these concepts found that they had a distinct market advantage because of their ability to focus the efforts of the managers and workers on common objectives. Hence they could not only control costs but lower them by introducing more scientific ways of performing work.

The integration of scientific management into manufacturing firms generated two business organization theories. The first was formal organization theory as discussed above, and the second was a theory of organization process and control. A need to explain process and control occurred when management took over control of the production operations. In so doing management became not only responsible for product and product design but also for production technology, particularly the design of work tasks, the selection of work tools, and the design and scheduling of work activities. The use of management specializations in these areas had the greatest impact on the manufacturing organization. The integration that took place during this period gave modern business its basic foundation and competitive strength. The organization chart of a typical company of the early twentieth century is shown in Fig. 1-2.

As in the other charts in this chapter, the organizational changes shown in Fig. 1-2 are vastly understated. This is done so that the impact of the changes on the organization of today can be more clearly seen. A major organizational adjustment of this era was the creation of line activities with supporting staff services. In our chart production is supported by engineering staff offices. The effect of this change on the organization extends beyond the creation of line and staff organization. The staff offices of this period were the product of the scientific management movement. The original staff officers in manufacturing were the technical-professional men who influenced the organization of the company and were the principal designers and developers of production as a line organization. Even today staff people tend to

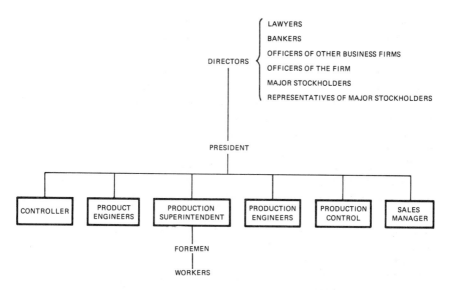

Fig. 1-2. Organization chart depicting an early twentieth-century company.

view themselves as of higher status than line men, and in general responsible for monitoring the performance of line activity.

This role of staff services in many firms has been reinforced by management expectations over the years, and is a source of frustration for the line managers who are ultimately responsible for the activities of their departments. A second effect of the existence of staff is that line managers find it difficult to justify their involvement in issues and problems that are not directly related to their department's immediate needs, for they feel that the larger organizational issues are within the purview of staff offices. The effect of this is that the organization is able to use only a part of its management capability to meet and resolve its needs in the present integration movement.

The Human Relations Era—Between the Wars

The growth and development of manufacturing technologies provided a sound base for competition within industries. Each company in attempting to obtain a differential cost, quantity, quality, or product advantage over its competition contributed to a general rise in the nation's technological capacity. Specialization of work tasks, assembly techniques, and mechanization were the leading competitive factors in the integration process. By the early 1920s the major technical breakthrough had occurred and business was finding it more difficult to obtain or retain a marked advantage over its competitors, and price competition was once again affecting the profits and progress of the technically advanced corporations. In the late 1920s Western Electric sponsored studies to determine if control of the physical environment was related to the productivity of its workers. The research was not successful in demonstrating that environmental control would yield higher productivity but did yield the unintended finding that treating the worker as a social being could lead to gains in productivity. The effect of these new findings was the beginning of the human relations movement in industry.

The new integration challenge to manufacturing was the absorption of man into the organization. Industry developed personnel programs and policy at the corporate level and management direction and development programs at the work level so as to better utilize its human resources. The social unrest of the 1930s quickly turned many of these programs from what many reporters of that period called "human engineering" to programs of defense and survival as trade unions and government made inroads into the work environment.

The attempt to integrate man into the formal organization led researchers into studying the work environment as a social setting. Organization theory had to expand to account for the unprogramed behavior of organization members and to help explain the success and failures of the organization in dealing with its members. From these studies organization scholars and leaders began to recognize that the real organization consisted of the formal structure and an informal structure that had great influence on actual operating practices. Management encouraged the development of human relations so that they might better work with the real organizational setting and gain the respect of the informal organization. The organization chart of our typical firm can be seen in Fig. 1-3.

The only major change in our typical organization is the addition of an industrial relations director. This change in the organization was the result of the union movement in the 1930s converting the emerging personnel functions from one of open inquiry and influence to one of representation of the official corporate position. This new department was responsible for dealings with the union, for the policing of corporate personnel policy and procedures, and for assisting managers in carrying out their employment functions. The effects of this enforced generation of an executive function is clearly evident in many firms where the industrial relations and personnel department is of very low status. Because of this low status it is unable to make substantive headway in assisting operating management in meeting the changes in employee attitude and work habits that are occurring within many sectors of the labor market and labor force.

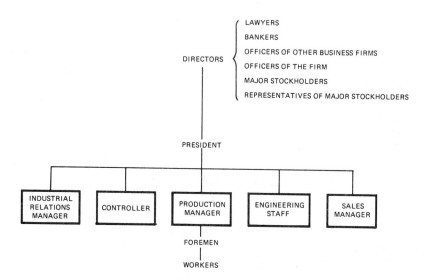

Fig. 1-3. Organization chart for a company of the 1930–40 period.

Administrative Era—World War II to Sputnik

The advent of World War II revitalized American industry, and the war's demands encouraged, indeed forced, manufacturers to advance production technology and to enlarge production capacity. After the war and particularly in the early 1950s the great buildup of our production capability in the first quarter of the century plus its rapid expansion during the war became somewhat of a burden on our competitive system. In addition manufacturing management had learned how to transfer the successful production experience of one company to another, and consequently a manufacturer found it extremely difficult to obtain and maintain competitive improvements in costs and productivity. Companies with management alert to what was taking place shifted corporate interest away from production and began to focus on their ability to attract and maintain markets for their products. The success of market orientation led administrators into investigating other tasks within the firm in search of new profit centers for corporate growth.

The challenge during this period was one of introducing administrative balance at the executive level in manufacturing companies. The ability to demonstrate growth both as a firm and as an industry as measured by increases in the gross national product now required competitive capability in a broad spectrum of business activities. The process of forming a competitive administrative balance required the introduction of nonproduction based skills at the executive level. These skills were equal in power and influence to those of engineering and production which had traditionally dominated industry. In order for the executive team to implement this new approach to competition it was necessary in many companies to make major organizational changes so as to integrate the operating organization with the executive leadership.

The scope and impact of this integration movement led both management leaders and business scholars to accelerate their study of management science, administrative science, and organization theory. These studies and theories were used to explain and to assist in the analysis of the increasingly complex industrial organizations. They called for integration of all the social sciences with those traditionally present from business, economics, and engineering to form a foundation for a new theory of administration. The impact of these changes in the integration process is evident in the lowering of the median age of executives in large firms as these firms expand their specializations at the executive level and as they require greater administrative sophistication of their corporate leaders. The organization chart of our current typical firm can be seen in Fig. 1-4.

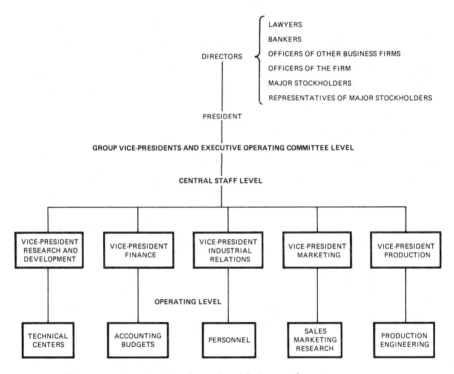

Fig. 1-4. Organization chart of a mid-nineteenth-century company.

The major organizational adjustment during this period was the centralization of administrative practices and the decentralization of operating activities. The day-to-day impact of this change is a movement away from a uniform corporate strategy to a number of project-centered strategies as the corporation interacts with its competitive environment. Members of the operating organization can observe these integration adjustments by increasing their awareness of changes in the formal organization, of changes in the status, prestige, and power of occupation specialties, of changes in their feeling of identity and contribution to the business, and of changes in the basic economics of the business. They can see where members of one project group are enjoying economic and administrative health while members of another group may be under strong pressures and fighting for survival.

Systems, Science, and Society—1957 to the Present

The success of the USSR's space program was interpreted by many Americans as a direct threat to the U.S. role in world leadership. The American response was political, social, and economic support for the rapid acceleration of space research and development activities under the coordination of the National Aeronautics and Space Administration. This agency demonstrated that systems management was a flexible and productive organization type that could unite a broad range of specialized interests into a common product objective with both the product and the objective subject to revision and change.

The space agency further demonstrated that science could be directly incorporated into production programs, and that applied science could through its research and development activities generate both its own conceptual base and new levels of product sophistication. Much of the work of NASA was subcontracted to private industry. The companies involved in these programs found that in addition to contributing to the space program they could apply the management systems, the direct use of science, and the product technologies they were learning to the private sector of the economy. Companies and industries that have learned to integrate management systems and science into their organization typology and into their product offerings have begun to replace high-production, cost-centered industries such as automotive and metals as leaders of advancements in the gross national product.

Evidence of this new integration process in manufacturing can be observed in the changes in education curriculum. Schools of business administration, who are the principal suppliers of management talent, have changed their programs from an information, case experience base to one oriented toward abstract and analytical concepts related to administrative and management sciences. Engineering curricula has changed from applied, technical objectives to theory and research objectives. Industry's need for universities extends beyond curriculum requirements and adjustments necessary to produce graduates who can cope with the current integration demands. Many companies have discovered that their product-centered technology centers are not geared to meet the competitive demands of the day and have turned to university scientists to conduct the research necessary for continued progress in their industry. Contract research within universities and the growth of research parks around universities indicate the rapid development of the integration movement in this area.

The constant growth of manufacturing through integration over these past seventy years has evolved around the development and refinement of products and production. The total impact of these activities on society has not been a central issue in industry, but by the late 1960s a fairly broad and representative sampling from society was seriously considering the social implications of manufacturing facilities and products. As manufacturing enters the 1970s it is faced with an additional dimension to the current integration movement, which is to use its new abilities of integrating science and systems to greatly lower the cost to society of manufacturing by-products, particularly pollution.

The evolution of manufacturing in the United States has been a series of integration movements each of which has increased both the complexity and the contribution of manufacturing organizations. The evolutionary stages have been:

1) Integration of natural and financial resources. This movement established the role and contribution of owners and executive officers in manufacturing.
2) Integration of organization concepts and engineering technology. During this period industry learned to absorb the technician into its competitive practices and development.
3) Integration of the human component into the organization. Here industry set the bases for obtaining improved productivity from its working members.
4) Integration of cosmopolitan specialists who could provide industry with a corporate, organizational, and administrative product that was greater than simply production.
5) Integration of the firm into the society. This movement directly integrates society's assets of science and technology and society's demands that industry must compute the environmental costs of its activities and products, formerly absorbed by society, into its

production costs. Effective integration calls for viewing manufacturing in a systems context rather than seeing it as a cloistered authority-oriented institution with environmental squatters rights.

The evolution of manufacturing demonstrates that the study of organization must be viewed in realistic terms for it is from operating reality that the forms, definitions, purposes, and challenges of manufacturing organizations are derived. The study of organization is and must be the study of reality, for it is in the real world that organization concepts are developed, tested, evaluated and, if necessary, discarded.

chapter 2

principles and practice

ACCORDING TO AN UNKNOWN AUTHOR "Theory without method is empty;/ Method without theory is blind;/Taken together they make a most formidable weapon." This is indeed true in the management of manufacturing enterprises. Sets of abstract principles do not provide all that is needed to build and maintain an effective organization. Likewise the manufacturing organization constructed without due regard for theoretical principles is likely to be ineffective. Ideally management should be guided by principles, but pragmatic concerns—the needs of the moment—must also be given consideration. This chapter is concerned with the principles of organization and the translation of those principles into practice.

An organization may be thought of as a system for directing the endeavors of two or more people working together toward a common objective. Accepting this definition, we recognize many kinds of organizations which vary significantly with respect to size, purpose, and complexity. Families, churches, businesses of more than one person, political parties, municipalities, fraternities—all of these are organizations, and each has developed to satisfy the need for system and order in some cooperative activity.

This chapter, however, is concerned with the development of organization as a means of improving man's ability to work together. The achievement in productive capacity of our society has depended to a large degree upon the development of effective organization in our large manufacturing firms, and we can expect continued improvement in production efficiency to accompany continued improvement in organization.

Too frequently organizations are thought of in purely structural terms. The establishment of an effective structure, however, is only the first step in providing for the organizational needs of a manufacturing company. Industry is dynamic; new methods of manufacture and improved concepts of administration require an organization that can be readily adjusted to meet changed situations. The organizational structure, even if perfectly suited to the needs of a particular enterprise, is only skeletal. Even the best organizational structure is worthless until it is implemented or put into effect; the structure must be made operational at the lowest levels of the organization where the products of the company are being made.

A well-planned organization is necessary for proper policy implementation. Lower levels of management are normally provided with the task of carrying out policies developed at higher levels. The difference in detail which exists in every situation requires policies to be developed in the form of generalities which can be adjusted to meet different challenges. Company policy is announced in broad terms because policy generally refers to the establishment of an objective or the administrative means of obtaining such an objective on a company-wide basis.

Organizational planning is essential in order to integrate line and staff functions. These functions should not be completely separate but should interlock. Because of these complexities, marginal areas tend to develop among components where authority and responsibility become overlapping, split, not understood, or not known.

1) *Overlapping*—Members of different components are assigned responsibilities which require them to work in the same area.
2) *Split*—A component cannot fulfill its responsibility to complete an assignment without specific performance by another.
3) *Not understood*—The extent of responsibility required of the component to bring an assignment to completion is not fully comprehended by all components involved.
4) *Not known*—Components are unaware of their own involvement in a specific situation.

Obviously such problems result in poor organization. An investigation into organizational thinking requires two assumptions:

1) That there is a mechanics of organization or, in other words, that there are structural characteristics of organization that can be considered separately from the dynamic characteristics that derive from the interactions of organizational personnel.[1]

---

[1] In regard to the structural aspects of organizations, see Daniel Katz and Robert L. Kahn, *The Social Psychology of Organizations* (New York: John Wiley & Sons, 1966), 71–109. According to these authors, traditional organization theory devoted primary attention to internal organizational structures to the neglect of the dynamic aspects of organization.

2) That there is a body of knowledge on the subject of organization, the constant elements of which may be called principles and which can be applied to some extent in all organizational situations. If we accept the existence of such principles, the problem becomes one of finding out what they are and learning how they may be best applied.

The term *principle* is used here in the same sense as defined by Henri Fayol:

. . . I shall adopt the term principles whilst dissociating it from any suggestion of rigidity for there is nothing rigid or absolute in management affairs; it is all a question of proportion. Seldom do we have to apply the same principle twice in identical conditions; allowance must be made for different changing circumstances, for men just as different and changing, and for many other variable elements. Therefore principles are flexible and capable of adaption to every need; it is a matter of knowing how to make use of them, which is a difficult art requiring intelligence, experience, decision and proportion.[2]

The purpose of organizing is to secure the maximum economies from the subdivision and specialization of effort while, at the same time, retaining unity of effort or coordination. A theory of organization can be established if we accept the condition that a distinction exists between the *mechanics* and the *dynamics* of organization. The basis of this distinction is the concept that there are some aspects of any organizational problem in which people, considered as individuals, can be ignored. These aspects relate to what we can call the mechanics of organization. Those aspects in which personnel must be considered as individuals constitute the dynamics.

Of course in practice the manager is continuously dealing with problems. But practice provides guidance only for problems that have arisen before. When faced with a new and different situation decisions must be made on a trial-and-error basis. Theory provides principles that hold true despite changed circumstances. These principles enable complications to be detected and eliminated and processes to be shortened and economized.

The literature on organization theory and management has become extensive, and each author submits his own "principles of organization." On the surface these principles appear different either in the method of explanation or statement of intent. Upon analysis of the

---

[2] Henri Fayol, *General and Industrial Management.* Translated from the French by Constance Storrs (London: Pittman, 1949), 19.

various lists, however, one finds striking similarities between the various sets of principles.[3] The reason for variances appears to be more semantical than real, and a good deal of ambiguity exists. It is worth remarking that in reading the literature in the field of management it is necessary to have a higher than usual degree of tolerance for the ambiguous.

Further analysis of the many sets of organizational principles suggests that they are all concerned with six major topics. These topics are:

1) Unity of objectives
2) Division of work
3) Delegation
4) Span of management
5) Unity of command
6) Organizational balance.

The text that follows takes up each of these topics in turn, presenting the formal principle relating to each and indicating the applicability of the principle to manufacturing organizations. Next the application of each principle to management practice is discussed. Of course a principle is not a rigid law to be applied in machine-like fashion to any existing organization; the dynamic aspects of organization must be kept in mind. Machine-like application of any principle can result in dysfunctional elements not originally anticipated.

UNITY OF OBJECTIVES

The organization and its parts should be a manifestation of the objectives of the company concerned, and organizational objectives should be established in keeping with societal and other restraints.

The word "objectives" refers to more than the goals of the organization. It also has reference to the personal goals of organizational members, which may be different from or may even be in basic conflict with company objectives. Additionally there is the implication that organizational objectives should be legitimate, that is, consistent with the objectives of the larger society within which the company operates.

---

[3] For these supposedly different principles of organization, see especially: Henry H. Albers, *Principles of Management: A Modern Approach* (New York: John Wiley & Sons, 1969); Chester I. Barnard, *Organization and Management* (Cambridge: Harvard University Press, 1952); Ernest Dale, *Planning and Developing the Company Organization Structure*, Research Report *Number 20* (New York: American Management Association, 1952); and Lyndall F. Urwick, *The Patterns of Management* (Minneapolis: University of Minnesota Press, 1956).

Objectives are not the specific qualitative or quantitative ends of an organization, such as a manufacturing company. A company's objectives should be stated in specific terms; they should be definitive, realistic, and attainable.

Societal Parameters

The fact that manufacturing companies exist as a part of the larger society imposes certain restrictions. The objectives of the organization must be consistent with the objectives of society. If these are disregarded then legal action can be taken to force the offender to conform. Legislation concerning labor relations, product safety, pricing and competition, and air and water pollution provide prime examples. Failure to obey established laws in these areas can bring punishment in the form of fines or even jail sentences for corporate officers.

Companies are wise to consider the effects their actions will have upon society even in the absence of specific laws. Irresponsible behavior—in wantonly polluting air and water, for example—can lead to the passage of unduly restrictive legislation.

Flexibility of Objectives

Organizational objectives cannot be established once and remain immutable; room must be left for change. It may become more profitable for a company to drop one product line and begin manufacturing different items; it may be advisable to cease manufacturing operations altogether and serve instead as a wholesale distributor for products manufactured by other companies. In the event of a significant change in the organizational environment, such as a change in federal or state laws, a breakthrough in technology, etc., review of objectives is called for, and modification may be necessary. This process of review and modification needs to be conducted on a continuing basis.

The Profit Objective

Profit may not be the only objective of a business organization, but it certainly is an essential objective if the organization is to survive. Koontz and O'Donnell have presented the case very well:

> A good argument can be made that in the United States all business enterprises have one and the same objective—to make a profit. This purpose is often obscured by platitudinous statements about service to the public and opportunity for employees. Not that these objectives are improper; certainly the profit-seeking enterprise will serve the public by producing useful and desirable goods and services at competitive prices. And a profitable, well-managed enterprise will provide good wages, security, and status for employees. But the common element in business enter-

prise, from the newsboy and peanut vendor to the largest bank or insurance company, is the pursuit of profit.

And yet, it seems inadequate to speak of profit as *the* motive of business, as though one merely said, "Business is business," when there have been so many cases of business owners with other incentives: power, social prestige, security, public acclaim, or any of the other strong motivations of human conduct. The business may be dominated by the desire to develop new things and try new ideas; . . . or to keep the business small, simple, and friendly—a sort of fraternal group; or to beat its nearest and largest competitor. . . . But in whatever terms objectives are stated, none is realizable without an actual profit.[4]

Perhaps it is accurate to say that profit is not so much an objective as it is the logical outcome of achieving such objectives as manufacturing a quality product, conducting an aggressive marketing program, and satisfying customers. By the same token, however, profit is a necessary prerequisite to the achievement of objectives such as organizational stability and market penetration. Profit then must be an ultimate goal for any business enterprise, but achievement of profitable operations requires the establishment and attainment of more specific, corollary objectives.

Personal Objectives

If the organization's overall objectives are to be met, they must be established with some consideration of the personal objectives of organizational members. If organizational objectives are in conflict with the objectives of the personnel responsible for achieving the aims of the organization, there will be many problems. What is needed is an integration of organizational objectives and personal objectives so that the two are mutually supportive.

Unity of objectives assures that organizational members will be working toward the achievement of socially acceptable company goals. Properly set objectives have the power to stimulate positive action. While the principle of unity of objectives has often been neglected, it offers a worthwhile challenge to management. The challenge is in identifying appropriate company objectives and relating these to the personal aspirations of the employees.

---

[4] Harold Koontz and Cyril O'Donnell, *Principles of Management,* 4th ed. (New York: McGraw-Hill, 1968), 111. Quoted by permission of the publisher.

DIVISION OF WORK

The activities of organizational members should be clearly defined and coordinated in order to contribute to the accomplishment of established objectives.

For an organization to function with a minimum of unnecessary duplication of effort, work assignments and other activities should be defined and arranged into a logical sequence. This is necessary if the organization's stated objectives are to be accomplished effectively.

This is the role of organizational documentation, as will be discussed in Chapter 8. At the moment we are concerned not with the whole of organizational documentation but with indicating the purpose and desirability of defining organizational roles through the tools of documentation such as position descriptions, policy statements, and organization charts. For purposes of this discussion we will refer only to the organization chart. Realize, however, that the organization chart is only one of several organizational documentation tools, and that taken alone it is insufficient to define and coordinate all the activities and functions of any given organization except the smallest.

Manufacturing organizations are composed of three major functions: finance, manufacturing, and sales. In a small company, one person may handle all three functions, but as company size increases it becomes necessary to divide the responsibilities among more people. Typically, the company evolves first to the state indicated by Stage I in Fig. 2-1.

The complexity of the company's activities then causes the evolution of numerous additional organizational units within each of the three functions. This growth for the manufacturing function is shown as Stage II in Fig. 2-1. The extent of growth of a function is dependent upon the nature of organizational work, the amount of this work, the degree of specialization practiced, and the personnel and workplaces available.

Continued organizational growth will require the addition of even more subunits for efficient organizational operations. Fig. 2-2, for example, indicates the evolution of a typical manufacturing function. Note that three subunits—manufacturing engineering, manufacturing, and manufacturing services—are utilized. This setup permits manufacturing engineering to perform the planning and controlling activities necessary in the manufacturing function. Materials management takes care of superintending the flow of materials into the plant and through the various production phases, and then, once the materials are in the final product state, on to the ultimate purchasers or customers. With the assistance provided by the manufacturing engineering and materi-

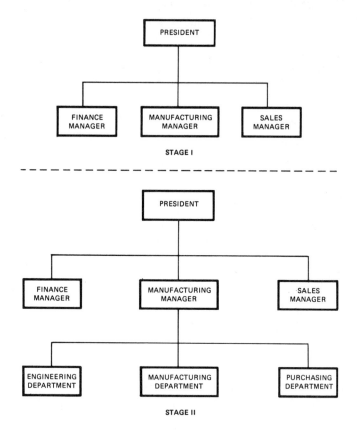

Fig. 2-1. Organization charts showing evolution and growth of a typical small manufacturing company.

als management groups, the manufacturing group concentrates on production, the task of fabricating the components and assembling the finished product.

The organizational structure described above illustrates the principle relating to division of work. Through such a division of organizational work, each individual task is accomplished more efficiently. Through this increased efficiency the achievement of overall organizational objectives is enhanced.

Looking again at the organization chart shown in Fig. 2-2, it can be seen that each new organizational subunit fits logically into the total organizational structure. The major task of manufacturing has been broken down into successively smaller task units. This process is known as departmentation. The consequence of organizational departmentation is the delineation and definition of executive responsibilities. This delineation and definition, when carried out correctly, contri-

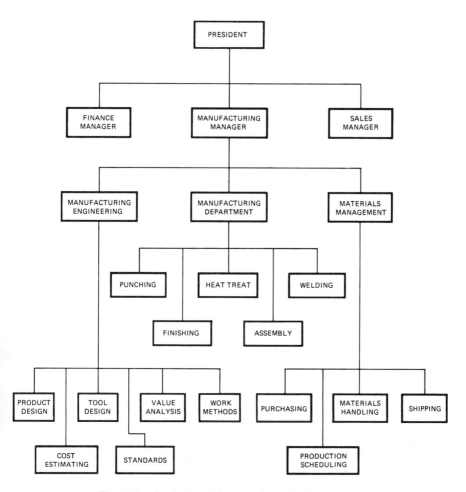

Fig. 2-2. Evolution of the manufacturing department.

butes to rather than detracts from the communication and coordination processes within the organization.

As previously stated, the activities necessary to achieve organizational objectives are a basic consideration in organizing, and the nature of these activities differs significantly depending upon the objectives. The process of departmentation is applicable to any organization, however, though a large organization will probably divide its work in many different ways. The functional method of departmentation, as illustrated in Figs. 2-1 and 2-2, is quite common. Many companies also find it advantageous to group manufacturing activities according to *product line.* A good example is the automobile industry. *Territorial* or *geographical* departmentation is used to some extent for manufacturing, especially when transportation costs are a major factor. Yet another method of work departmentation is according to the type of *process* or *equipment* being used. This method is most common for large job shops or in other manufacturing companies when more than one part of the product is fabricated using a given process or piece of equipment. These methods of departmentation or organization will be described in detail in the following chapter.

For now let us say that division of work is an important method by which the manager can build an effective organizational structure. Through the use of departmentation he can arrange manufacturing activities in such fashion as to arrive at a structure that is simple, logical, understandable, and efficient.

The management job is far from complete, however. The largest problems relate to organizational staffing, giving life to the structure. The manager must determine the *personnel* needed and clearly specify the requirements and qualifications necessary for each position. This topic is covered in Chapter 6 and is mentioned here only as a reminder that once departmentation is completed, the easy job is finished.

DELEGATION

In any organization there must be a clear line of delegation of authority from the ultimate source of authority to every individual in the organization.

Many managers encounter their first real problems in dealing with the concept of delegation. The greatest cause of difficulty in this area is the misunderstanding and misinterpretations of such terms as *delegation, authority, responsibility,* and *line-staff.* The reason for this misunderstanding and misinterpretation is at least partly the lack of consistent definitions. This is nothing really new for the field of management, which has always been plagued with inconsistent terminology.

When they think in organizational terms, many managers refer mentally to the organizational structure or framework. For many managers this organizational structure is depicted by the organization chart. Managers tend to have a negative attitude toward this chart. It places constraints on their behavior and their relationships with other people in the organization, and often specifies these constraints in ways that do not conform to the real organization.

Most organization charts confound three important dimensions of organizational structure, trying to describe all three with one set of lines and boxes. First, they say something about *authority structure* or relationships, usually by locating particular boxes at higher or lower positions on the chart. Second, they say something about the flow of *communications* by drawing lines between boxes. The lines connecting the boxes thus join organizational positions together in a hierarchial fashion, since some boxes are higher on the chart than others. The chart makes no provision for lateral communication networks, and it is assumed that one does not communicate with people with whom one has no authority relationship. Third, the charts say something, in a shorthand type of way, about the *roles* of persons in the organization. There are titles in the boxes that indicate the kinds of activities carried on by the occupants.

The following paragraphs discuss the concepts of authority, delegation, responsibility, line-staff, and the informal organization. This discussion seeks to define the concepts and suggest how they can contribute to organizational success.

Authority

Organizational structures are designed with authority in mind. We build organizations in the shape of pyramids because that shape makes the exercise of authority easier. Pyramids create differences in rank and status, and the people in the higher ranks supposedly can use their authority to influence lower ranks. Under the influence of the pyramid designation of authority, superiors almost naturally turn to authority whenever problems arise with subordinates. The very idea of delegating authority rests on the assumption that authority can help people who have more of it to change the behavior of those who have less of it. In fact, the superior is usually defined in a relationship as the person with more authority.

Like other tools, authority can be used expertly or clumsily. And like other tools, it must be used by men. Top managers have long since unhappily recognized that the delegation of considerable authority to middle and lower management is no guarantee of effective management. Indeed, some managers seem to supervise better with less authority than with more. And, conversely, some supervisors function better with more of it than less. The issue is not only how much authority but how it is used and by whom.

To clarify the concept of authority, perhaps it would be helpful to try to define the term. Sometimes when we talk of authority, we are thinking about a formal designation such as that denoted by rank. For example, authority can be defined as one's military rank. The captain may not know exactly how much authority he has or even what it is, but he knows he has more than the lieutenant and less than the major.

Authority also has something to do with power, sometimes formal power, again like military rank; power that can be formally changed or delegated. "They," the "top brass," or "somebody up there" can change one's rank and thereby one's authority and thereby one's power. Sometimes, we use the words authority and power differently. We speak of someone with an authoritative personality. Here we mean "influential" or "respect-evoking," but we do not mean "formally delegated." We mean something intangible the person carries around inside him, not the insignia he may wear on his shoulders.

Besides this confusion between formal and personal authority, another confusion results in the use of the word because authority may be viewed from the perspective of the manager who uses it as well as from the perspective of the subordinate upon whom it is used. When we identify with the user, authority appears to be a mechanism for coordination and control. When we take the perspective of the subordinate, however, authority seems more like a mechanism to punish or reward.

Authority might be defined as the power to command, or to cause others to take actions considered appropriate for the achievement of an objective. Implied in the definition is the responsibility for making decisions and seeing that they are carried out.

Compliance as a result of sufficiently applied power is also included in this concept. This compliance, however, can be gained in various ways—persuasion, sanctions, requests, coercion, constraint, and force. Today's trend seems toward greater use of persuasion and requests. Typically managers refrain from the use of coercion. They even avoid the use of the word authority because to many it simply means the ability to force compliance.

Delegation

Delegation of authority is essential to the existence of an organization. Without it the chief executive would be the only management member of the enterprise. There would be only one department, and there would be no organizational structure.

To delegate simply means to grant or confer authority in order to accomplish particular assignments. It does not mean to surrender authority. In delegating a manager always retains his overall authority for the assigned functions whether he wishes to or not. Delegation does not mean permanent release from these obligations but rather the granting of rights and approval for others to operate within prescribed areas.

George Terry suggests several steps to assist towards effective delegation:

1) *Make the potential delegator feel secure.* Typically the nondelegator is a hard worker, fully competent in his field but he feels insecure in

his job. This is partially the reason why he surrounds himself with mediocre people or in any event those who lack the courage to challenge him. He wants to continue as the superior and to be looked upon as a necessary man on the company team.

2) *Realize the need for delegation.* As long as a manager is limited to what he can accomplish himself, he will always be short of time and limited in his achievements. . . . A manager's need is to multiply himself. The only alternative is to acquire helpers, train them, and permit them to contribute in full measure.

3) *Establish a work climate free from fear and frustration.* This is essentially psychological and social in character. The executive must have a feeling of confidence that delegation of authority will reward, not penalize, him. It must represent an opportunity for growth, not the certainty of getting bawled out.

4) *Encourage a deep belief in delegation.* A manager must want to make delegation successful and strive to make it succeed. He must view delegation as the way to develop his subordinates, to liberate their energies purposively, and to build a real management team. He must realize that these goals are elusive and to win them takes time, effort, and persistence.

5) *Tie-in with intelligent planning.* Authority should not be delegated to the management team before goals are clear. To delegate without knowing and keeping in mind objectives leads to chaos. Authority is utilized to achieve goals, and the extensiveness of the authority should be in keeping with the type of activities performed in attaining the goals.

6) *Determine how the delegator keeps his hand in it.* Since the delegator retains his overall authority for delegated duties, he is always interested in keeping himself well enough informed to protect his own accountability and to be fairly certain of the outcome. Few managers want to be merely the depository of the result. The delegating method followed should provide the means for informing the delegator of the status of the assignment in time to take corrective steps, if needed.

7) *Determine decisions and tasks to be delegated.* A simple and direct means of solving this is for the delegator to list all the various types of decisions and tasks that must be performed and then rate each one in terms of (1) their relative importance to the total enterprise, and (2) the time required to perform. These data serve to determine what type of decisions and tasks should be delegated. In most cases, those that are relatively less important and most time consuming may be delegated.

8) *Choose the delegatee wisely.* This might well be the man with unused and the not so obvious abilities. . . . the assignment should be measured to the man. It should be challenging but not too tough to finish.

9) *Delegate authority for whole job.* It is advisable to give the delegatee a choice to participate in a complete undertaking. Broad rather than narrow projects best serve to whet the imagination and stimulate

ingenuity. Such assignments serve as an effective means of testing a man's ability to manage and of building his confidence. Too frequently the delegated work constitutes what the manager himself doesn't want to do. He uses delegation of authority to rid himself of unpleasant tasks, and often such delegation is performed without adequate thought.

10) *Give assistance to delegatee.* Delegation is not a matter of giving a subordinate an assignment and necessary authority and letting him on his own succeed or fail. The delegating manager does not assume the role of a helpless onlooker. Typically, the delegatee is going to require some assistance and commonly goes to the delegator for help. . . . The delegator makes himself available for discussions, counsels the delegatee, lends encouragement, and maintains a helpful, continuing relationship with the delegatee.[5]

Responsibility

Responsibility, like authority and delegation, is an important concept affecting organizational relationships. Responsibility may be thought of as the obligation of an individual to carry out assigned tasks to the best of his ability. It is what a person is expected to assume in order to carry out his assigned activities.

Responsibility comes into existence because a person with authority requires assistance from an individual and delegates authority for performance of needed specific work to the individual—the acceptance of the obligation by the individual to perform the work creates his responsibility. Since a delegator of authority does not relinquish any of his authority, the manager is ultimately responsible for what the individual accomplishes or does not accomplish. As with authority, a manager cannot refuse to accept responsibility for the mistakes of his subordinates by placing the blame for failure on them.

For sound organizational relationships the authority and responsibility of any manager should be coequal. Since a manager's authority gives him the power to make and enforce decisions concerning his assigned duties and his responsibility by the obligation to perform these duties by using his authority, it follows that authority and responsibility are closely related.

Authority without responsibility lacks an ultimate purpose or justification for existing. Likewise, responsibility without authority to carry out the assigned duties has a hollow ring. A manager cannot expect performance of assigned duties from a subordinate who does not have the necessary authority to see that the work is accomplished. Or con-

---

[5] George R. Terry, *Principles of Management,* 5th ed. (Homewood, Ill.: Richard D. Irwin, 1968), 343–46. Quoted by permission of the publisher.

versely, when authority is delegated to a subordinate who fails to accept it by assuming responsibility we have an equally bad situation.

Line-Staff

In considering the enterprise as a whole, *line* refers to the basic functions or activities of the organization. The authority of the line is the prime authority of the organization. If the authority over the activities is directly related to the accomplishment of the major objectives of the firm, then, these units are line units.

Staff refers to the supporting activities within an organization. The staff authority is to recommend, persuade, and advise the line. In other words, if the authority over the activities is indirectly related to the accomplishment of the major objectives, such units of the organization are considered staff units.

An additional word must be said about line authority, particularly when considering whether a working unit of an organization is to be considered line or staff. Characteristic of vertical growth is superior-subordinate authority relationship; that is, a superior delegates authority to a subordinate who in turn delegates authority to another subordinate and so on forming a line from the very top to the very bottom of the structure. The authority relationship is a direct line between superior and subordinate. Each member should know from whom he receives orders and to whom he reports. The manager of any organizational unit has authority over his unit whether the unit is considered as line or staff in the total structure. Even the manager of a staff department has what is sometimes called "thin line" authority and is responsible for the work of his unit and its contribution toward the objectives of the enterprise.

A totally different point of view that is worthy of consideration is proposed by Mason Haire:

> It is constantly repeated that the staff's function is to provide advice and support to the line. It persuades on the basis of its expertness in its specialized function. It has no authority to put its point of view into practice. The authority belongs to the line—the line authority. If we put these notions together, we reach a strange conclusion. If the staff has no authority and we maintain a balance between authority and responsibility, surely it follows that the staff has no responsibility! But no organization plan ever envisaged this. We just keep the two concepts simultaneously by maintaining them in logic-tight compartments while we think about the organization.
>
> Again, the problem seems to be in what we mean by "authority" and "responsibility." The staff's persuasiveness arose from its expert understanding of its specialized function and its ability to point out that if we want a certain goal we must take certain actions to reach it. The line, on

the other hand, had the "do it or else" authority. But the staff's persuasiveness arising out of expert knowledge sounds more and more like the line manager's "law of the situation." The line manager progressively gives up the "or else" and his persuasiveness arises from the process of managing itself—from the fact that what he asks people to do is seen or believed to be the appropriate thing to do. The two kinds of influence come closer and closer together. Staff and line "authority" become indistinguishable. It's probably time to stop trying to distinguish them.[6]

Informal Organization

The formal organizational structure sets up the levels of the organization hierarchy and establishes the formal relationships between people in the system. But people have their own motives, abilities, likes, and dislikes, and they build up within the system a social structure of their own. In daily contacts they form ways of working together that are different from the ways provided by the formal organization. They establish short cuts and do favors for one another. They work more easily with certain people, and they build up friendships with some and antagonisms toward others. People who give and receive help become bound together by shared work experiences and attitudes. They construct detours around people they dislike and around inadequate superiors.

These complex relationships that form among organizational members create working procedures and task groups that are known as the informal organization. Some groups are large, others are small. Some follow the lines of the organizational structure, and some develop within other groups or even overlap other groups.

The significance of a manager's recognizing the informal organization is, of course, so that he may utilize these groups to accomplish the work objectives. It is a grave error to ignore the social entities of the informal organization or to believe that they are necessarily bad in their effect. The obvious desirable goal for the manager is to organize formally in such a way that the influences and activities of the informal organization tend to support the formal structure.

THE SPAN OF MANAGEMENT

As additional people are added to an organization, the number of relationships increases at a greater rate than the number of people added.

---

[6] Mason Haire, *Psychology in Management*, 2nd ed. (New York: McGraw-Hill, 1964), 210–11.

There are too many variables in a management situation to conclude that there is any particular number of subordinates which a manager can effectively supervise. Such things as the type of work—whether routine, repetitive, or homogeneous in nature—the ability of the manager, his relative position in the organizational structure, faith in subordinates to perform satisfactorily, and the degree of teamwork that is present make it difficult to say a manager should have only a given number of subordinates.

More specifically, when subordinates are well trained the span of management can be relatively large. Presumably a well-trained subordinate is able to initiate the proper action quickly. Companies in which the work remains essentially the same and is repeated over and again with slight, if any, change are also usually successful in using greater spans of management than are companies with dynamic and volatile activities.

An interesting theory that recognized that the problem of managing others is both an individual and a social problem was devised by the French management consultant, V. A. Graicunas.[7] His theory emphasizes the complexity of managing more than a few subordinates and concerns the superior-subordinate relationships in an organization.

Graicunas defined three types of superior-subordinate relationships: (1) direct single relationships, (2) direct group relationships, and (3) cross relationships. It is noted that there are other possible relationships apparently overlooked by Graicunas: (1) either one subordinate or another may initiate action from the superior, or (2) the superior may assume the role of an equal in group relationships with one or another subordinate.

Consider a superior A as having three subordinates, B, C, and D. In this instance there are three direct single relationships. The direct group relations exist between A and every possible combination of subordinates, B, C, and D. These relationships include between A:

and B with C
and B with D
and C with B
and C with D
and D with B
and D with C
and B with C and D
and C with B and D
and D with C and B.

[7] V. A. Graicunas, "Relationship in Organization," *Papers on the Science of Administration* (New York: Institute of Public Administration, Columbia University, 1937).

Cross relationships occur when B, C, and D must confer with one another:

B to C
B to D
C to B
C to D
D to B
D to C.

From these various relationships Graicunas developed a formula that yields all possible types of superior-subordinate relationships requiring management attention. If n equals the number of people in a group, the total number of possible relationships can be computed by use of the following formula:

$$r = n \left[2^{n-1} + (n - 1)\right]$$

To realize the overwhelming increase of relationships as subordinates are added, see Table II-1.

TABLE II-1. Possible Relationships Between Superior and Subordinates.

Size of Group (n)	Number of Relationships (r)
1	1
2	6
3	18
4	44
5	100
6	222
7	490
8	1,080
9	2,376
10	5,210
15	245,970
20	10,486,140

UNITY OF COMMAND

As the reporting relationship an individual has to a single superior becomes more complete, there will be fewer conflicts of orders and a greater feeling of personal responsibility for achieving results.

Unity of command means that each person, from the bottom to the top of the organization, has just one superior, and only that superior is authorized to give him direct orders. In the average company this principle is violated frequently and flagrantly. Organizational structure may be properly designed and policies and procedures carefully set up, but the principle on which the whole structure is built—and the principle with which everyone agrees—is violated left and right.

A superior has direct authority and responsibility for his subordinates; he is responsible for their actions. If someone else gives orders to them, that manager has assumed authority over them, taking the authority away from their superior and leaving him with the responsibility. This is contrary to the principle that authority and responsibility should be coexistent. A manager giving directions to another manager's work group is violating the chain of command.

Such violations make managerial work more difficult and less effective. The organizational structure becomes distorted, and authority and responsibility are no longer commensurate. The manager finds it difficult to plan and organize the work of his department under these conditions. He cannot direct his men effectively if they are receiving direction from another manager, especially if they choose to accept the outsider's orders and reject his own. Coordination becomes next to impossible if other managers are issuing orders, assigning work, and interfering with the planned flow of work while the superior is trying to set up priorities and schedules. Controlling the work of the department becomes impossible when the people issuing orders do not have the responsibility for carrying them out.

ORGANIZATIONAL BALANCE

Organizing should be dynamic; it should take into account all changes in the company; organizational changes should be planned and directed toward the achievement of established objectives; and organizational principles must be applied in light of the overall objectives of the organization.

In every structure there is need for balance. For example, there must be balance in the centralization and decentralization of authority. Many matters, for example, require adequate authority at the level of the foreman or the district manager. On the other hand such matters as control over capital expenditures and the overall level of operating expenses may properly be centralized in the upper levels of management. Moreover, the inefficiencies of broad spans of management must be balanced against the inefficiencies of long lines of communication.

The organizational inefficiencies of multiple command must be balanced against the gains from expertness and uniformity in applying functional authority to staff and service departments. The savings of occupational specialization in departmentizing in accordance with enterprise function must be balanced against the advantages of better management obtained by establishing profit-responsible, semiautonomous product or territorial departments.

As there is the need for such balance, there is also a need for maintaining the organization in a dynamic state. Normally there is no clear indication signaling the precise time at which an organizational change should be made. Terry presents five key factors that indicate when a change is in order.

1) *Growth of the company.* As an enterprise grows, additional organizational levels are added, functions multiply, more products are taken on, and the spans of authority widen. Action tends to slow up, becomes inflexible and cumbersome, and decision making is retarded.

2) *Market and product considerations.* Change in the markets and products of an enterprise commonly suggest changes in the organizational structure. Market characteristics such as size, location, number of potential customers, outstanding preferences of buyers, pricing problems, and channels of distribution help determine what type of organizational structure should be attempted. In some instances there are marked differences among local markets, with the organization being constructed to meet best these specific requirements. When there is a variety of products, the problem of decision making and coordination can become quite complex. In such cases, divisionalization in organization may help supply the solution. For the marketing efforts of each product to succeed in its own competitive market, expeditious decisions by managers completely familiar with the unique marketing problems of that particular product are often required. Diversification of products appears vital in this area.

3) *International markets.* Normally foreign sales and frequently foreign manufacturing are handled by different units than those of domestic sales and production. . . . When production is performed in foreign countries, the tendency is to divisionalize by a territory basis. Other considerations such as taxes, currency control, import-export restrictions, and quota systems suggest the desirability of keeping foreign operations separate, and this, in turn, results in separate organizational units for foreign operations.

4) *Production characteristics.* When the raw materials utilized in the production process are readily accessible, bulky, or heavy, or freshness of products to consumer is important, then adoption of a divisionalized organization by territory is often helpful. In contrast, products requiring relatively high capital investment, unique processes for manufacturing, and a great deal of engineering skill usually indicate product divisionalization. The choice, or as a matter of fact the change, is not

always clear cut. Separation of the physical production facilities offers one approach, or, as an alternate, the use of separate cost systems for each product or group of related products can be followed. When separation is not feasible, a common practice is to have one production unit sell to other production units at competitive prices or to distribute production costs on some predetermined and equitable basis.

5) *Cost.* As a result of organizational dynamics, there are adjustments and changes that must be made for the organization to remain effective in light of new circumstances. To implement reorganization entails cost for administrative expenses, for personnel, and for additional plant and facilities. The organizational change should always be appraised in terms of what will the change cost and what benefits can be reasonably expected from the change. This is difficult to answer, but reorganization is usually in order if efficiency costwise can be bettered.[8]

THE APPLICATION OF PRINCIPLES

Until now we have concentrated on demonstrating that there are principles of organization and that they are widely accepted—although not always stated in the same way. As Drucker states in the Preface to his book *The Practice of Management,* "There is probably no field of human endeavor where the always tremendous gap between the knowledge and performance of the leaders and the knowledge and performance of the average is wider or more intractable."[9] Management must use these principles as guides in attempting to solve organizational problems.

Again as Drucker states: "Good organization structure does not, by itself, produce good performance—just as a good constitution does not guarantee great presidents, or good laws a moral society."[10] One of the most significant of the other needed factors is favorable attitude, that is, favorable attitude toward the structure by the men who make up the organization.

Favorable attitudes can mean many things. The aspects that have meaning for management are the will to make the organization work and the willingness to make constructive recommendations for changes in structure. Organization must be seen as the solution to problems of human cooperation. It is important to note the difference between making constructive suggestions for the improvement of the organizational structure, and using the structure as an excuse for performance failures.

It is important that management investigate problems with the possibility of organizational causes in mind. Recognizing that a diffi-

---

[8] Terry, *op. cit.,* 411–13. Quoted by permission of the publisher.
[9] Peter F. Drucker, *The Practice of Management* (New York: Harper, 1954), *vii.*
[10] *Ibid.,* 225.

culty can be structural opens the problem to new solutions other than those that could be applied to personality conflicts, incompetence, lack of personnel, etc. Another point which is more a technique than a principle is realization of the need to settle problems in the early stages before responsible managers become committed to different solutions.

Another feature of the complicated problem of applying principles effectively to management problems lies in the dynamic character of organization. No book on organization has ever been written that can be applied dogmatically to any given company. A theoretically sound and logical organization setup can and often does founder on the hidden shoals of human nature.

While the progressive manager will seek guidance from the textbook, he must remember that he is dealing with individuals and not with theoretical abstractions. Organizations are nothing more or less than groups of people with a common purpose. These organizations must be rearranged from time to time so that the skills and abilities of the management personnel are used to the greatest effect.

Principles of organization are principles of action. Principles as stated in the abstract apply only for an instant in a hypothetical or historical situation, in the same sense that the organization chart is only a picture of the company at rest. It is the function of the manager to solve the dilemmas of operation. His response to organization ranges from attention to the structure to inventive and independent action performed intuitively. Good judgment and a sense of proportion enable him to apply principles to specific situations.[11]

THE MANAGER'S JOB

One of the significant challenges confronting the free world is the development of greater managerial capability. The objective is to solve human problems of production at their source of origination—among those who work together, regardless of level. The alternative is to manage them through governmental intervention or political legislation. The former is, of course, the more flexible way. If it can be accomplished, it ensures continuing grass roots vitality because men have vested interests in their own efforts.

Every person in a management capacity bears the responsibility for solving the human problems associated with achieving maximum production through the productive utilization of people. The concept that a manager manages only the factors of production, without regard for people, is obviously a far too limited definition of his task. Likewise

[11]For a current overview of organization theory, see Peter F. Drucker, *The Age of Discontinuity* (New York: Harper, 1969), Chap. 9. In particular, Drucker discusses organizational performance, organizations and the quality of life, and the legitimacy of organizations.

the concept that production will take care of itself when the manager successfully communicates with and motivates his people is a too limited picture of the requirements for achieving true competence.

The most reasonable point of view is that a manager's task is one of developing and maintaining an environment that promotes work. Maintaining this type of environment requires far greater skill than is necessary to use either of the other two approaches. The manager must combine the best of both managerial concepts, balancing the good and bad features of each. Mature, skillful management demands an awareness of and a capability in dealing with the total complex of forces which constitute the work environment. Yet in the final analysis, organizational environment determines the degree of effectiveness actually achieved.

Thus the manager's job is to provide an environment which (1) promotes and sustains efficient performance of highest quality and quantity; (2) fosters and utilizes creativity; and (3) builds enthusiasm for experimentation, innovation, and change.

SUMMARY

The efficiency with which employees perform their work, the degree to which they work harmoniously with each other, and the satisfaction that they derive from their jobs can be no greater than the organization permits. The organization thus provides the foundation for the management of people since it is the basis for the establishment of individual job requirements and since the nature of authority, responsibilities, and formal relationships are dependent upon it. It is necessary then, to have an understanding of the principles of organization. Consideration is given these "principles" from the viewpoint that they are fundamental truths that are, because of continued research and updating of concepts and ideas, flexible and subject to change. Specifically, the principles of (1) unity of objectives, (2) division of work, (3) delegation, (4) span of management, (5) unity of command, and (6) organizational balance are discussed.

This chapter has also been concerned with the dynamics of organization. Because organizations are dynamic, attention is devoted to the interrelationships between organization and human behavior. Such interrelationships have become the subject of increased emphasis and research. For example, the size and shape of the structure, and the extent to which authority is centralized, can have a significant effect upon the people within the structure. Improper organization can result in conflict and feelings of pressure and frustration on the part of organizational members. The organization of the future will have to be more human oriented and will likely recognize the importance of creating a desirable psychological climate within which people may work satisfactorily rather than being concerned primarily with the improvement of production technology.

chapter 3

types of organization

THIS CHAPTER DESCRIBES the forms that organizations of at least moderate complexity may take and reviews the circumstances which will lead designers of organizations to choose a particular structure. The general form may be described by referring to a particular type of organization (hence the title of the chapter), but very rarely is a given organization a pure type. It is common practice to label organizations as *functional, product,* or *regional* types because of their bases for primary division. As will be seen later, however, functional divisions may be subdivided territorially, product divisions can include functional units, and regional divisions are frequently organized in ways that do not depend upon their physical location.

Such terms as *structure, type,* and *primary division* were used above in certain special senses. It may be well at this point to provide some definitions for these terms and take a preliminary look at the problem of typifying organization structures.

ORGANIZATION STRUCTURES AND DEPARTMENTATION

Certain theories and principles were introduced in Chapter 2, and it has been shown that organization planning is essentially the translation of principles into practice. The end product of the translation, of course, is the web of relationships that delineates the delegation of authority from the top to the bottom of the organization and concomitantly divides up and assigns the work. "Organization structure" is merely shorthand for "the structure of organizational relationships and allocations of responsibility for activities." An organization "type" is a structure that implements some consistent rules of formation.

Unfortunately, the structure of an organization is not describable simply in terms of shape or pattern. There is still much to say beyond the fact that an organization is narrow and deep when it has multiple levels of authority and little differentiation of function, or that it is wide and shallow when there are few levels. The boxes on the typical organization chart could be filled in many ways, and the lines connecting the boxes are subject to multiple interpretation. It is more meaningful to examine, first, how the choices can be made in assigning tasks to the organizational units (groups of people and facilities) which the boxes represent, and how performance is affected and, second, what is the meaning of the relationships the lines represent.

In any formal business organization there is a first level of separation into divisions; this is what is meant by "primary division." Logically, primary division is related to primary purpose so that the various product lines are frequently the determinants of the structure of the organization. Successive repetitions of the process of division below the level of primary division provides the final elaboration of the structure. For want of a better term, both the process of segmenting an organization vertically at all levels (creating divisions, departments, and further subunits) and the resultant structure are called "departmentation." Types of organizations, so far as vertical division is concerned, are then identified according to the scheme of departmentation they follow.

Clearly, vertical division is not all that determines organization structure. As earlier discussion of line and staff relationships has shown, the manner in which authority is distributed provides yet another dimension to be considered. Since there are at least these two dimensions to organizational structure, complete typification of an organization requires us to say something like, "The XYZ Corporation's organization is the line-and-staff type with product departmentation at the division level and functional departmentation at subordinate levels."

There really are but two major questions in departmentation: What are the alternative bases for action? How can these be used in organization planning? Before examining the alternatives, let us review what we are striving to accomplish in organizational planning by adopting a "systems view" and seeing where departmentation fits.

THE SYSTEMS VIEW OF ORGANIZATION

Systems analysis has great power primarily by virtue of its generality. In viewing organization from the systems point of view we take advantage of the fact that the essentials of analysis are the same for all systems and that these essentials embrace relatively few principles. The principles to be applied here, moreover, are consistent with the principles of organization presented in Chapter 2.

While definitions of the term *system* vary, virtually everyone easily grasps the concept and sees that any set of interacting components may be regarded as a system. The various notions that a system must have boundaries, that the environment of a system is whatever is relevant to it that is outside its boundaries, that a system typically is viewed as performing some process by accepting inputs and transforming them into outputs, and that complex systems are composed of assemblies of subsystems are all natural extensions of the basic concept. Obviously organization planning as a system-type problem is concerned with designing an effective system, i.e., selecting components and arranging relationships among them so that the system performs well.

What help does systems theory provide? A minimum list of guidelines would be:

1) The proper unit of analysis is the whole system. It is an error to analyze a part of a system without consideration of its effect on total system performance or the effect on the part of its interaction with other parts.

2) Optimal system design is design which optimizes some measure of system performance. What a system is should be related to what it is supposed to accomplish, and it does not follow that separately optimizing each component and relation yields an overall optimum.

3) Structure is a determinant of system performance. Selection of functions of components and the modes of interaction among them (for example, whether functions are mutually augmentative, regulative, complementary, supplementary, etc.), is crucial, since a system's behavior is more than the summed independent behaviors of its parts.

While these guidelines are by no means exhaustive, they indicate the direction of systems analysis, and they do tie directly to some workable principles for departmentation.

DEPARTMENTATION PRINCIPLES

Probably the most important implication of the systems approach is that if the *whole* organization is considered, complicated structures reduce predictability and simple structures are to be preferred. Control is facilitated by reduction of the quantity of interaction and associated communication processes necessary for performance by organization elements.

Assignment of Functions

Closely allied with the principle of simplicity is one of clarity of assignment of functions. Unless duplication of function is necessary for security or safety, it is to be avoided. In order to be able to understand how the organization works, it is necessary to know with a minimum of uncertainty how the parts work, i.e., which organizational unit is responsible for each activity and in what terms. Assignments which leave responsibilities uncovered are no more justifiable than those which overlap.

Rules for Grouping Activities

While it is easy to see that departmentation should result in clear-cut organizational relationships which can be interpreted without difficulty, this is at best an indirect aid to the *act* of departmentation. The need for a more definitive prescription has led organization theorists such as March and Simon[1] and Parsons[2] to propose principles or rules for grouping activities. A simplified set of rules might consist of the following:

1) *Association or similarity principle.* On the grounds that like things belong together, activities which are essentially the same should be collected into one unit. The first question, of course, is what attribute or attributes should be used for judging likeness? Since any activity may be characterized according to what it is (i.e., what operations it comprises), who does it, how it is done (i.e., what methods are employed in performing the operations), where it is done, when it is done, and why it is done, any one or any combination of these may be selected as the basis for collection. Nearly all accepted forms of departmentation come from such sorting of activities into organizational units. The second question, naturally, is: How much similarity is required? Deciding whether most of an activity in a group is "like" the activity in another group often will be a difficult decision. Any principle, however, can be expected to extend but part of the way to practice, and the way it works out in particular cases is shaped by circumstances peculiar to the individual case.

2) *Interaction principle.* Here the reasoning is that the relationships between activities should govern their grouping. Generally tasks which have little to do with each other (despite their similar nature) become organizationally separable, and those which affect each other strongly become candidates for grouping. For the most part, recognition of interaction consists of departmentation by work flow. Thus activities which are sequential are grouped to bring a complete sequence within an organization unit

[1] James G. March and Herbert A. Simon, *Organizations* (New York: John Wiley & Sons, 1958).
[2] T. Parsons, *Structure and Process in Modern Societies* (New York: Free Press, 1960).

or arranged to give organizational separation between work stages. Where activities are parallel rather than sequential, organization boundaries logically should exist so that work-oriented interactions will be weak across the boundaries and strong within them.

3) *Managerial principle.* Shifting the focus from activities to their management, this basis for grouping relies upon application of general principles of organization and management to secure particularly desirable features such as controllability, balance, flexibility, potential for growth, or others (see Chapter 2).

TYPES OF DEPARTMENTATION

As noted earlier, the two main departmentation questions concerned identification of the bases for activity grouping and the method of employment of these bases. Up to this point the emphasis has been on the latter question, by means of examination of principles which with intelligent application would yield effective forms of organization. But what are the organizational possibilities? To answer, it is necessary to describe departmentation alternatives and discuss the factors influencing their selection.

Functional Organization

Of course, all organization structures are functional in the sense that they convey purpose and indicate the functions performed by the parts of the organization. This, however, is not what is meant by functional organization. Unfortunately, confusion continues to persist in the literature of organization because of the advocacy by F. W. Taylor in the early 1900s of what he called the "functional form of organization."[3] Under Taylor's concept several specialized departments exercised authority over the specialties for which they were responsible wherever they occurred, i.e., each exercised authority in respect to one function over workers in other departments. While this method of organization rarely has been applied to entire organizations and is more an interesting relic than a practical method, the principle of specialization it embodies continues to be applied in some organizations where staff departments have a "functional authority" over their area of interest.

The modern meaning of functional organization literally is "organization by function" or departmentation at the level of primary division or below according to the business function performed. For further clarification, see Fig. 3-1. When the departments are for the execution of essential or "organic" functions of the business (such as manufacturing and sales) they are line departments, and when their purpose is

---

[3] Frederick W. Taylor, *The Principles of Scientific Management* (New York: Harper, 1947).

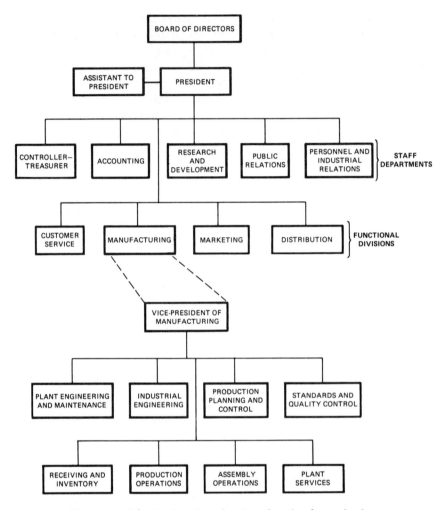

Fig. 3-1. Organization chart showing a functional organization.

ancillary (such as personnel administration) they are staff departments. This type of organization is one that most often evolves when organizational differentiation is rudimentary, and although it may continue to be the principal basis for primary departmentation, with company growth and organization expansion it is likely to be supplanted or supplemented by another method of departmentation.

It is the inadequacies of the entirely functional approach which impels more sophisticated departmentation. As an organization achieves a scale at which subdivision is extensive, several varieties of ills begin to appear. If, for example, organization growth is accomplished only by adding levels which are successively finer redivisions of the primary functions, the results will be over-centralization, inflexible bureaucracy, or an excessively hierarchical structure. The shortcomings of monolithic structures as manifested in faulty coordination and lack of control can largely be avoided by establishing smaller autonomous units more closely adapted to needs.

Product Organization

Departmentation by product brings together activities which are essential to or mainly related to the production and distribution of a particular product or class of product. Since the products of an organization can be either goods or services, or combinations thereof, (e.g., activities of installation, maintenance, repair, and provision of information and instructions which accompany sales of products), departmentation by service is the logical equivalent of product departmentation.

Product division may be complete or partial, and primary or secondary. Complete division exists when all aspects of administration and operation necessary for the handling of the product at an organizational level are contained in a single department. The division is primary when a product department is neither a section of a more inclusive department nor subordinate to another department. Fig. 3-2 shows

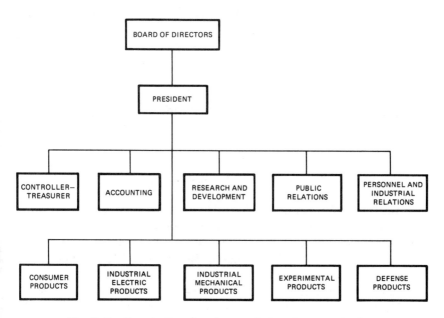

Fig. 3-2.   Organization chart for a typical product organization.

a typical product division-type of organization. The principal reasons for product organization are:

1) To secure through product-centered structuring the general advantages of specialization and division of labor. This motive will be strongly persuasive where application of personal attention and expertise promise substantial return.
2) To solve problems of coordination arising from multiple interdependencies in the activities involved in conceiving and designing a product, preparing production facilities, planning and controlling manufacturing operations, and marketing and distributing the product.
3) To produce in the organization a needed emphasis on the product. Such stress may be vital in a competitive environment where research and development efforts for the creation of new products and improvement of old ones are highly important, where an opportunity to exploit a basic process or material with a variety of products is present, or where product proliferation may inhibit proper attention to the requirements of individual products.

In general, product organization will be most advantageous when there can be considerable independence of facilities so that the departmentation provides logical administrative units and minimizes potential conflict. For this reason, complete product division typically goes with multi-plant operation which allows all of the activities in a location to come under the direction of one administrative group. An even more convincing case can be made for product organization when distinct separations can be made in several directions—if markedly differing technologies are inherent to different product classes, if the products are sold in different kinds of markets, and if different marketing approaches are taken for different products.

Regional Organization

When the activities of an enterprise are geographically dispersed, a departmentation which conforms to physical distribution of personnel and facilities often appears desirable. Terms used for this regional grouping are geographic, territorial, or area division, each connoting that activities are assigned to organizational units according to where they take place. The regional organization type of departmentation is illustrated in Fig. 3-3.

That an organization's work is done in scattered locations is not sufficient reason in itself for adoption of regional organization, for unless it offers some definite and significant advantage, an alternative

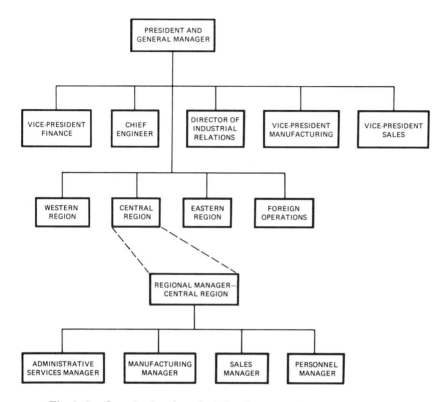

Fig. 3-3. Organization chart depicting the regional type of organization.

basis for grouping may still be preferable. The same kind of economic analysis which aids in solving problems of plant location is applicable here. Whether administrative activities should be close to or remote from the site of operations and whether contiguity should be given primary consideration in the composition of the organization units are questions of gain and loss as functions of location.

Handling problems at the local level has much to recommend itself, but sensitive response to local conditions and close coordination of all functions in terms of regional outlook may not always be possible. Autonomy may prevent the effective use of the type of organizational specialization offered by departments whose concentration is a function rather than a region. Against the gain of "good local picture" must be offset the cost of a "poor big picture."

Since ability to define territories clearly and associate costs and benefits with how boundaries are drawn is instrumental in choosing regional departmentation, there are a few prime characteristics which should be aimed for:

1) *Difference of context.* The presence of real regional distinctiveness is conducive to regional organization. At the extreme of foreign operations, sharp differences of language, law, and culture require organizational recognition. In many firms whose basic departmentation is other than regional, overseas operations are grouped separately.
2) *Localization.* Operations may be localized because they are materials-bound or because the nature of products or markets restrict distribution territorially. Whether regional boundaries are the natural ones provided by geographic features or the artificial ones of political units, their organizational impact is plain.
3) *Duplication.* If common operations and problems of administration appear in various regions, the establishment of a standard structure in each may be quite effective. Normal practice in this case is to have subdivisions of the regional departments corresponding to home office departments so that some of the advantages of functional, product, or other types of specialization may be realized.

Profit Center Organization

This type of departmentation represents a serious attempt to apply with minimum restriction the departmentation principle which urges reduction of the quantity of interaction necessary for effective performance. In its pure form, profit center organization would make departments virtually autonomous units responsible to higher levels solely in terms of profit and loss. It has even been suggested that the ideal is an association of independent enterprises under common ownership—a form approached at the corporate level by some modern conglomerates.

Since departmentation approaches are practically oriented, profit center organization within firms is likely to stop well short of the ideal by recognizing that there are services which can be furnished by specialized departments more economically than by the individual departments. Similarly, profit and loss accountability typically is obscured by arbitrary pricing for exchanges between profit centers and by arbitrary valuation of resources of the enterprise employed in operations by profit centers. In addition profit centers are sometimes established at levels below primary division in situations where there cannot be clear-cut separation of the activities of one department from those of others. Also the proportion of all operations influencing a department's performance which is under the department's control may be insufficient to make profitability a meaningful measure.

The internal structure of a profit center is unlikely to differ much from other types of departments; any of the bases of departmentation may be applied for subdivision. Externally, by virtue of their special responsibility, the relations of profit center departments with others are likely to differ sharply from those existing in other types of organizations. If the separate product divisions of a firm are treated as profit centers, competition among them may inhibit cooperation. Unless incentives for taking into account the total organizational effect of the profit center's action are present as well as the profit incentive which has been built into it, departmental decisions will tend not to be coordinated with those taken elsewhere.

An obvious advantage of profit center organization is that its organizational units function under an unequivocal measure of performance so that their size, composition, scope of activity, and other attributes are to a degree self-adjusting, as managers do those things which raise profit and avoid those which lower it. It is often asserted that this is an organizational form with high potential for developing self-reliant managers who thrive under continual evaluation and respond positively to financial incentives.

MISCELLANEOUS AND COMBINED TYPES OF ORGANIZATION

It was noted earlier that the rules for grouping activities are based on a few broad principles. Because of this, there are almost limitless possibilities for applications in specific cases suggested by certain features of organizations' activities. In some cases types of organizations may be evolved which are offshoots of those already discussed. In other instances the basis for departmentation may be unique to the situation and the resulting organization form a novel one.

There are a few well-recognized types of organization used other than the ones mentioned up to this point; a brief examination of them will suggest the direction this further classification can take. The customer groups or clienteles that are to be served may provide the rationale for departmentation, activities connected with the requirements of each being grouped together. Similarly, the means by which a service is provided or the institutional arrangements which facilitate it may be the criterion for collecting tasks into manageable sets, e.g., wholesale versus retail sales or professional versus nonprofessional items.

At the operating level the means of performance may be a determinant of structure. Organization by process, by equipment, or by material are elementary possibilities. Production stages, craft groups, recurrently applied operation sequences, or assemblages of associated tasks can be the link between technical arrangements for work and organization for its management. Such variants are often lumped under the heading of "functional organization" and with reason, for they may be regarded as the basic units which are aggregated to compose a business function.

There is no requirement that any organization must be designed throughout according to a single scheme, and combined types of organization are more the rule than the exception. At the division level, different modes of organization may be adopted for the several divisions, and it is not unusual to find more than one basis for grouping within a division. Multiplication of organization types clearly ought to be done with caution, however, and insistence that forms be closely associated with the activities they contain should not be pushed too far.

Grid and Matrix Organization

Adjustment of organization to cope with the requirements of major projects or missions may be secured by the use of several devices. First, a "committee" may be charged with developing a solution or providing the mechanism for discussion of the aspects of a problem affecting various parts of the organization simultaneously. Second, a "task force"[4] may be established which draws its personnel and resources from permanent organizational elements and which is dissolved when its objective has been accomplished. Finally, a modification of the formal organizational structure may be made which recognizes the special requirements of a project while retaining most of the advantages of departmentation.

If a project cuts across organizational lines and requires managerial representation from several specializations, a "grid" form of organization may be selected. This form of organization is shown in Fig. 3-4.

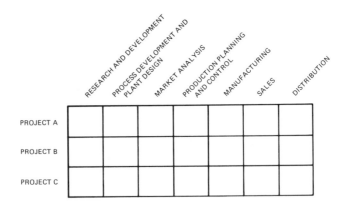

Fig. 3-4. Representation of the grid type of organization.

---

[4] Definitions for "committee" and "task force" are given in Chapter 4.

The project becomes temporarily the basis for creation of an organizational unit, but the members of the unit are also members of departments. While this form plainly violates the principle of unity of command, it is done with a purpose. The purpose is to escape some of the rigidities of the permanent organization and assure, hopefully, that the project is treated as an entity rather than in a piecemeal way.

When more than one dimension of division is crossed by project organization, the more general designation of "matrix organization" applies. It is possible to conceive of separate projects—sequential or parallel—being set up for development of a particular product or product group. At the same time, just as in the "grid organization," each project may draw its participants from a number of departments. One team from a department may be working on a certain Project A directed toward a given problem. Another team from the same department may be working on Project B, directed toward a different problem. Still another team from the same department may be working on Project C, directed toward solving in a different way the problem of Project A. These posibilities are illustrated in Fig. 3-5.

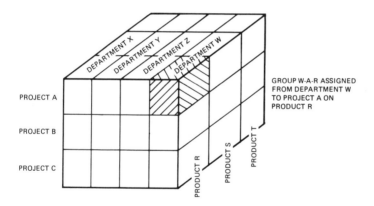

Fig. 3-5. Representation of the matrix type of organization.

Line and Staff and Organization Form

Everything that has been said in this chapter applies with minor variations to the design of staff departments, though we have referred almost entirely to line departments. While the internal organization of most staff departments tends to be functional or functional-regional, there is no theoretical reason why staff activities need be treated differently in deciding how they are to be grouped for performance.

Identification of activities as line or as staff, however, is itself a basis for departmentation. When there is any question of a department's responsibility for results shaped by the actions of those who are not in that department, the subject is immediately line-staff relations. It is sufficient to say here that "line and staff" is a type of organization, but a "type" in a different sense than that word is used in this chapter. Because the line and staff relation is so important a topic in its own right, the reader is referred to the coverage it has been given briefly in Chapter 2, and in more detail in the literature.[5]

SUMMARY

The forms taken by organizations of at least moderate complexity have been discussed at some length. Organizations have been described as being most often of the functional, product, or regional types. The systems approach was noted as being an effective method for viewing the problems of organizations with regard to structuring them for optimum efficiency. Departmentation was defined as both the process of segmenting an organization vertically at all levels, thus creating divisions and departments, and the structure resulting from the application of the process.

The principal reasons for *product* organization were found to be: (1) to secure through product-centered structuring the general advantages of specialization and division of labor, (2) to solve problems of coordination arising from multiple interdependencies in the activities involved in developing, manufacturing, and marketing a product, and (3) to produce in the organization a needed emphasis on the product.

The principal advantages of *regional* organization are that it permits making a sensitive response to local conditions and that it allows close coordination of all functions. There is, however, the gain in achieving a "good local picture" to be balanced against the possibility of a "poor big picture" for the overall company.

The advantages of the *profit center* type of organization are found to be that of permitting each unit to operate under an equivocal measure of performance so that their size, composition, scope of activity, and other attributes are self-adjusting.

The *grid and matrix* and *line-and-staff* types of organization were discussed. The grid and matrix type of organization was noted as being particularly well adapted to the operations of the firm with a large number of project type activities.

---

[5] Louis A. Allen, "The Line-Staff Relationship," in Max D. Richards and William A. Nielander, eds., *Readings in Management*, 2nd ed. (New Rochelle, N.Y.: South-Western, 1963), 715.

chapter 4

specialized
types of organization

THIS CHAPTER DISCUSSES some of the organizational forms and techniques that have been developed to serve the unique or special situations that arise in manufacturing. Most of these are departures from the traditional bureaucratic form of organization used in the majority of manufacturing companies, at least in the older established industries.

It is not surprising that specialized adaptations of the traditional, or classical, structure have been felt necessary to handle current organizational problems. The traditional structure which dominates 'the manufacturing industry was well suited to serve the needs of its time. In recent years, however, technological and environmental changes have presented problems that traditional organizations were not designed to handle. Of even greater importance are the changing attitudes of employees, customers, government, and the general public. These changing attitudes have a significant influence on a company's efforts to reach its objectives, and consequently upon the organizational structure employed.

BACKGROUND

We can understand better the relevance and the necessity of organizational innovation if we review briefly the background of manufacturing organization and the rationale for the conceptual changes that have taken place over the years.

Development of Value Systems

The broad value system prevalent in nineteenth-century America was the individualistic ethic. This stemmed from the ideas of economic freedom and the Protestant ethic and the expanding frontier with its seemingly endless opportunities for individual accomplishment.

The twentieth century brought a new value system to society, a system which is generally termed the social ethic. The growth of urbanization and industrialization and the resultant close contact of people, particularly employees, created increasingly complex problems of interdependency. Also during this period there began a significant shift from owner-managed firms to absentee ownership with hired, professional managers operating the enterprise. It was natural that the value system would change, with decreased emphasis on individualism and greater focus instead on the collective well-being of society. New attention had to be given to working together in a cooperative relationship, and new types of organizations had to be developed to accomplish this.

Early Organization Theories

It was this emerging social ethic that fostered Taylor's scientific management. Taylor's ideas were directed primarily to manufacturing operations. He pictured man as an economic being, motivated to attain his fair share of society's economic output. As such, man was interested in economic efficiency and was willing to work in a manner to maximize this economic efficiency. Taylor developed the theories and concepts of scientific management on this, by today's standards, narrow concept of man's wants and needs. Division of labor and scientific methods would produce the efficiency while wages based on productivity would produce the motivation.[1]

This was generally recognized as sound theory for its time and is still followed with little change today in many manufacturing companies, particularly in production operations.

In the 1920s, however, there began to appear evidences of democratic liberalism among workers. The first significant revelation of this was made by Elton Mayo and his colleagues from Harvard with their publication of the results of studies conducted at the Hawthorne (Illinois) Works of the Western Electric Company.[2] These studies challenged the machine theory of economic man and spearheaded the human relations movement. The human relations movement challenged the concepts of the scientific management school and shifted some of the focus away from the man-machine theory to consideration of the importance of the interrelationships among individuals within the organization. This was the first significant recognition of the open-system concept of organization, wherein it is recognized that any orga-

---

[1] Frederick W. Taylor, *The Principles of Scientific Management* (New York: Harper, 1947).

[2] F. J. Roethlisberger and W. J. Dickson, *Management and the Worker* (Cambridge: Harvard University Press, 1939).

nization is only a part of a whole organization system, and is affected by changes in other parts of the system.

Modern Organization Theories

Rensis Likert, Douglas McGregor, and Chris Argyris, among others, have developed revisionist theories of organization.[3] The central idea of their approach is the necessity for commonality in organizational and personal goals. Their concepts are not easy to describe in brief terms, but for our purposes it is sufficient to say that they stress participative management and mutual trust as being the means to attain this commonality. According to Likert:

> The organizational structure and its manner of functioning must insure a maximum probability that in all interactions each of the individuals involved will, in the light of his background, experience and expectations, view the interaction as supportive and one which contributes to his sense of personal worth.[4]

Chester Barnard, as far back as 1938, introduced the concept that organization should be concerned with the processes of decision making as well as with the processes of action.[5] Herbert Simon has expanded on the framework introduced by Barnard and presents the concept of ". . . a hierarchy of decisions—each step downward in the hierarchy consisting in an implementation of the goals set forth in the step immediately above."[6] Simon rejects most of the traditional concepts and places emphasis on the problem-solving process. One effect of this type of thinking on organization structure is to encourage the design of organizational structures to accommodate the flow of information needed in the decision-making process.

A further extension of the decision-making concept has developed into management science. Included in this general term are such techniques as operations research and industrial dynamics.

Open-System Concepts

The early traditional, or classical, organization theories may be classified as *closed-system* concepts. That is, it is assumed that the organization has control over or can reliably predict all of the outside

---

[3] Rensis Likert, *New Patterns of Management* (New York: McGraw-Hill, 1961); Douglas McGregor, *The Human Side of Enterprise* (New York: McGraw-Hill, 1960); Chris Argyris, *Personality and Organization* (New York: Harper, 1957).

[4] Rensis Likert, "A Motivational Approach to a Modified Theory of Organization and Management," in Mason Haire, ed., *Modern Organization Theory* (New York: John Wiley & Sons, 1959), 191.

[5] Chester I. Barnard, *Functions of the Executive* (Cambridge : Harvard University Press, 1938).

[6] Herbert A. Simon, *Administrative Behavior,* 2nd ed. (New York: Macmillan, 1957), 5.

forces acting on it. These organizations are designed to follow a completely rational approach toward their goals.

The first significant questioning of this approach came with the human relations movement when it was recognized that the employee would not necessarily perform predictably, and that variations in employee behavior had a significant effect on the attainment of goals by the organization. Subsequent findings have revealed that there are an almost infinite number of environmental influences that affect an organization's performance. Even when identified, it is difficult if not impossible to predict their effect and even more difficult to control the result.

Modern organization theories emphasize different aspects of these environmental influences, but all recognize that they have a significant effect and cannot be ignored by the organization if it is to attain any degree of competitive efficiency. Modern organization theories have borrowed heavily from an evolving *general system theory* which applies to many systems, whether physical, biological, behavioral, or social.

Sir Arthur Eddington expressed the systems concept in terms easy to understand when he wrote:

> We often think that when we have completed our study of *one* we know all about *two,* because "two" is "one and one." We forget that we still have to make a study of "and." Secondary physics is a study of "and"—that is to say, of organization.[7]

Eddington's "and" suggests that we have much to gain by considering organizations in larger frames of reference. What he is saying is that the whole is greater than the sum of its parts.[8] If we focus on an analysis of minute segments of the organization, i.e., the "micro" approach, we will be overlooking important cause and effect factors. Systems theory, in considering a larger frame of reference, takes the "macro" approach by looking at the whole system including the relationships of the separate elements.

Open Systems Versus Closed Systems. An important aspect of systems theory is the distinction between closed and open systems. Organizations have dynamic interactions with many elements of their environment—employees, labor organizations, governments, customers, suppliers, dealers, competitors, etc. Within the organization the various parts (departments, divisions, etc.) are interrelated with each

---

[7] Arthur Eddington, *Nature of the Physical World* (Ann Arbor: The University of Michigan Press, 1958), 5.

[8] Eddington's concept that the whole is greater than the sum of its parts is currently being studied in management circles under the term "synergism."

other in the accomplishment of the organization's goals. The failure to recognize the effects of these interactions (closed system) is one of the greatest weaknesses of the traditional models of organization.

This is not to say that a closed-system strategy has no place in today's manufacturing organizations. Where there is a routine, recurring operation with largely predictable and controllable problem areas it may be most efficient to organize this particular operation as a closed system within the larger organization, provided adequate buffering is maintained to shield the closed system from the environmental influences. The operation can never be a true closed system, however, so long as there are people involved, since human beings, as employees, are one of the greatest sources of uncertainty in an organization.

James Thompson treats this subject in his discussion of *technical cores,* or islands within the larger organization that are sealed off from environmental influences in order to attain maximum technical efficiency.[9] He points out that the closed system can never be completely attained but that organizations operate under the assumption that steady conditions exist. This is done by *buffering* the inputs and outputs of the technical core. In manufacturing, for example, buffering of inputs is accomplished by stockpiling of materials and supplies to assure a steady stream into the core, preventive maintenance of facilities and equipment to minimize the uncertainties of breakdowns, and employee training to bring the workforce into similar patterns. Buffering of outputs is accomplished through warehousing of inventories which permits the technical core to produce at a constant rate. Such buffering, of course, is not as feasible when dealing with a perishable or seasonal product.

While spelling out this practice, Thompson makes an important point that is easy to overlook if we are not alert for it. He states that while buffering to protect the steady state of the technical core has considerable advantages, these advantages are often outweighed by added costs to other parts of the organization. An example of this is the cost of maintaining both input and output inventories and the chance of costly obsolescence of inventories. A natural answer to these problems is to attempt to smooth out the supply and demand markets so that inventories may be minimized while still maintaining a steady state within the technical core. At some point, of course, such protection ceases to pay off, and the operation should then be reorganized in such a manner as to be able to cope with the shifting environmental influences, in other words, to recognize the reality of an open-system situation.

---

[9] James D. Thompson, *Organization in Action: Social Science Bases of Administrative Theory* (New York: McGraw-Hill, 1967).

Coordination. While large and complex organizations often contain specific operations which are organized as closed systems, the organization as a whole generally recognizes and responds to the environmental influences. Many of these influences penetrate into the organization itself and reveal themselves in the form of uncertainties with which the organization must cope. A common response to these annoying problems is to create a new organization to solve the problem or to "coordinate" two or more parts of the organization in a united effort to avoid or solve the problems. As a result, in too many large organizations there is a proliferation of coordinating activities which sometimes, in turn, require the establishment of activities to coordinate them. This situation is, indeed, occasionally carried to ridiculous extremes.

One of the greatest benefits that an attitude based on the systems concept can offer us is the realization that we should look at the entire organization when considering a solution to a specific organizational problem. We should not lose sight of a key point in systems theory; all parts affect all other parts. Every action taken has repercussions throughout the organization. All elements of an organization, both human and non-human, are linked by an extremely complicated interdependence. When the initial reaction to a relationship problem is to establish a third party to coordinate it, we are setting in motion another variable within the total system which may have a more undesirable effect than the original problem.

Katz and Kahn in their excellent book make several points in this regard.[10] They point out that, typically, organizations respond to problems with a tightening of integration and coordination to improve stability. However, there could well be a much greater requirement for flexibility which tighter integration and coordination restricts. Coordination may even become an end in itself rather than the most expeditious means to an end. In this situation every attempt at coordination may produce several new organizational problems.

It may well be that, for a particular problem or conflict, the establishment of a coordinating activity is the best solution. As Katz and Kahn make clear, however, a characteristic of all open systems is that there does not have to be a single method of achieving an objective. What this tells us is that we should consider the sympathetic effects of any organization change throughout the whole organization and thoroughly consider reasonable alternatives.

The following pages discuss some of the more useful organization techniques which can be considered in answering coordination problems between the various elements of the total system. It will be evi-

---

[10] Daniel Katz and Robert L. Kahn, *The Social Psychology of Organizations* (New York: John Wiley & Sons, 1966).

dent that in all of these examples coordination is the central problem. In other words, they recognize the pervasiveness of the open-system concept by attempting to bring together, or coordinate, the various elements of the system.

SYSTEMS ENGINEERING

Systems engineering involves the development and integration of the necessary components to produce a larger product as the final objective. It is concerned with developing sub-systems and systems to come up with the overall larger system which is the final product. The term is used to describe engineering systems which are of great complexity. Oftentimes there is no assurance that the required sub-systems are, at the moment, feasible. In this context, it can involve the research and development of components and methods as well as the integration of these components into the overall objective through the production process.

The wide range of functions which are necessarily a part of such a complex process, as well as the often lengthy time sequence, requires the devotion of special attention to the organizational process. The organization must provide for the efficient coordination of the decision process and the flow of information which is so vital for the decision process. Systems engineering is an important part of the concept of project management, discussed in the next section of this chapter.

The Coordinative Aspect

An important feature of systems engineering is its coordinative process. As is the case with a number of organizational terms, systems engineering has many meanings and is discussed in many diverse ways in the literature. In this chapter, systems engineering is differentiated from design engineering, which is the design of specific components. Systems engineering, as we are using it here, is concerned with the integrating of the *components* into a total system, the final objective. The systems engineer is a coordinator, a monitor, a reviewer, an evaluator, an expediter and above all, a communications link between all the elements of the process. The range of his involvement extends not only across traditional functional lines but also covers the entire time sequence—from "cradle to grave."

Operation and Structure

It will be helpful to have an idea of the way a systems engineering organization operates. Depending upon the complexity of the system under development, individual systems engineers, or sub-organizations of the systems engineering function, may be assigned to a specific subsystem. There may be a half-dozen sub-systems or upwards of a hundred. These individual sub-system engineers must be coordinated by successive levels of supervision until reaching the manager responsible for the total system. The number of levels of such a hierarchy should be kept to a minimum in order to facilitate communications. This idea of a minimum of levels is extremely important, since the essence of systems engineering is communication.

Communications

Communications is the transmission of information. The information we are talking about here is *all* information concerning the product. This brings us into a whole new field—the Management Information System. Since this topic is treated in Chapter 7, it will not be discussed here, except to say that such an information system must provide information on a real-time basis in the following areas:

1) Reliability experience, cost, forecasts, and objectives
2) Testing information
3) Piece costs, tooling costs, engineering costs, and other fixed costs
4) Component information relative to part number, weight, material, source, etc.
5) Standards data
6) Names of responsible systems engineers
7) Approved design changes
8) Timing objectives.

Depending upon the system involved, this list can be expanded. The amount of information, and the frequency of change in the data, will require the aid of a computer even in cases of a relatively simple system. Certainly, in the case of a complex system, the systems engineering concept cannot be followed without a computer data system.

The organizational location of the systems engineering function should be influenced by the pattern of information flow and decision making in the organization. March and Simon, supported by an increasing number of present-day scholars, build their whole theory of organization on a decision-center model.

The organization structure itself is greatly influenced by the pattern of information flow. Pfiffner and Sherwood emphasized this as follows:

It is quite apparent that information is a principal basis for decision. The information needed in making a decision is likely to exist in many places with the result that facilities must be provided for transmitting that information to the decision centers. The conduits for such transmission may or may not follow hierarchical channels. One writer distinguishes between structure and dynamics stating that dynamically "administration appears as a patterned whirl and flow of communications . . ."

It is at this point, of course, that some of the new concepts come most directly into conflict with one of the dominant aspects of traditional organization theory, the requirement that communications shall flow through command channels. Today we find that such a precept is no longer as sacred as it once was. No less an administrator than Ralph J. Cordiner has insisted that communications should never bog down in channels. A person in one division is expected to seek information from another division by calling "straight across the company" on the telephone.[11]

Systems Engineering Functions

Systems engineering is a prime example of an open-system method of organization. The traditional bureaucratic model is antagonistic to its operation, particularly in regard to its principles of unity of command, separation of functions, and lines of communication. An examination of the typical functions of systems engineering will make clear why an open-system type of organization is required:

1) Guide the advanced engineering effort toward forward objectives, and ensure that the various parts of the system will mesh when advance components are available.
2) Establish objectives and specifications for the system. This requires involvement in cost and marketing assumptions, as well as manufacturing feasibility and capacity planning.
3) Monitor performance against objectives throughout the "cradle to grave" sequence.
4) In the course of monitoring performance, identify problems and initiate corrective action to solve the problems.
5) Synthesize the information regarding the system and serve as the focal point for action and decision-making resulting from such information. Initiate switches to alternative courses of action if required.
6) Concur in final engineering approvals.
7) Advise higher management on the progress of the program.

Relationship to Other Types of Organizations

A function such as this fits easily into a project management type of organization. However, it is not so simple to adopt it in a more traditional form of organization. Following the concept of an open system, where a change affects in some manner all other parts of the organiza-

---

[11] John M. Pfiffner and Frank P. Sherwood, *Administrative Organization* (Englewood Cliffs, N.J.: Prentice-Hall, 1960), 303.

tion, a traditional form of organization could not receive a systems engineering function without considerable change in the interfacing organizations. This applies not only to the existing structure but to the "state of mind" of the organization as well. When unity of command, separation of functions, and strict adherence to hierarchical lines of communication are inherent, it is obvious that the systems engineering concept can introduce serious conflicts unless the total organization is prepared for change.

PROGRAM MANAGEMENT

As was stated, systems engineering fits easily into a program or project type of organization, but the traditional bureaucratic model is antagonistic to its operation. According to Johnson, Kast, and Rosenzweig "the program management concept has evolved from systems—engineering approaches employed to meet complex industrial- and military-product applications over a number of years. In general, program management includes the combination of systems engineering—the integration of the physical components of an assembly—and information systems—the establishment of a communications and informational network between the various functions whose performance is necessary for a successful product mission."[12]

Scientific and technological advances have led to increased specialization in men and organizations. These technological advances have led to the development of complex products. The traditional forms of organization have been hard pressed to provide the integration among functional components that is essential to the successful management of the resultant complex systems. This has led to the emergence of the systems concept in general and program management in particular.

Organizational Structure

Johnson, Kast, and Rosenzweig describe program management as the establishment of centralized management agencies whose primary responsibility is to provide overall integration on a systems basis of many diverse functional activities.[13] The centralized management agency, termed the program or project manager, generally is superimposed upon the functional organization as shown in Fig. 4-1.

The program management organization shown in Fig. 4-1 is simplified for discussion purposes. The basic organization is functional. There are three functional operating components (Engineering, Manufacturing, and Sales) and three staffs (Industrial Relations, Finance,

---

[12] Richard A. Johnson, Fremont E. Kast, and James E. Rosenzweig, *The Theory and Management of Systems* (New York: McGraw-Hill, 1967), 139.
[13] *Ibid.*

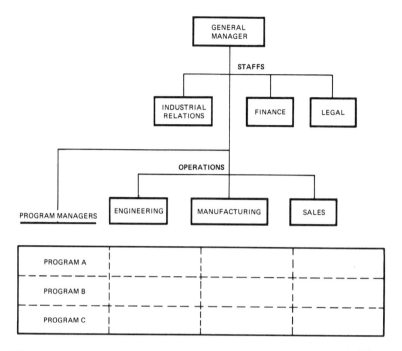

Fig. 4-1. Program management superimposed upon a functional organization.

and Legal). The organization is unusually large and is engaged in a number of complex projects. Each of the projects is assigned to a program manager, shown on the left side of the figure. The personnel in the three functional operating components are responsible administratively to their line supervisors. Like any line executive, the functional unit head is responsible for hiring, evaluating the performance of, and compensating his subordinates. The functional head is responsible for how and where the work is performed.

The Program Manager

The program manager is responsible for the overall planning, coordination, and the ultimate outcome of the program, sometimes called the product mission. The five functions necessary to successful mission accomplishment are perception of need, design, production, delivery, and utilization.

The special role of the program manager is described by David Cleland as follows:

> The project manager acts as a focal point for the concentration of attention on the major problems of the project. This concentration forces the channeling of major program considerations through an individual who

has the proper perspective to integrate relative matters of cost, time, technology, and total product compatibility. The project manager is personally involved in critical project decisions concerning organizational policy including: cost and cost estimating; schedules; product performance (quality, reliability); commitment of organizational resources; project tasking; trade-offs involving time, money, and performance; contract performance; and total production integration.[14]

In the example of program management discussed here, each program manager is a "lone operator." This is the usual case, though in some instances program managers are provided with limited staff support. In any event, it is obvious that the addition of program managers to the organization tends to create more complex relationships and to provide at least the potential for organizational and interpersonal conflict. For one thing, each functional specialist assigned to a program has two bosses—his functional head and his program manager. Authority and responsibility are not so well defined as in the straight functional organization, nor is there a clear-cut hierarchical relationship between the functional heads and the program managers. These need not be serious disadvantages, however, if there is a spirit of cooperation among the program managers and the functional heads on such matters as the allocation of personnel and the appraisal of performance. Conflicts that cannot be resolved can be referred, in our example, to the general manager.

There are, then, trade-offs between the purely functional organization and the program management organization. Program management is designed to overcome the weakness of the functional organization in providing effective coordination and integration over the many functions and specialists involved in any complex program, but program management tends to complicate organizational relationships and may diminish somewhat the performance of the specialized functional components over the broad range of programs.

Success and Failure

Program management occasionally does fail. According to Ivars Avots:

> The most common reasons for project management failure are: the basis for the project is not sound; the wrong man is appointed project manager; company management fails to provide enough support; task definitions are inadequate; management techniques are not appropriate; or project termination is not planned.[15]

---

[14] David I. Cleland, "Why Project Management?" *Business Horizons* (Winter, 1964), 83.

[15] Ivars Avots, "Why Does Project Management Fail?" *California Management Review* (Fall, 1969), 78.

For program management to be successful, judgment must be exercised with respect to its application, and planning must precede its implementation. Program management should be considered for one-time projects that are complex but well defined, such as development of a new product, installation of a computer system, or construction of a new facility. It should be considered when there is a convergence of a number of complex projects, or one extremely large and complex project, that may be too much for the existing organization to assimilate. The advantage is that such complex projects can be carried out with minimum disruption to the organization.

RHOCHREMATICS

The material flow process is one of the systems within a manufacturing operation. The material flow system spans the entire operation —from the input of raw materials to the distribution of finished products to the ultimate consumer. The term *rhochrematics* is used in referring to this system. Rhochrematics has been defined by Johnson, Kast, and Rosenzweig as:

> . . . the science of managing material flow, embracing the basic functions of producing and marketing as an integrated system, and involving the selection of the most effective combination of sub-functions such as transporting, processing, handling, storing, and distributing goods.[16]

Organizational Interrelationships

There are innumerable and intricate interrelationships among the many functions of the organization that in many ways affect the material flow process. Production schedules affect both the prices the purchasing activity pays for production parts and materials and the modes of transportation the traffic activity selects for the parts and materials. The mode of transportation and in-plant material handling requirements affect packaging of incoming materials, and advertising and product identity considerations affect the packaging of finished products for the customer. Sales forecasts by market area affect production scheduling and transportation patterns from the plants. The economies of relatively long production runs influence finished product inventories and the distribution of finished products through warehouses, wholesalers, and retailers.

Product Variety. There has been a trend over the past several decades toward increased product variety and this, in turn, has expanded geometrically the problems associated with effectively

---

[16] Johnson, Kast, and Rosenzweig, *op. cit.*

managing the production and distribution of goods. This increased product variety results from a shift in emphasis in most companies during the past several decades from a manufacturing orientation to a marketing orientation and an attendant concern with the needs and likes of customers, increased use of a range of products as a sales promotional tool, and greater market segmentation as the size of markets grows and market researchers discover the preferences of submarkets. The production and distribution of this increased variety of products involves anticipating demand, locating inventories on a geographic basis, maintaining adequate stocks, controlling inventories, and planning production. All of this underscores the growing importance of rhochrematics—a systematic and integrated approach to the total material flow system.

Coordination and Change. As in the case of program management and task forces, the application of the systems concept to the material flow process stems from the need to coordinate the various elements of a system that cuts across the traditional lines of the functional organization. Unfortunately, many activities that are part of the material flow process analyze problems and make decisions with little regard for the effects of these decisions on other activities. As a result, decisions are made that may optimize a segment of the flow process but not the system as a whole. This suboptimization, or emphasis on a segment rather than the whole, may not be so much a matter of self-interest on the part of middle management as inability to see clearly the full scope and complexity of the system.

Three alternatives for integrating change brought about by new technology into the organization were described by Frank Jasinski as follows:

1) Changing the technology to conform with the existing organizational structure.
2) Changing the organization so as to define and formalize the relationships required by the technology.
3) Maintaining both the existing organization and the existing technology, but introducing mechanisms to reduce or minimize the discrepancies between the two.[17]

Implementation of the Rhochrematics Concept

The essential first step in dealing with the material flow process on a systems basis is for top management to be convinced of the value of the total systems approach and to support its implementation. This

---

[17] Frank J. Jasinski, "Adapting Organization to New Technology," *Harvard Business Review* (January–February, 1959), 80.

support is needed because there likely will be a need for changes in policy, practices, organization, and attitudes. Top management support is needed to overcome the natural barriers that exist between specialized functional areas, particularly between the production and marketing organizations, that must coordinate their natural flow activities if the systems approach is to be effective.

Several organizational actions can be taken to facilitate the systems approach to material flow. One such action is to set up an operations research group responsible for bringing to bear on the material flow system all the management science techniques that are available. From an organizational standpoint, it would be advisable to establish the research group as a staff activity because, as we have seen, its work should encompass the entire system from raw material stage through production of finished goods and the flow of the finished goods to the final consumer.

Another organizational action that can be taken is to group together many of the material flow functional components, if not centrally, at least within the production and marketing areas. An example of such a grouping in the production area would be consolidating purchasing, traffic, production control, and perhaps production scheduling under a materials manager. According to Dean Ammer, "this change is easy to make and yields substantial benefits: forced cooperation between purchasing and production control; tighter inventory control; efficiency in coordination; and better communication."[18] Ammer states that managements that adopt a systems approach will prefer some such form of materials or supply organization since it forms a natural subsystem with fairly well-defined objectives and channels of communication.

The materials organization in production could then coordinate its activities with a similar grouping on the marketing side, such as sales forecasting, order processing, and physical distribution. Committees may also be used to assist in the coordination of the material flow system. For example, a scheduling committee can be established to bring together representatives from the various activities that are both affected by and can contribute to the scheduling process.

TASK FORCES

A specialized type of organization that is being used to an increasing extent is the task force. Looking ahead into the 1970s, Courtney Brown, formerly dean of the Graduate School of Business, Columbia

---

[18] "Materials Management as a Profit Center," *Harvard Business Review* (January-February, 1969), 73–75.

University, believes businesses will organize "constellations of task forces" that will solve one problem and then move to another, crossing traditional functional lines as they operate.

The task force or team is formed to accomplish a particular objective or purpose. The task force members usually are selected from various components and specialized functional areas within the organization, although certain members may be hired from the outside. The makeup of the team depends upon the particular nature of the task force's mission. Since the task force is set up to accomplish a specific mission, its life span, like that of the program or project manager organization, is the time required to complete the mission. Then each member of the task force returns to his regular position or perhaps becomes a member of another task force constituted to accomplish another mission.

Task Force Uses

Before considering a number of factors relating to task force organization and operation, let us first examine some situations in which task forces have been or can be employed:

1) A company may plan to submit a bid for the design, development, and manufacture of a relatively complex product. A task force may be established to develop all facets of the bid. Such a task force might be made up of team members from finance, purchasing, engineering, manufacturing, material control, legal staff, and personnel. Should the contract be received, the planning team can then form the nucleus of the operating organization.

2) Particular problems may arise with respect to scheduling of production and the control of material inventories. A task force in this case would be set up to define the specific problems and develop recommendations for resolving them. This team, in all likelihood, would include representatives from production scheduling, production control, purchasing, traffic, finance, and systems.

3) In a somewhat narrower context, a task force may be established to select a site for a new plant. The functional specialties that would be represented on such a task force would include, among other, traffic, labor relations, plant engineering, purchasing, finance, and public affairs.

The Task Force as a Temporary Integrative System

The task force, like program management, is a specialized way of integrating the efforts of various technical specialists in the resolution of complex problems or in the accomplishment of tasks that are broadly based and cross many of the traditional functional areas. Problems and tasks seldom can or should be viewed in the narrow context of any one function such as engineering, production, or marketing. The systems concept or view is essential if all relevant factors and effects are to be properly analyzed and evaluated. The task force is a type of systems approach to a specific problem or task.

The task force is a *temporary* system. Warren Bennis characterizes the current era as the "temporary society" and, in order to help with the rapid changes in the environment, temporary systems are a necessity in an organization. Bennis writes:

> The key word is "temporary." There will be adaptive, readily changing temporary systems. These will be task forces organized around problems to be solved by groups of relative strangers with diverse professional skills. . . . The tasks of the organization will be technical, complicated, and unprogrammed. They will rely on intellect instead of muscle. And they will be too complicated for one person to comprehend, to say nothing of control. Essentially, they will call for the collaboration of specialists in a project or team form of organization.[19]

The unprogramed and temporary nature of the tasks of the organization leads to the concept of "floating task forces" or "constellations of task forces" mentioned earlier. Task forces are formed and disbanded as various needs arise. Several task forces may operate at any one time, that is, as "constellations." Certain task forces may move from one problem to the next, that is, "float." Task forces do not displace or replace the existing organization. They are superimposed on the traditional, hierarchical organization structure.

The flexibility that the task force brings to the base organization structure also can be extended through the "structural fluidity" of the membership of the task force itself. In an article entitled "Management by Task Force" Wickesberg and Cronin make this point:

> Structural fluidity is the theme for any task force. The heart of the concept rests in the ability to add new members when their potential contribution is high and to subtract members from the core group when specific contributions have been secured and no further need of these particular talents is foreseen in the immediate future. In this way, the team approach permits rapid adjustment to changing demands and requirements. It provides the means whereby a company can take prompt and maximum advantage of significant changes or modifications in mission, technology, and market requirements. Diverse technical individuals and

---

[19] "Organization Change—Operating in a Temporary Society," *Innovation* (May, 1969).

units are tied together by a common purpose. Sense of accomplishment is achieved as results, tangible results, accumulate from team efforts.[20]

Flexibility between the "planning" and "doing" of a project can be attained by shifting the strength of team membership from the competent and experienced planners in the early stages to the operating types as the project moves into the "doing" stage.

Crucial Factors

A number of factors are crucial to the success of task force organization. First is a clear definition of the task itself—the specific objective that the task force is to achieve. Related to this is the need for a clear delineation of the authority and responsibility of the task force manager and his team members. The unique role of the task force manager is such that considerable thought must be given to selecting the best possible manager for the position.

The task force manager generally is responsible for directing a high proportion of professional people from various technical specialties and from differing levels of the organization. As stated earlier, the essential tie between planning and doing in knowledge work must be understood and properly managed by the task force manager. The task force manager must be able to deal with the conflict that inevitably will arise as the project progresses through its various stages, and he must be adept at making cost-time-effectiveness decisions for the good of the project. As Paul Gaddis sees it, the temporary life of the task force constitutes another challenge to the task force manager:

> . . . the project manager must trust his corporate management, implicitly in most cases, to provide him and his forces with continuity of work on successive projects. Needless to say, the record of top management in achieving this continuity will affect the peace of mind, if not the performance, of the project manager and his entire staff.[21]

As the role of the task force manager is unique, so also Bennis sees the role of the executive or "manager of task force managers" as changing:

> The executive becomes coordinator or "linking pin" between various task forces. He must be a man who speaks the polyglot jargon of research, with skills to relay information and mediate between groups. People will be evaluated not according to rank but according to skill and professional training.[22]

---

[20] A. K. Wickesberg and T. C. Cronin, "Management by Task Force," *Harvard Business Review* (November-December, 1962), 113.

[21] Paul O. Gaddis, "The Project Manager," *Harvard Business Review* (May–June, 1959), 91.

[22] Bennis, *op. cit.*

COMMITTEES

There is no more controversial organizational device than the committee. Critics of committees are legion. "A camel is a horse designed by a committee" is one of the more popular critical remarks, but there are others just as poignant. Consider, for example, "the most effective committee size is three with one member out of town and the other home sick in bed." In fairness to the committee form of organization, however, it should be understood that these are not valid criticisms of committees per se, but criticism of committees that are misused or ineffective.

Committees are a specialized type of organization in the sense that they are established to fulfill a specific purpose or objective. Committees also are specialized in the sense that they may be used extensively by one company and hardly at all by another company comparable in size, product, and geographic dispersion.

Discussion here will be limited to the various types of committees and the use which is made of them. In general, however, it can be said that committees are formed for much the same reason as the other specialized organizations that have been discussed—to provide a means of integrating the various functional specialties of an organization.

Types of Committees

One distinction in types of committees is in level. At the top is the board of directors, which is the legally constituted governing body of a corporation. The board may delegate specific authority to special and permanent committees of the board. At the corporate level, the president and other top executives may establish committees to assist them in the performance of their duties. For example, a manufacturing committee may be established to advise on manufacturing problems and to assist in formulating policy. At the division level, a general manager may form an operating committee primarily as a means of communication on important problems, plans, and objectives. At the plant level, the plant manager may hold daily operating meetings which are, by their very nature, committee meetings.

Another distinction in the type of committee is in its authority. Some make decisions, others are advisory, and others are formed purely to receive information. A committee that has authority to make decisions affecting subordinates responsible to it is termed a plural executive and is a line committee. A committee that serves in an advisory capacity is a staff committee.

Committees may also be formal or informal. A committee that is established as part of the organization structure and has specific, ongoing responsibilities is a formal committee. One formed to help resolve a particular problem is an informal or ad hoc committee that passes out of existence when the problem is resolved, similar to a task force.

Advantages

The committee form of organization, properly managed, has a number of strengths. A problem may require coordination and the application of a variety of specialized knowledge areas such as engineering, production, and sales. A committee facilitates integration of varying viewpoints and may provide more balanced and reliable judgments. As stated earlier, committees can serve as an effective means of solving the problem of coordinating among separate but interrelated functional activities. Committees permit wider participation in decision making and can, if properly directed, be used to motivate managers and promote group rather than individual effort.

Example

An example of the use of committees at the operating level is provided by a large food company that has used a Junior Board of Directors since the early 1930s. This board is composed of assistant department managers and selected other lower-level personnel. The purpose of the board is not to supplant the judgment of the more mature managers, but to provide the company's senior executives with new ideas. In addition to the junior board, this company has a number of functionally constituted boards, including a production (factory) board.

ZONE MANAGEMENT

A specialized organizational arrangement having some application in manufacturing at the plant level is zone management. This section first describes how zone management differs from the more typical plant organizational alignment. Next are discussed the objectives of zone management and the factors that should be evaluated when deciding whether to use a zone management organization rather than the more typical alignment.

The "typical" or standard plant organization is shown in Fig. 4-2. The plant staff departments (the plant controller and the Industrial Relations Department) report directly to the plant manager as do those more technically oriented departments that support production on a plant-wide basis (such as the Material Department and the Manufacturing Engineering Department). In this example, the Plant Engineering Department and the Tool Maintenance Department report to the production manager and have plant-wide responsibility in their functional specialties. Each production supervisor under the production manager (superintendents, general foremen, and foremen) is responsi-

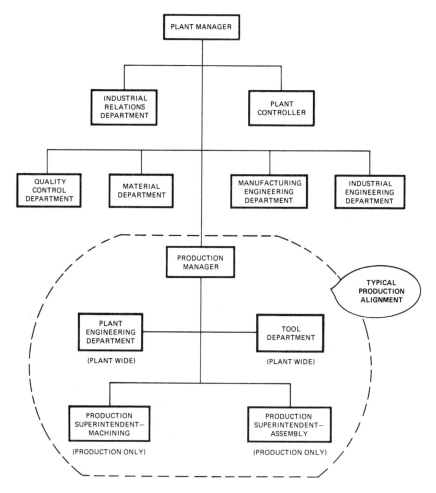

Fig. 4-2. Typical plant organization.

ble solely for supervising the production work force in a particular part of the plant operation.

The same plant organized along zone management lines is shown in Fig. 4-3. The plant is divided into three zones, and a zone manager is made responsible for each zone. In addition to having responsibility for production operations, each zone manager is also responsible for plant engineering and tool maintenance within his zone. The plant-wide Plant Engineering and Tool Maintenance departments do not exist in the zone management organization; these responsibilities are divided among the three zone managers.

The essential difference between the two alignments described

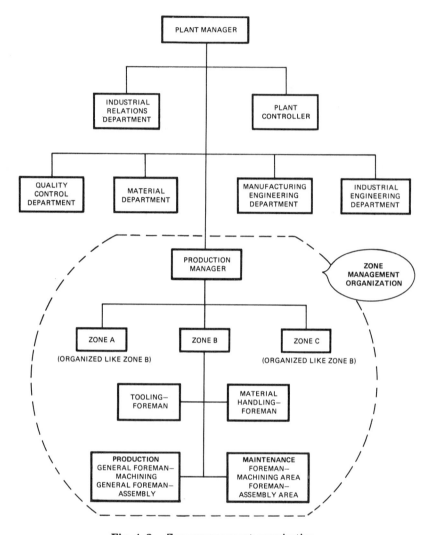

Fig. 4-3. Zone management organization.

above is the organizational level which is responsible for production operations and for functions that directly support production. In the typical organization the production manager is responsible; in the zone management organization the next lower level is responsible. That is, the zone managers are responsible in their respective geographic areas.

Zone management constitutes a move away from the purely functional organization (activities grouped on the basis of specialized technical skills) to the "product" or "purpose" type of organization (activities necessary to accomplish a purpose or produce a product are grouped together under the supervision of one person).

The objective of the zone management organization is to divide the management task under the plant manager and to reduce, to some extent, the coordination required among functional specialties. Each of the zone managers is responsible for production in his area and, unlike the production superintendent in the typical organization, has control over many of the tools (support services) directly affecting production. Responsibility is pinpointed to a greater degree. Healthy competition can develop among the zone managers, particularly if their responsibilities are relatively comparable. The zone managers get broader experience and, other things being equal, should become better qualified for the position of plant manager than the more specialized heads of the various functional activities in the typical organization.

There are a number of points to be evaluated when considering a change to zone management. For one thing, the typical functional organization makes maximum, and probably more economical, use of technical skills, machinery, and equipment. It may not be feasible, for example, to divide all tool maintenance, especially major work, among the tool activities in each of the zone organizations.

As in any situation in which there is a choice to be made between two or more organizational alternatives, careful consideration needs to be given to the advantages and disadvantages of each alternative. There are always trade-offs. Given the right size of plant, the appropriate product mix, and management personnel who are both technically qualified and sufficiently adaptable, zone management has much to offer.

PLANNING

Planning has been a recognized function of management since the French industrialist, Henri Fayol, first referred to planning as one of the five key functions of managing. Fayol saw planning as a process: "The plan of action is, at one and the same time, the result envisaged, the line of action to be followed, the stages to go through, and the methods to use."[23]

Other traditional organization scholars, in setting forth their various *principles* of management, also included planning as a vital element of the management process. Koontz and O'Donnell follow Fayol's basic definition when they describe planning as: "An intellectual process, the

---

[23] Fayol's five functions of managing were planning, organizing, command, coordination, and control. Henri Fayol, *General and Industrial Management* (London: Sir Isaac Pitman & Sons, 1949), Chap. V.

conscious determination of courses of action, the basing of decision on purpose, facts, and considered estimates."[24]

Planning is a function of all levels of management, from the top of a multi-division corporation down to a foreman in a plant. Brian Scott presents a good description of the different types of plans generally found in business:

1) *Goals:* statements of the primary purposes for which the firm (or a component part of it) is being operated.
2) *Policies:* understandings (written, oral, or implicit) designed to set perimeters as guides to the thinking and action of subordinates within an organization.
3) *Budgets:* statements of expected quantitative results for some future period.
4) *Procedures:* statements which provide details of the way in which specific plans are to be accomplished.[25]

As we have seen, planning has for over fifty years been considered a necessary function of business. In the 1970s, however, planning will be an even more necessary part of management if a firm is to survive. Important environmental and technological developments are occurring so rapidly, and the elements of a business enterprise are so complex and costly, that planning, particularly long-range planning, must be a continuous process if a firm is to remain competitive.

Planning itself is an extremely complex subject since it, too, requires consideration of the entire system of which an organization is a part. The planning process will not be covered here, but some *organizational* aspects of planning will be discussed.

A basic organization question on which all managers must make a decision concerns the relationship of "planning" to "doing." There is no consensus, even today, concerning the relative merits of the two schools of thought: Should "planning" be performed by the same persons responsible for "doing," or should they be two separate tasks performed by different people. Until an organization resolves this question to its satisfaction the organizational arrangements for planning cannot be determined.

The case for separating planning and doing was forcibly expressed by Taylor:

All of the planning which under the old system was done by the workman, as a result of his personal experience, must of necessity under the new

---

[24] Harold Koontz and Cyril O'Donnell, *Principles of Management,* 4th ed. (New York: McGraw-Hill, 1968), 42.
[25] Brian W. Scott, *Long-Range Planning in American Industry* (New York: American Management Association, 1965), 23.

system be done by the management in accordance with the laws of the science. Because even if workman were well suited to the development and use of scientific data, it would be physically impossible for him to work at his machine and at a desk at the same time. *It is also clear that in most cases one type of man is needed to plan ahead and an entirely different type to execute the work.*[26]

While Taylor was writing in terms of the production worker, his ideas have been extended to all types of operating management by later writers.

The opposite view is held by equally distinguished scholars. In a recent paper, Peter Drucker discusses planning in terms of productivity of the worker:

. . . to make knowledge productive will bring about changes in job structure, careers, and organizations as drastic as those which resulted in the factory from the application of scientific management to manual work. The entrance job will, above all, have to be changed drastically to enable the knowledge worker to become productive. For it is abundantly clear that knowledge cannot be productive unless the worker finds out who he himself is, what kind of work he is fitted for, and how he works best.

In other words, there can be no divorce of *planning* from *doing* in knowledge work. On the contrary, the knowledge worker must be able to plan himself; and this the present entrance jobs, by and large, do not make possible. They are based on the assumption—valid for manual work but quite inappropriate to knowledge work—that anyone can objectively determine the "one best way" for any kind of work. For knowledge work, this is simply not true. There may be one best way, but it is heavily conditioned by the individual and is not entirely determined by physical (or even mental) characteristics of the job. It is temperamental as well.[27]

The answer to this dilemma is probably the answer for so many other organizational questions—it depends on the situation. It is possible, for example, that in a particular company a significant number of managers are not competent to plan but are only fitted for "doing." One thing is clear, however. Planning must include both decision making and fact finding. Much of the intelligence about environmental changes and reactions to organizational programs is obtainable only by the "doers." If the decision-making aspect of planning is separated from the fact-finding aspect, there certainly must be a coordinating organization that ensures a full exchange of views and information between the two parts.

---

[26] Taylor, *op. cit.*

[27] Peter F. Drucker, "Management's New Role," *Harvard Business Review* (November–December, 1969), 53.

Katz and Kahn suggest that planning can be separate from doing, but that decision-making and fact-finding functions still should not be combined:

> Programmed planning can be implemented through two auxiliary or staff functions, one to develop specific alternative courses of action for anticipated changes in the environment, the other to gather intelligence about environmental changes and reactions to organizational programs. Both these functions are generally combined in a single staff group, to the great neglect of the intelligence function. Guesswork replaces exact knowledge of environmental trends.[28]

Following the open-system philosophy, there appears to be a necessity for some centralization of the planning function. Further, there are many valid reasons for active participation in and support of the planning function by top management. At the same time, planning often requires certain information and decisions to be kept confidential at least to the point of limiting the number of people involved. These considerations suggest that planning will be ineffective on a highly decentralized basis.

In the light of the foregoing expressions of divergent thinking we propose a planning organization based on the open-system concept which centralizes the *coordination* of planning activities but that makes use of the "doers" as a committee or task force to contribute information and assist in its analysis and interpretation. Decisions must necessarily be made by top management, but the "doers" should be listened to and given a chance to react to the decisions before they are finalized.

COORDINATION CONCEPTS

Throughout much of the previous discussion in this chapter we have made references to coordination. In a large sense coordination is what organization is all about.

Exponents of traditional organization have provided us with several alternatives in regard to structuring our organizations. For example, Luther Gulick offers four alternatives for grouping sub-organizations:

1) By common purpose to the overall organization
2) By common process
3) By type of clientele
4) By geographic area.[29]

---

[28] Katz and Kahn, *op. cit.*

[29] Luther Gulick and Leland Urwick, eds., *Papers on the Science of Administration* (New York: Institute of Public Administration, 1937).

Gulick would have us organize according to the alternative which applies to our situation. In modern complex organizations, however, all of these bases are important. If we were to organize according to geographic area, for example, we often find common processes required in each area. Also, in previous pages, we have emphasized the importance of communication flow in the decision process to the particular form of organization structure.

Such a multi-dimensional view of the interrelating pieces of an organization brings out the necessity for devising coordinative processes. It also indicates the numerous opportunities for costly inefficiencies if we fail to coordinate properly. This multi-dimensional view is another example of the recognition of the open-system concept in organizations. The almost infinite number of variables to be considered leads naturally to a consideration of the heuristic approach of March and Simon, which they term "satisficing."[30]

The idea of satisficing recognizes the humanly impossible task of pursuing every alternative before selecting the best one (maximizing) and instead proposes to select an alternative that will do the job required without continuing to search for the best alternative. As March and Simon put it, we should search through the haystack to find a needle that is sharp enough to sew, without trying to find the sharpest one in the whole haystack.

Thompson presents the basic ideas of March and Simon in a particularly understandable way.[31] He offers three forms of coordination for different situations:

1) *Coordination by standardization.* This involves prescribing rules and standard operating procedures for all similar components within the organization. Obviously, this programed kind of coordination is suited primarily for situations that are relatively stable and repetitive, or for components that have similar functions but are not directly interrelated, such as sales offices organized by geographic area.

2) *Coordination by plan.* This involves the establishment of programing and timing schedules linking interrelated components. It is particularly suited to organizations that are departmentalized by process, such as relating procurement components, parts plants, and assembly plants. Here the flow is sequential, with one component dependent upon the performance of another component before it can serve the third component in the process.

3) *Coordination by mutual adjustment.* This involves the exchange of "feedback" between interrelated components and is best used

---

[30] James G. March and Herbert A. Simon, *Organizations* (New York: John Wiley & Sons, 1958).
[31] Thompson, *Organizations in Action,* 56.

when there is a two-way relationship between components, such as the plant maintenance department and the production department. The maintenance department is dependent upon the production department for maintenance assignments, and the production department is dependent upon the maintenance department for keeping its equipment operable.

Of these three forms of coordination, coordination by standardization is the least costly, while coordination by mutual adjustment is the most costly. It would seem desirable, then, to group components in a manner that allows coordination by standardization if possible. Often this is not possible, so more costly coordination forms must be used. It becomes evident, however, that careful consideration should be given to the organizational structure so that components are positioned in the structure to facilitate the implementation of plans or mutual adjustment.

It is this kind of consideration that has developed the materials management concept, whereby all the functions related to the materials flow, i.e., purchasing, warehousing, traffic, shipping and receiving, materials handling, material follow-up, etc., are grouped into one department in some companies. In other companies, however, we may find that shipping is related more closely to the production component than to the procurement function. In this case it may be advisable to place shipping under production rather than materials management in order to make use of the least costly form of coordination.

Bringing together separate but interrelated functions, such as under the materials management concept, introduces an additional level of management which acts as a resolver of conflicts between the separate functions.

Harold Leavitt points out the diminishing role of classic authority in the design of organization structure.[32] Traditional organization is influenced by the military view of authority, but modern organization practice has shown that control can be maintained with much less use of this type of authority. The authority role is being replaced by the roles of communications and coordination, and organizational structures are reflecting this change in thinking. Organizing around work flow to facilitate communication and coordination is antagonistic to the traditional view of organizing around lines of authority.

Horizontal communication—disregarding hierarchical lines of authority—is more and more prevalent in our organizations. A dramatic example of this is presented by Melville Dalton in his report of

---

[32] Harold J. Leavitt, *Managerial Psychology* (Chicago: The University of Chicago Press, 1964), 381.

his study of an industrial firm which he gives the fictional title of Milo Fractionating Center.[33] Dalton shows two organization charts for Milo—one based on formal authority relationships and one based on communication and informal influence. The two charts bear almost no resemblance.

Likert introduces a means of horizontal communication and coordination in his "linking-pin" concept, whereby each component is linked to the total organization by means of an overlapping structure.[34]

No one has devised a formula of coordination for universal use. An effective approach depends upon many variables. Coordination is not without cost, but there can be many gains. We must select the form of coordination that results in overall gain. Generally speaking, the simple creation of an add-on organization to coordinate is not productive. It is generally more productive to look into the structure itself, analyze the work flow and communications channels, and adjust the structure to this reality.

SUMMARY

The common characteristic appearing throughout the various types of organization considered in this chapter is that of coordination. These specialized types recognize differing needs to bring together at some point two or more elements.

Coordination costs money, but it saves money, too. Through systems engineering and program management it is possible to coordinate highly complex systems without increasing the levels of management. Implementation of the concept of rhochrematics permits economy of effort through the recognition that common purpose is as important as common function in attaining an objective. Through the use of task forces and committees purpose is recognized as being as important as function in determining the division of labor. Zone management also deviates from the strictly functional approach.

These techniques make use of the open systems viewpoint, which can be helpful in solving the operational problems of efficiency and effectiveness through organizational means. This viewpoint enables us to focus on the *macro* approach to objectives, whereby duplication of effort can often be eliminated in separate parts of the organization.

---

[33] Melville Dalton, *Men Who Manage* (New York: John Wiley & Sons, 1959).
[34] Likert, *New Patterns of Management.*

chapter 5

organizational
documentation

THE HISTORIC VIEW of organizational documentation stresses charts and position descriptions. The perspective taken here is that the entire management process and its underlying structure or framework is the proper scope of organizational documentation. There is no single type of documentation, nor any single manual, which can cover such a wide area. And therefore the subject is treated as a set of basic elements which can be combined as needed to form an integrated and complete body of documentation.

The first volume of this management series pointed out that there are three major elements existing in any organization:

1) Personnel
2) The management process
3) The operating structure or framework in which personnel function. [1]

Organizational documentation has historically communicated all three, although the stress has been primarily on organizational staff, reporting relationships, and job responsibilities. These are, however, only a small part of the three areas enumerated above. Moreover, these traditional areas may be viewed as the "static" element whereas the dynamic aspect of organization—the process of task accomplishment—is emerging as the area in which documentation can ultimately make the greatest contribution. The underlying causes of this change transcend manufacturing, even the whole of business. They stem from the accelerating rate of change in the environment within which

---

[1] Ivan R. Vernon, ed., *Introduction to Manufacturing Management* (Dearborn, Mich.: Society of Manufacturing Engineers, 1969), 11.

commercial organizations operate, the necessity for better means of communication and faster learning, and the simple fact that no business can afford to face each decision by reexamining its basic policies at the highest corporate levels.

In today's complex environment documentation is essential to define and communicate the major elements of the organization and thereby improve each individual's contribution to the major tasks of the business. Through accurate documentation the relationships and interactions of organizational elements may be comprehended more easily. The interaction of organizational elements is shown in Fig. 5-1.

Fig. 5-1.   The interaction of organizational elements.

PURPOSE AND OBJECTIVES

Effective documentation starts with a need to communicate and the realization that as an organization grows it must perpetuate sound policies and practices, define the areas of responsibilities, authority, and reporting relationships of personnel, and ultimately address the principal operational tasks.

Present Attitudes and Practices

Presently, organizational documentation is usually done on a "just enough to get by" basis. It is probably accurate to say that no area of organizational work receives less professional attention than formal communication. The reason is that complete organizational work is laborious and necessitates a stringent commitment, often more specific than management is really willing to make. In addition, the "payoff" is intangible, and delay of organizational documentation does not usually produce immediate crises.

Typically, top management in any organization believes that authority, responsibility and, in fact, the entire management process are clearly stated and generally understood, while the lower levels think that clarification is needed. As a result, higher levels of management frequently believe organizational documentation is unneeded, while lower levels would like to see better clarification of their roles. In addition, many managers do not want excessive restrictions placed upon their actions by the levels above. Therefore, upward views may differ greatly depending on whether the viewer prefers a structured and well-defined environment or a loose organization with maximum latitude and little predetermined responsibility or guidance. Lastly, documentation, to many, means bureaucracy, particularly the "rules" that come from several levels above which often appear without warning, understanding, or justification.

Future Needs

The underlying question is whether increased communication on the subject of organization is essential to, or at least, contributory to, improved manufacturing management. Every organization has a modus operandi, and there exists an extensive body of knowledge about it—in the minds of the more experienced members. The communication process is, therefore, a matter of disseminating this knowledge and also providing a means for change that is fast, clear, and uniform. The need for improving communication and providing direct access to the lore of business operations is greater today than ever before. The typical undisciplined, on-the-job training approach will surely have to be supplemented with documentation in matters unique to the business that are not covered by external publications such as books and articles.

Thirteen basic principles of organization have been cited as essential.[2] Of these, the following five depend on the effectiveness of documentation and communication:

1) Clearly understood objectives
2) Unambiguous assignment of managerial duties and responsibilities
3) Precise statements of authority
4) Plainly stated chain of command
5) Proper delegation of authority.

---

[2] *Ibid.*, 18.

If, in fact, management has not communicated these five points to the satisfaction of the organization below, this failure may imply that management is not sufficiently committed to them.

While undeniably important, these items are largely static in that they are seen in terms of individual jobs. As the manufacturing organization becomes more complex, as a result of greater size, increased interaction, or wider scope of responsibility, it can no longer be viewed merely as a static structure defined by individual jobs and the reporting hierarchy. An organization must be dynamic and concerned with accomplishing tasks. It is in these terms that the organization can most effectively be studied and described. Unlike the first aspect of organizational documentation, which is focused on structure, responsibilities, policies, and objectives, the second or dynamic aspect addresses the actions, ground rules, and responsibilities relevant to the activity.

As industry grows and becomes more integrated, the dynamic task-oriented description of responsibility will be an important and often necessary aspect of documentation (for example, in starting up a new plant or transferring a major product to another location). That is, it will be insufficient for manufacturing management merely to be skilled in the basic technical aspects of manufacturing (e.g., manufacturing engineering); a thorough understanding of the total interaction will also be required. An interesting analogy can be made with a football team. Although each player is skilled in his particular position, the team would not be successful without plays that are carefully worked out and practiced. In fact, the primary emphasis in training the team is perfecting the interaction of the players.

The dynamic and static aspects of organizational documentation are shown in Fig. 5-2. Vertically the organization is viewed in terms of position responsibilities and policies. Horizontally it is depicted as a series of tasks made up of relevant responsibilities and policies. In addition, the task view adds the dimension of time and interactions not easily visible from the static view.

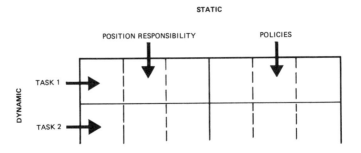

Fig. 5-2. Dynamic and static matrix of documentation.

Acceptance of Documentation

Not every manufacturing organization is ready to accept and utilize a wide range of documentation even though the need is there. To be sure, announcements of important changes in personnel or reorganizations and a new set of charts are universally interesting, even intriguing. These documents do not guide or control individuals, however; they only state who and where the personnel are. Other areas of documentation aim at guiding and directing people or establishing and protecting a policy. When they are told how to act, many of the very best managers will resist regardless of the quality of the guidance. As in accepting any control, motivation to want it—recognition that it is needed and helpful—is essential.

The support that management gives will markedly affect the value of documentation. People will sense fairly quickly whether those who issue documents really believe the things that are said or have mindlessly subscribed to pleasant sounding platitudes. This support must start at the top!

Support, or lack of it, can show up in many subtle ways, but once credibility becomes doubtful organizational members will soon disregard the guidelines. A common example is for a manager to bury a position description in the bottom drawer and *then* decide what role the current occupant of the particular position is to perform. This is such a frequent behavior pattern that most people in manufacturing (and other fields as well) have experienced it at least once, if not many times. A more serious situation exists when top management either disregards the policies, principles, and responsibilities it supposedly fostered or does not even appear to know them. In such an environment a general approach to documentation is probably without value, and effort would be better spent on solving this problem or on selected items. These are items which are either free from the credibility problem (e.g., organization charts) or in direct fulfillment of policies that the manager of the effected area will actively support.

Before implementing any new documentation, it is essential to know where support exists and whether it is sufficient to gain total acceptance. (Here is meant support for the medium of communication apart from the message. An active disagreement on the latter is often a sign of involvement and interest.) One might hypothesize a plant in which there were no position guides and considerable problems of responsibility among basic functional departments, for example, among the Industrial Engineering, Production Control, and Assembly and Testing departments. To initiate position guides as a means of solving the responsibility problem would normally require support from the plant manager or from the managers of the subordinate functions. There are, of course, occasions when it is desirable for a staff area or a line manager to create or demonstrate a type of documentation, in an effort to sell it, without any prior support.

Procedures Versus Organizational Documentation

Everybody has seen, read, tried to follow, and finally laughed at a procedural memorandum or instruction both in and out of business. This kind of communication is characterized by the intent to eliminate judgment on the part of the follower. A pure procedure tells how to do something. Of necessity, a business procedure will contain responsibility assignments of a very specific nature which are usually "how" oriented and do not address total activity or accountability. Organizational documentation as covered here does not include procedures. One must be wary, however, for the writers of procedures rarely have a broad management perspective and may easily end up defining organization responsibilities by assignment of actions. This may be contradictory to fundamental assignments already worked out. Worse yet, many managers consider all documentation, other than organization charts, "procedures." It is reasonably safe to assume that they also think "management" does not need procedures. In this case, the best approach is to stress the differences between them and the importance of keeping procedures separate from organizational documentation. Since there is no absolute definition to separate the two, each organization must arrive at its own criteria, police itself accordingly, and be agile at defending distinctions.

How Much Documentation?

Documentation is not an end objective of a manufacturing firm. It is doubtful, however, that anything but the smallest organization could do without some written delineation of responsibilities. The real challenge is how much and what type of documentation is appropriate for a specific organization. Ideally, the documentation "system" should contribute to achieving those objectives of the business which could not be achieved as well without the documentation. The prerequisites for achieving these objectives can be stated in the form of desirable or necessary conditions, and the extent to which they are met then becomes the basis for documentation. Following is a sample of conditions which a typical organization would want to foster:

1) Sufficient knowledge of "who's who" and of the overall organizational structure to communicate efficiently. (Organizational documentation covers this area in several ways, charts, directories, and announcements, for example.)

2) Maximum delegation of authority consistent with meeting job performance. (Lack of delegation may arise from failure to inform people clearly that the task is theirs or from unwillingness to delegate because it is believed that the lower level does not have the knowledge or capability. Both situations will respond to documentation.)

3) Effective execution of jobs coupled with a feeling of confidence in position responsibilities. (This directly relates to position descriptions and to general task-oriented guidelines.)

4) Consistent application of policies, principles, or common activities. (Documentation transmits decisions made in advance or guidelines to be used in making decisions.)

5) Effective communication of "permanent" directives. (Verbal communication is not always effective as a substitute for documentation; memos are not much better: they get lost, filed away, are not updated as times change, and may not have adequate distribution.)

6) Minimum number of unresolved questions of responsibility. (In any large organization there are responsibilities which nobody wants or which the only person capable of handling is reluctant to accept. In addition, it is not unusual to find tasks which are continually being debated and reinterpreted. Organizational documentation serves the purpose of recording such understandings once they are hammered out.)

7) Providing the means for people new in their positions or in the organization to educate themselves in their area of responsibility. (Complete organizational documentation, as depicted in this chapter, can provide a significant body of educational material.)

DOCUMENTS

One of the few *musts* in documentation is that each type of document must adhere to a consistent objective or subject area. Uncertainty of purpose or misuse of the media leads to confusion, conflict, and questioning among the users. Before discussing the specific documents, we will look at the primary *messages*. It should be understood that several documents may be needed to cover an area or that on occasion two subject areas can be combined in one document without confusion.

Basic Areas

Policies, Objectives, Beliefs, Philosophies, and Missions. This covers a large set of fundamental principles which guide the business. Typically they would transcend manufacturing and apply at the top level of the corporation or at a level where profit and loss is determined—a subsidiary or division encompassing sales, engineering, and manufacturing. There is good reason, however, for manufacturing to have some of its own policies.

Management Practice. This covers the vast subject of operations management in the sense of organizational function rather than procedural steps. Generally speaking, this area needs subdivision of its own. Subclassifications could be:

1) By single "function" such as personnel, quality control, finance, etc.
2) By major tasks of manufacturing, normally involving many areas, either day-to-day or occasional events (for example, scheduling or starting a new plant).
3) By grouping items of limited scope but uniquely manufacturing (for example, vendor relations and contacts).

Position Objectives, Responsibility, Authority, and Skill Requirements. This covers the set of information relevant to planning a job, fitting it into the organization, setting skill level requirements for the position, locating and selecting candidates, providing the man, his manager, and others with specific knowledge of the job, and setting performance standards and appraising. This is also the area in which territorial issues can be resolved in writing.

Organizational Structure. This covers reporting relationships, position titles, and names of incumbents.

Interorganizational Agreements. These are special documents, normally written to settle disputes, and often covering only a single topic, that define responsibilities, resolve new matters before they become problems, or formalize changes or agreements.

Specific Documents

Due to the wide variety of names used for documents, there may be some confusion between the titles used here and those familiar to the reader. Exact titles are optional so long as they are in keeping with the message and not too similar to each other.

Statements of Beliefs and Principles. Every rational course of action or decision derives from an accumulation of facts, assumptions, and objectives. And no matter how factual or analytical decisions may seem, if traced back far enough, there will usually be a point where judgment was employed. This in turn was a function of deep-seated values; a matter of what people believe in or what they think others believe. Beliefs can be established by an organization and made part of the environment. They can relate to many topics, such as people, quality, customers, suppliers, community image, or social service. Not all of these relate to organization, of course, but many affect responsibilities. For example, assume that a belief expressed by the company is that quality is its basis of success. Organizationally, this suggests a strong quality control department with widespread responsibility, which may include the area of customer satisfaction.

Obviously many companies have been highly successful without ever writing down a statement of their beliefs. In some cases verbal communication can do the job better, particularly if the influx of new people is not rapid nor the organization large. Should written statements of beliefs be considered necessary they must come in a personal manner from the recognized leader. In a tightly integrated company the leader will tend to be the president or chairman whereas in a decentralized organization the leader could be the head of an operating unit. The form of such a statement is unimportant as long as it is sincere, has conviction, and is personal in feeling. When put in writing, beliefs should be available to every employee.

Policy and Staff Letters. No organization can afford to spend time remaking decisions. Aside from being a wasteful use of resources, the results are often inequitable because the decisions are inconsistent. A prime purpose of the *letter* is to make a decision in advance on common or recurring problems. If not the total decision, then the deciding factors at least are spelled out to give the necessary consistency to decisions. The second function of the letter is to establish an operational practice, requirement, or guideline. Lastly, a letter may be used specifically to delegate authority.

Depending on the organizational structure, publication may come from staff heads or from the single head of the organization (plant manager, division president, etc.) where an appropriate staff structure is not present. Regardless of point of approval, all line and staff organizations should have the responsibility to propose and draft letters. In companies with organizational planning departments, this department should review them for consistency with all existing guidelines and job responsibilities. Each document should cover only one subject and should be self-explanatory except for specific references to other documents.

Practices or Management Guides. The subject of a practice is a task, major or minor, continuous or intermittent. Unlike a procedure, the practice deals with a task which requires extensive management judgment and involves complex decisions. The practice aims directly at the management process and must structure the process in terms of major events, activities, inputs, outputs, risk assessments, specific management controls, and the management responsibilities for these events. Addressing the business as a series of tasks is profitable because it focuses on the dynamic interactions within the organization and between major functions; it also surfaces problem areas needing resolution and provides a basis for educating people in the management of the organization and its activities.

An effective way of opening a practice is to start with a short list of the major responsibilities or actions covered by it; these would be the items of importance to the highest level of plant (or division) management. The remainder of the document is then organized by subtasks. Thus a practice on production cost management might have four primary divisions:

1) Establishing the product cost objective
2) Estimating the cost when designed
3) Targeting or setting objectives for a particular year
4) Measuring and reducing the cost.

A primary objective of a practice is to expand the capability of management to carry out complex interfunctional activities without having constantly to consult with higher levels of management to resolve issues or "straighten the mess out." It delegates authority and at the same time provides knowledge to do the job.

Position Guides (Position Descriptions). One of the few axioms of organization theory is that everyone should know what his job is. Occasionally this is self-evident or can be stated verbally, but for management and professional positions it is invariably desirable to write down the job description. Proper documentation permits the total work to be clearly and completely divided without overlooking some tasks or allowing others to become the subject of territorial disputes. When used fully, the position guide can be the basis for setting specific objectives and for evaluation of salary level, skill requirements, and experience for the position.

The essential part of such a guide is a set of responsibilities. It can be written with short terse statements in as little as half a page or in a broader paragraph style taking several pages and providing some deeper "interpretation" of the responsibilities. No matter which approach is used, the guide must be thoroughly free from "method" statements and qualitative adjectives. The only exception should be when such phrases are really part of the position responsibility rather than related to performance standards, practices, or procedures. These should be separate from the guide. (For example, the manager of the cost estimating department is primarily responsible for estimates. His guide should *not* discuss the quality of an estimate nor even state that they should be "accurate," etc. It might, however, include the responsibility to measure actuals against estimates and analyze variances.)

It is generally recommended that guides be no more than one page long and that they be divided into short paragraphs. This form is easier to write, follow, and maintain. Jobs that are complex organizationally, however, may require position guides which not only define responsibility, but outline how the job relates to others. It is helpful, if not essential, to start a guide with a summary statement of two or three sentences. Many jobs fall into a group which itself has a lengthy list of responsibilities which are standard for the set. For example, all managers have common responsibilities, relating to subordinates, which nonmanagers do not have, such as hiring, appraising, and recommending salary increases. The sets of common responsibilities should be listed separately from the guide and merely referred to for reasons of efficiency and also because individuals do not have the option of changing them. Certain types of positions can best be covered by two position guides (or a combination guide-description where the description part is constant) when that position is based on a standard classification. Thus manufacturing engineering might have five technical levels from "junior" to "consultant" and for each a generalized description designed to stress the differences in responsibility and qualifications. At any time, however, each engineer has a specific assignment for which there is another guide. The dual concept is most valuable in controlling job levels in regard to salary and ensuring an equitable structure within and across departments for positions which need the same types of skill and experience (but in greater or lesser degree).

Organization Directory. A directory is a broad-based "who's who" in the company and covers many more people than should be put on charts. As a minimum, it must have position title, name of incumbent, and person to whom he reports, preferably in that order. Other things can be added such as telephone number and exact location for mailing purposes, although each addition increases maintenance. It is useful but not essential to list all members of the organization alphabetically.

The value of a separate directory will not be realized in a small organization; even a plant of several thousand employees may not need a full separate directory but instead can use a part of the plant telephone book. The directory will make its greatest contribution in multilocation organizations which might comprise several manufacturing plants, or a combination of manufacturing, engineering, and sales locations. It should be organized by "functions" and laid out to maximize "search efficiency" by judicious use of vertical space breaks, indentions, and upper and lower case letters when available. Major subunits (such as plants) should have authority over their own parts of the directory, whether the system uses only a typewriter or employs tele-processing and computers. Dividing the directory over the various sub-units facilitates changes and improves the accuracy of titles, spelling, and other such matters.

Fig. 5-3 shows a typical organization directory layout. The section of the directory shown is organized according to personnel job func-tions. In a large directory a second section in which names are listed alphabetically is helpful.

TITLE	NAME	REPORTS TO
Plant Manager	F. Smith	F. Jones
Assistant	J. Doe	J. Smith
Works Manager	T. Brown	F. Smith
Manager of Manufacturing Engineering	G. Green	T. Brown
Special Projects Manager	M. Grey	G. Green

Fig. 5-3.   Sample layout for an organization directory.

Since everybody cannot normally be in the directory, it is necessary to make some touchy decisions. A practical ground rule for some organizations is to include only managers, superintendents, and fore-men. Nonmanagers who have key jobs as assistants or specialists, such as a legal counsel, should naturally be included, but the list must be controlled. The presumption is that by reaching the manager of the organization one can make the appropriate contact.

Organization Charts. A chart is a highly informative yet very lim-ited depiction of an organization. It is much like a map in which all roads have been drawn alike; thus the reader cannot distinguish the turnpike from the back road except by inference. Despite the limita-tions of charts in depicting the degrees of delegation, actual working relationships, and size and status, the organization chart is still the single most important document.

In theory, charts could carry a great deal more information than they typically do. As on a road map, color, line width, coding, etc., could depict all types of factors such as staff-to-line relationships and true profit/decision centers. While these possibilities exist, and deserve further application, it does not seem likely that even a detailed chart can be an adequate substitute for the documents discussed previously.

There are many variations and features which add to the versatility and usefulness of a chart. A discussion follows of some possibilities.

Boxes and their contents. The rectangular box is standard, but ovals and circles may be employed to present an image of breaking with tradition. The box may contain:

1) Position title
2) Function, activity, or area of the business (for example, manufacturing, personnel, and foreign operations) when not implicit in the title
3) Name of the incumbent.

A chart need not include personal names when the use is primarily to study and evaluate the organizational structure. In addition, condensed charts can carry multiple items in one large box. For example, such an arrangement might be used to indicate that the purchasing manager has five main buyers who procure distinct groups of items.

Words without boxes. A variation on the use of multiple names within the box is to leave out the box lines altogether. This makes the chart easier to prepare, can be just as readable, and saves space. Perhaps the most effective approach is to combine boxes at the top of the organization with titles only at the lower levels.

Committees. When a standing committee is actually part of the organization it should be included in the chart. Many corporate charts, for example, show an "executive committee." If the committee only makes recommendations, the line(s) can go to the principle area(s) receiving the recommendations.

Dotted lines. Whereas a solid line means a true reporting relationship, a dotted line denotes direction and/or control only. It should be used sparingly on a standard organization chart (but perhaps liberally on a special chart designed to show actual working relationships) and not as a means of showing staff direction to line. A suitable application of a dotted line might be to connect a domestic employee assigned to work at a foreign location with someone in the foreign organization.

The basic methods of diagramming a chart are shown in Fig. 5-4. Methods 1, 2, and 3 can be combined in a single chart, with Method 1 being used at the top of the chart and 2 and/or 3 used lower in the chart. Method 4 is more compact because it greatly reduces the number of boxes. It is used most effectively in combination with Method 1.

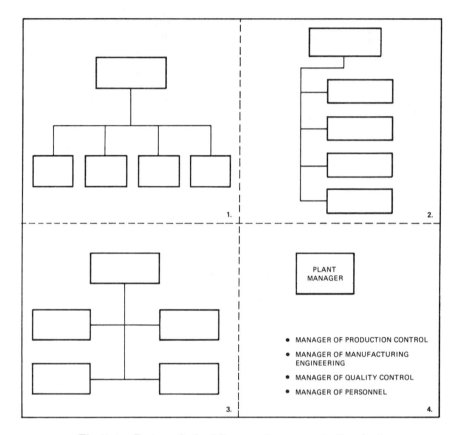

Fig. 5-4. Basic methods of diagramming an organization chart.

Organization Announcements. A few basic rules can go a long way in avoiding problems with announcements:

1) Everyone involved should know of the change, as it affects himself, before the announcement is made public.
2) People should not be left stranded, a situation which results when they are removed from one organization but not attached to another.
3) All aspects of the announcement must be approved since later retraction or change is embarrassing.
4) A consistent practice should be followed on the use of "promoted to." A sound practice is to use it only for the promotions. An alternative is to use "has assumed" for *all* people going to a new job.

5) A consistent policy should be established regarding what position levels are to be covered by announcements.

Organization Manual. A typical manual is composed partly of the items already covered, such as charts, and partly of material unique to organizations such as the items in the following list. Major subdivisions of the manual should be divided into "sections," which in turn are subdivided into "part" and page. The sections will normally be separated by tabs.

Essential items:
    Mission, charter, objective of organization
    Organization charts
    Position guides
    Basic responsibilities of managers, supervisors, foremen.

Optional items:
    Charts of higher levels within the company
    Beliefs and principles, general
    Organizational guidelines, concepts, principles, standards
    Organizational changes or additions, control and approval of
    Titles, definition and use of, for organization and for positions.
    Committees, use and authority of
    Interorganizational relationships
    Delegation of authority and powers reserved
    Escalation and resolution of conflicts
    Appointments to positions; selection, approval
    Salary changes; guidelines, approvals
    Employee relations, general matters
    Definition of terms such as *approve* and *review*
    Communications and primary written documents
    Organization directory.

Each organization must determine which of the optional items are important and establish a logical grouping into sections. Staff letters, instructions, and practices have not been listed above because they tend to form a homogeneous group of their own dealing with operational matters. It is often desirable to have a second manual on operations or if the total quantity is small to use one binder clearly divided into two halves to cover all organizational and operational material.

One acceptable way of organizing a manual is shown in Fig. 5-5. Note that most of the documents discussed in this chapter are included. The items omitted are lower level position guides, announcements, and the more complex task-oriented practices. These could be included in a second manual.

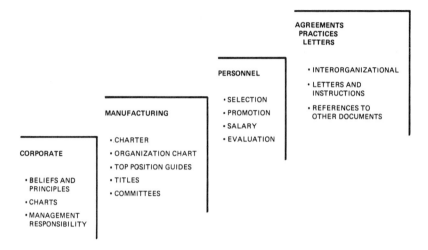

Fig. 5–5.   The organization manual.

PUBLICATION, CONTROL, AND USE

This section covers matters essential to the disseminating administration, and use of organizational documentation.

Mandate Versus Guideline

The primary purpose of documentation is to further the end objectives of manufacturing (usually related to delivery, cost, and quality). This cannot be at the expense of individual initiative, creativity, and risk-taking since these are essential to a vigorous organization. On the other hand, there would be little reason in directive documentation if it were not intended that people conduct themselves or act in the prescribed way. (A chart is an example of nondirective documentation; a policy statement is directive.) There are several ways to overcome this apparent dilemma. First of all, good documentation extensively delegates authority and provides guidelines while minimizing rules about making decisions. Secondly, where specific rules are needed to define final authority or ensure strict adherence in certain matters, then the documentation should clearly say so. In short, there must never be confusion between guideline areas and requirements. If a man is assigned an area of authority, that is specific. In exercising his authority he may have many alternatives but not the option to ignore it or try to avoid it. Higher management in the organization must assume the responsibility for establishing the desired interpretation of documentation between the extremes of unquestioned acceptance and disregard.

Preparation and Approval

Organizational documentation does not appear naturally and spontaneously. In the normal course of business, memos will appear from all directions, each adding a little piece or perhaps making a major addition to the responsibility structure or management system. The total job of weaving these into a solid set of documents should ideally be assigned to a specialized team close to the top of the organization (for example, for all manufacturing in a major corporation this would be the corporate staff, whereas for a large plant this team would report to the top of the plant organization). High placement, however, must be tempered by the work scope anticipated. If documentation is limited to charts and directories, then this is a "clerical" service since line management will be making the decisions and changes. That job could best be done in the personnel or administration department. As the work scope expands it becomes increasingly difficult and pointless to separate the documentation from the analysis. It should be readily agreed that a position responsible for organizational structure and effectiveness needs to be placed high in the staff. The documentation, being an integral part of the job, is the responsibility of the same persons.

When a single staff team has overall organizational responsibility, it should undertake all documentation tasks which cross functional areas (for example, charts, directories, a manual, broad policy, and general agreements with external organizations) and must review and resolve conflicts in position guides or other areas where interorganizational problems can arise. Ideally, position guides should be prepared by the person occupying the position and his manager and only approved by the central staff, and any other documents which pertain to only a limited scope of operations should be prepared by the staff or line management serving the area.

Maintenance

Organizational documentation is like a yacht—if you can't afford to maintain it, you can't afford to buy it. Change is natural to business, and the documentation and the real world must be kept in close match. Changes are not always transmitted initially by the documentation; major changes are often stated verbally or in a memorandum. If documentation cannot be kept reasonably current, then it is better to drop it altogether or cut back on the sensitive, ever-changing items (if separable) and stay with more basic points. In addition, many little things can be done to facilitate maintenance, such as:

1) Avoiding more detailed references than necessary, so that minor changes in titles, etc., do not create a problem

2) Subdividing the text and laying out pages to facilitate replacing the minimum number of pages at one time
3) Cross-referencing items sensitive to change so that only the primary entry would need to be changed.

There is no exact timetable for maintenance, though the following guides can be a starting point. It is assumed that any known specific change will be picked up and either be marked on a master maintenance copy or, if very significant, the document will immediately be changed.

1) All documents should be reviewed once a year even if there is no known change. This should be done by a person thoroughly versed in the subject who can assess total implications rather than details.
2) A position guide should be reviewed whenever a new person assumes the position and in conjunction with changes in surrounding positions.
3) Organization directories should be brought up to date on a fixed schedule permitting a maximum of 5 to 10 percent error but should not be updated more than once a month.
4) Charts should be changed whenever changes occur in top positions. Since the cost of total instantaneous change is normally prohibitive, changes in lower level positions are normally accumulated until several can be made at once.

Formats and Headings

Formal communications, those which are controlled and updated, require an appropriate printed heading and "section, part, page" numbering system. The objective is to create an image for the document which clearly and quickly identifies it and conveys a sense of authority. Written documents more than several pages long will usually benefit by paragraph numbering, either the all numerical system (1.1, 1.2, 2.1, 2.2, 2.2.1, etc.) or the number and alphabet method (I.A, 1.a,b; II, etc.). This facilitates reference, search, and indexing since reference is to topical material rather than page numbers which have a way of changing during maintenance.

Recipients and Acceptability

It is neither practical nor desirable to direct documentation to everyone. Generally, the audience is middle management or higher. The primary users should be understood in terms of their prior knowledge, their information needs, and their position or organization level. This determines the distribution of the document, its content, editorial arrangement, and style. Attention should always be given to making the document attractive and pleasant to read. Length itself is a drawback as are long unbroken bodies of text and overcrowded pages. Usage can be enhanced by having a summary which contains the most significant points, not just a rundown of the content but items significant to higher management. A good guide for increasing acceptability is to keep paragraphs shorter than one-third page and to use visible subheads for each new topic.

In the final analysis, acceptability will depend on how well the documentation fulfills the three basic needs of:

1) Defining the organizational structure and the role of personnel
2) Transmitting a body of guidelines and directives
3) Establishing the areas of responsibilities, interactions, and controls associated with major tasks.

SUMMARY

While organization documentation in the past has been chiefly a matter of preparing charts and position descriptions, a wider perspective is urged. Organization documentation should be concerned with the three major organizational elements—personnel, the management process, and the operating structure or framework—and should recognize and define the dynamic nature of these elements.

Effective documentation is a means of communicating and perpetuating sound policies and practices, and the process of documenting in itself contributes immeasurably to the development of good policies and practices. Through documentation organizational members are made aware of their own authority, responsibilities, and reporting relationships as well as those of other members of the organization. Although many organizations perform the task of documentation very poorly, there is a real payoff for proper accomplishment in this area.

The specific documents employed are identified as:

1) Statements of beliefs and principles
2) Policy and staff letters
3) Practices or management guides
4) Position guides
5) Organizational directory
6) Organization charts
7) Organization announcements
8) Organization manual.

Each of these documents has a place in the documentation of organizations, though not all of them may be necessary for any one organization. Indeed, it is unlikely that a given organization would require all of them. The final judgment must be in terms of the effectiveness of the organization in accomplishing its primary mission.

chapter 6

organizational staffing and development

THE HUMAN ELEMENT CONSTITUTES the basis for success in any organization. The degree to which an enterprise is able to attract, develop, and motivate personnel at all levels determines the extent to which organizational goals can be established and attained. This is particularly true in the present era of rapid technological change where the ability to meet today's problems must be coupled with the capacity to plan for and to meet the challenges of the future. Success in such a dynamic environment demands progressive forms of personnel staffing and development which serve the dual needs of the organization and the people who work in it.

Programs of personnel staffing must assure that the organization is supplied with the types, numbers, and levels of skills necessary to assure the success of present as well as anticipated business undertakings. This demands that current talent be properly utilized and that the organization develop its capacity to attract new skills as needed.

Next there must exist a strong and constant management emphasis in the area of personnel development. One of the greatest concerns of most forms of enterprise is obsolescence, not just the obsolescence which develops from worn-out machines and facilities, but the type of obsolescence which may develop in people. The type of individual who fails to grow and develop constantly, who applies yesterday's knowledge to today's problems, who spends his time reflecting on past successes instead of present challenges, is embalming his own future as well as that of his company. Preventing such obsolescence requires considerable attention both in analyzing new and changing skills and technologies and also in keeping human resources as competitive as possible.

This chapter covers the responsibilities which all managers share in the areas of personnel staffing and development.

STAFFING THE ORGANIZATION

Of constant concern to any manager is the staffing of his organization. Maintaining a force of the correct size, together with the required combination of skills by type and level, is a never-ending activity. Turnover, transfers, promotions, demotions, and other factors all combine to cause a constant shuffle of talent and consequent readjustments in any operation.

The staffing function is very closely linked with the total personnel development process. It is a basic truth that one cannot succeed in developing people without first having the right type of people. A company must attract the kind of talent required to fit its job specifications; the people hired should possess the experience, education, personality, and interests necessary to perform present tasks and be developed for more responsibility in the future.

At one time staffing was not a difficult problem. Industry did not require the thousands of separate skills needed by large concerns today. Instead of employing persons with given skills, it was customary to consider hiring so many "hands." The foreman or "gang boss" of the day would line up an ample supply of candidates and simply pick out the ones he wanted—usually the healthiest looking specimens with the most brawn.

Today the problem is decidedly different for manufacturing companies. Getting the right person for a particular job can place stringent demands upon the managers throughout an organization. Locating sources of talent, attracting personnel in a highly competitive market, and effecting proper utilization of present talent all combine to make staffing a real challenge, requiring the close cooperation of personnel specialists and line managers.

Manpower Planning

A sound staffing program begins with a well-thought-out manpower planning program. Manpower planning should be a part of an organization's short-term as well as its long-term plans. Customarily, the initial manpower plan is quantitative in nature and is derived largely from the present and projected business base. As a part of the overall financial estimate of work volume, a manpower or labor estimate is derived. Usually this is the result of a considerable amount of preplanning throughout the organization by management personnel in marketing, engineering, manufacturing, and other areas. The resulting budget figure shows the dollars it is possible to spend for direct and overhead labor; this figure is usually converted into actual manpower numbers and is broken down to individual departments.

In addition to quantitative manpower planning, the organization should examine the qualitative aspects of manpower requirements. There are numerous aspects in this area which may have an impact on any enterprise. For example, new or changing technologies may create a demand for skills not available internally. Manpower capability deficiencies may call for strengthening segments of the organization through internal or external staffing actions. Retirements, voluntary turnover, and other depletions may also create a need for special actions. The condition of the external labor market also is a factor to be considered.

It is important not to restrict a manpower plan to a mere prediction of numbers of "heads" required, but to look in advance at the whole problem of numbers, talent mixes, and levels, plus manpower competence and potential. Much of this can only be done by the individual departmental manager. The industrial engineer, the estimator, and the financial planner are helpful in furnishing data on business volume and workload, but it is only the individual manager who really knows his personnel and their abilities and potential. He must make the judgments and initiate the action to ensure that his staff is ready to cope with the demands of both present and future workloads.

In performing qualitative manpower planning, special attention should be given to those skills which are in short supply or which take a considerable amount of time to develop. For example, such skilled craftsmen as machinists and toolmakers are often hard to find. Engineers and other professional skills also pose a problem, and finding management personnel, from the first-line level to the executive levels, may be most difficult of all.

An important aspect of manpower planning is to provide for early identification of future staffing problems rather than waiting for the sudden emergence of serious talent shortages. Once quantitative and qualitative manpower plans have been made, the manager has the initial guidelines within which to operate. He knows what he will need to get his job done in terms of numbers, levels, and types of skills. At this point, however, he must rely on data from several other sources which should exist within his organization.

Job Classification Structure

Job classification systems are invaluable in assuring that jobs are evaluated properly and that wages and salaries are administered equitably. Such systems are aimed at determining the relative worth of jobs in relation to other jobs within the organization and comparable jobs in the geographic area and throughout the given industry. Any organization which displays indifference to relative wage or salary levels is inviting low morale, inefficiency, and high turnover rates.

Job classification systems do more than determine the economic value of individual jobs, however; they also establish the ladders of work within the organization according to job specialties. Through describing jobs, they establish the benchmarks which guide the manager in the effective utilization of his personnel. Job classification systems also form the basis of the promotion system, establish standards by which employees can be evaluated, and set criteria for use in making job assignments.

Proper utilization of personnel in accordance with job classifications accomplishes several objectives:

1) Increased efficiency
2) Greater economy
3) Improved morale
4) Better labor relations.

Each of these is discussed below.

Efficiency. In general, it can be stated that people perform best when working within their proper classification, assuming that they have been properly trained and classified.

Economy. Work requiring low skill levels should be assigned to relatively unskilled and lower paid personnel. Obviously, it is not economical to pay a highly trained individual to perform a task that could be accomplished by lower paid employees. A well-designed job classification system minimizes such mis-assignments.

Morale. Most people prefer to operate at their full level of capability. A skilled employee assigned unskilled work for a period of time loses his drive and enthusiasm. The situation is analogous to that of a major leaguer given the same salary but assigned to the minors. The baseball player, like the industrial worker, loses a certain amount of stature, which can be attributed to the lower level at which he is operating.

Labor Relations. Mismatching of job assignments and personnel classifications causes trouble with organized labor. This is particularly true when the employee is assigned higher graded work than that for which he is being paid.

The job classification system must not be allowed to become outdated. The complexity of industry's products and services increases constantly, and this is likewise true of the individual jobs which combine to create these products and services. Classification systems must be kept up to date so that they are representative of actual demands upon the individual employee in terms of individual responsibility, mental and physical requirements, and skill requirements.

People are also changing constantly. The concept of job simplification, of breaking down the total effort into its smallest components, is under challenge today. Most of the behavioral scientists working in industry are encouraging the use of "job enlargement" and "job enrichment." Evidence exists that many of today's employees are not content to perform simple repetitive tasks but want to make a broader and more creative contribution to the organization. They want a meaningful job, not one that has been simplified into a dull routine. They want to participate in decision making and make suggestions concerning work improvement. There is a growing understanding that the work itself is the real motivating influence behind human effort and that job content, individual responsibility, and freedom to participate are productive desires of employees which can be channeled and utilized to the advantage of the organization as well as the employee. In situations where employees have been allowed greater participation, results have been achieved in terms of increased output, reduced costs, lower turnover, and so on.

In summary, it is vital that the formal job classification system and the assignment and responsibilities extended to the employee not be overly confining. No worker wants to be regarded and treated as no more than a mere pair of hands and feet with his every motion defined and his creative ability thwarted. People have much to offer at every level; it is up to management to bring out their potential.

Personnel Appraisal

Job classification systems define organizational positions and are essential in establishing a proper frame of reference in personnel staffing. Another valuable tool is a sound personnel appraisal system.

As was stated, the manager must be aware of the individual jobs making up the manpower plan; in the same vein, he needs to know the capability and potential of his people to fill these jobs. A good appraisal system not only helps to match men with jobs, but it also is the core of personnel development since it enables development efforts to be focused on the defined needs of the individual.

Types of Systems. There are many types of personnel appraisal systems in use today. Perhaps the most common is the "trait" approach which attempts to evaluate the personality and performance factors affecting job success. Plans based on this approach attempt to measure such factors as initiative, quality and quantity of work, dependability, ability to deal effectively with others, etc. Fig. 6-1 shows an appraisal form used to evaluate these traits. Using this form, the appraiser (usually the supervisor) merely checks the phrase which best describes the person being evaluated, then adds a few comments.

PERFORMANCE APPRAISAL

RATER WILL PLACE A CHECK (√) ABOVE THE PHRASE THAT BEST DESCRIBES THE INDIVIDUAL BEING APPRAISED.

JOB KNOWLEDGE

( ) OFTEN REQUIRES ASSISTANCE   ( ) OCCASIONALLY REQUIRES ASSISTANCE   ( ) ADEQUATE FOR JOB   ( ) GOOD KNOWLEDGE   ( ) THOROUGH KNOWLEDGE

PLANNING AND ORGANIZING

( ) OFTEN UN-SATISFACTORY   ( ) USUALLY ACCEPTABLE   ( ) CONSISTENTLY SATISFACTORY   ( ) OFTEN SUPERIOR   ( ) CONSISTENTLY SUPERIOR

ABILITY TO INFLUENCE OTHERS

( ) EXCEPTIONAL ABILITY   ( ) OFTEN OUTSTANDING   ( ) CONSISTENTLY ADEQUATE   ( ) USUALLY ADEQUATE   ( ) OFTEN INADEQUATE

EMOTIONAL CONTROL

( ) CANNOT BE RELIED UPON IN A CRISIS   ( ) EMOTIONS SOMETIMES HANDICAP DEALINGS   ( ) USUALLY EVEN TEMPERED   ( ) MAINTAINS GOOD CONTROL   ( ) ALWAYS MAINTAINS SELF-CONTROL

SELF-EXPRESSION

( ) CONSISTENTLY SUPERIOR   ( ) FREQUENTLY SUPERIOR   ( ) CONSISTENTLY ADEQUATE   ( ) USUALLY ADEQUATE   ( ) OFTEN INADEQUATE

DEPENDABILITY

( ) INADEQUATE   ( ) NOT TOO SUCCESSFUL   ( ) ADEQUATE   ( ) GOOD   ( ) EXCEPTIONAL

JUDGMENT

( ) POOR   ( ) SOMETIMES ACCEPTABLE   ( ) USUALLY ACCEPTABLE   ( ) ALMOST ALWAYS ACCEPTABLE   ( ) EXCEPTIONAL

COOPERATION

( ) EXCEPTIONAL IN DEALING WITH OTHERS   ( ) COOPERATES WILLINGLY   ( ) COOPERATES FAIRLY WELL   ( ) COOPERATES SOMETIMES   ( ) UNWILLING TO COOPERATE

INITIATIVE

( ) COMPLETELY LACKS ENERGY   ( ) SOMETIMES ADEQUATE   ( ) USUALLY ADEQUATE   ( ) OFTEN SATISFACTORY   ( ) EXCEPTIONAL DRIVE AND AMBITION

WHAT INCIDENTS OF THIS EMPLOYEE'S PERFORMANCE DURING THE RATING PERIOD INDICATE ABOVE-AVERAGE CAPABILITIES?

WHAT INCIDENTS OF THIS EMPLOYEE'S PERFORMANCE INDICATE AREAS IN NEED OF IMPROVEMENT?

BASED ON YOUR APPRAISAL AND YOUR INTERVIEW WITH THE EMPLOYEE, WHAT SPECIFIC ACTION WILL YOU TAKE TO HELP IMPROVE HIS PERFORMANCE?

WHAT SPECIFIC ACTION HAS HE AGREED TO TAKE TO IMPROVE HIMSELF?

Fig. 6-1. Performance appraisal form based on trait evaluation.

Customarily the employee's supervisor discusses the rating with the individual employee and offers advice on how he can improve himself.

The problem with rating systems based on the trait approach lies in the fact that the appraisal traits do not always correlate with job success. Assumptions made in defining the rated traits are not always valid. For instance, we may include "initiative" in a rating form when little initiative is really required in the job. Or a trait such as "self-expression" may be used in rating a worker whose responsibilities for communication may be almost nil. Or, a rating on the trait of judgment ability may be applied to an individual whose decision-making responsibilities are very limited. In short, such systems impose common rating factors on people in diverse jobs with varying responsibilities.

As a result of such imperfections in trait-rating systems, there is a definite trend toward evaluating each individual in terms of what is expected of him in his particular job assignment. Such systems depend upon a measurement of actual results against pre-set objectives or standards. Some of the considerations involved in making such "results oriented" appraisals are discussed below.

Establishing Objectives or Standards. It is essential to good appraisal that the subordinate be well aware of the objectives or standards against which he is being measured. The degree of formality involved in the process may vary depending on the level of the individual and type of activity in which he is engaged. At higher levels it has become customary to establish specific objectives, to work out implementation plans in detail, and to disseminate these throughout the operation. This enables subunits of the organization at successively lower levels to develop their own goals in accordance with the overall objectives, thus providing a common sense of direction to the organization as a whole.

In addition to keeping everyone on the same track, established objectives provide excellent criteria against which to measure performance. In the case of nonsupervisory salaried and hourly employees, it becomes more difficult to set specific objectives over a long time span since jobs and assignments vary from day to day. Nevertheless clear job assignments and goals with expected *standards* of performance should be set by the supervisor for *every* subordinate. Often the subordinate can contribute to the establishment of these assignments and goals.

Without established objectives or standards, the appraisal process loses a significant amount of strength. The danger is that it may become merely a "rating" tool instead of a stimulant to improved performance.

Observation of Performance. Observation is the process of giving one's attention to the action and output of a person in order to gain knowledge of him and his demonstrated ability and potential. Observation is naturally sharpened if objectives or standards are pre-set. The appraiser then knows what to look for and what specific items to measure. He is in a better position to gain an accurate appraisal based on measurement of *results* rather than a subjective measurement based on *impressions.*

One difficulty in summarizing our total observations over the appraisal time span is the natural tendency to forget performance during the early part of the appraisal period, thus basing the whole evaluation on recent performance. Particularly in the case of employees performing complex functions it is wise to record, in a simple and informal fashion, performance which is either substandard or above expectations. If such recordings are made during the entire course of the rating period, they help to supplement the appraiser's memory when he prepares the evaluation report.

There are a number of errors commonly made in observing performance which should be guarded against. Some of these with their suggested solutions are listed below:

Errors	*Solutions*
Jumping to conclusions on the basis of poor evidence.	Get the facts first.
Distorting what is observed because of bias, interests, or attitudes caused by threats to self-esteem, "pat" ideas, or reflection on the supervisor's ability.	Learn to be impartial and to check with someone else if in doubt.
Seeing or hearing what is expected rather than what occurs.	Again, get the facts.
Failure to observe the supervisor's influence on the man being observed.	Check first to determine if you are at fault.
Using memory rather than observation.	Practice observation and record the facts immediately after observing.

Recording Performance (The Appraisal Itself). In completing the appraisal form, care should be taken to ensure that judgments cover the complete evaluation period and not just the past several weeks or months (continuous recording of performance data will help here). It should be remembered too, that the appraisal should be based on measurement of *results,* not on personality traits or characteristics.

Naturally, if personality factors which are correctable are detracting from job results, these factors should be brought to the individual's attention. The standard for measurement, however, is still the result measured against the goal or assignment.

Post-Appraisal Interview. All of the work that has gone into the appraisal up to this point—making observations, recording them, and evaluating performance—has been preliminary to the most crucial step of the whole appraisal process, the post-appraisal interview.

The goal toward which the appraiser has been working is to instill in the subordinate an awareness of his own relationship to his career and to the welfare of the company. If the interview produces a subordinate better equipped to take on new responsibilities, happier in his work because he understands what is expected of him, and more eager to accept challenges than in the past, then real results have been achieved in the appraisal process.

The post-appraisal interview involves discussion of the appraisal with the employee and any follow-up which may be done as a result. The interview includes laying intelligent plans for the man's development. Properly conducted, the interview affords the supervisor and the employee with a common understanding of the evaluation that has been made and paves the way for clarifying differences of opinion. The interview provides a time for making practical plans for helping the man improve and plotting his development.

In preparing for the interview, the interviewer should review the employee's record thoroughly. What are the factors about which you feel confident? What do you have questions about? What seems important? What should you praise him for? What factors should be discussed for improvement?

Try to predict how the employee will react to your information. Put yourself in his shoes. Are there parts he will resist strongly? How will you handle this type of reaction?

In general, a post-appraisal interview involves communicating your evaluation, coming to an understanding about problems, and planning for the future. More often than not, your interviews will follow this pattern. The following suggestions may prove helpful:

1) Let the employee know the purposes of the interview well in advance. This lets him gather his thoughts and prepare for areas in which he is afraid of an unfavorable evaluation.
2) Arrange the time and place of the interview to be as free as possible from interruption. Choose a time when you are both in a good mood.
3) In opening the interview, put the employee at ease. A person is

more likely to relax and be in a position to discuss his performance if you are relaxed yourself.

4) Introduce the session by describing its purpose in your own words, and explain what time period and job assignments are covered in your evaluation. Outline the general approach which you have planned and ask whether this approach looks helpful to him.

Beware of the following common mistakes:

1) *Talking all "sweetness and light."* This prevents the person from knowing what you really feel, from explaining his behavior, and from getting whatever help you might offer.

2) *Talking about little things while ignoring big ones.* An employee is usually ready to face his record directly, and he expects the same from you.

3) *Telling the employee how you would handle the situation if you were in his shoes.* After all, he has to do the job with his own resources, not yours. He has to find a method available for him. You and his job set the standards, but the method of attaining them is for him to discover with your help.

4) *Not making clear what you expect of the employee, or not having the same standards for everyone.* It may not be possible to have precisely defined standards, but in evaluating a person a manager inevitably uses *some* standards. He owes it to the employee to try to spell these out as clearly as possible.

In discussing your evaluation, explain the basis on which you have made it. Cite some specific observations which guided you. If the employee has done a good job, point out that his high performance is related to his own job satisfaction and his future with the organization. If he has done a poor job in some respect, take the attitude that this is a problem that you share with him.

In interpreting the employee's performance, the manager should compare his ideas with the interviewer's explanations. In the process of trying to reconcile the differences, a perceptive manager can often discover some basis to assist the employee in improving his performance.

In laying plans for the future, the interviewer's role in this important phase of the program is to suggest possibilities, raise questions, and generally stimulate the employee to consider his own goals and methods of achieving them. The following elements are usually essential if any change is to occur:

1) A goal for self-improvement must be set by the job holder himself. It is appropriate to suggest outside reading or participation in training or educational courses.
2) Accurate feedback to tell the employee how well he is proceeding in achieving his goals.
3) Additional energy. Before an employee will spend his energy, he must be motivated to achieve his goals by changing his behavior. Obstacles to any change, and the increased skill necessary, require increased energy output.
4) Changed opinions of the man by others. What other people expect us to do has some bearing on what we are able to do. Before any change can be permanent, a change in other people's expectations is necessary.
5) Assistance from you. From time to time your support, suggestions, cooperation, etc., will probably be required.
6) Recognition of limitations. The limitations of one's self, of others, and of one's job must be taken into account.

The interview should be terminated when it is no longer productive. Close by summarizing the entire discussion with special emphasis on any agreements that have been reached. Also include disagreements; agree, however, to investigate them in the future in order to discover the source of the disagreements and to achieve a better understanding of them. You can also include one or two significant points which have not been covered in your discussion in your summary.

Personnel Inventories

Many organizations have set up systems to catalog their available skills, and they use such information in selecting and utilizing their human resources. These systems range from simple hand-operated files to those employing complex mechanized techniques. Such systems are usually aimed at:

1) Inventorying existing manpower capabilities
2) Identifying qualified individuals to fill vacancies
3) Evaluating the organization's capability to take on new business
4) Projecting future skills requirements
5) Evaluating staff proposals and new programs.

Data collected on organizational personnel usually includes current job title and assignment; social security number; company service date; formal education by type of degree, year, and institution; informal education, such as company courses; military service and draft status; membership in professional organizations and level of participation; patents; professional licenses; papers and publications; foreign language fluency; past experience by title, date, assignment, project, and company; and skills ranked in order of proficiency. In addition, other information is sometimes inventoried. This might include: results of latest personnel appraisal; current salary and recent salary history; job and skill preferences; and potential for promotion.

Personnel inventory systems must, of course, be kept up to date. Updating requires constant attention and is usually the responsibility of the personnel department. Periodic tab runs can be made showing information of general benefit to the organization such as the number of employees with certain skills; the number of academic degrees by level and academic specialty; number of employees in various grade levels; names of promotable individuals; number of employees eligible for the draft; and so on. Also, internal searches can be made to discover individuals with specific qualifications to be assigned to new tasks. Some organizations also like to know of current employees who have experience in other companies.

A typical "skill catalog" or "talent bank" questionnaire is shown in Fig. 6-2. The individual completing the form is given a code book to use in completing the questionnaire. The information is then key punched and can be retrieved from computer storage as desired.

Managerial Personnel. In addition to systems that provide information on the overall employee population, special purpose personnel inventories may also be used. One such special purpose inventory is the Management Development Planning or "backup" chart. An example is shown in Fig. 6-3. This chart is used to show the depth which exists within the management structure; they are of great assistance in pointing out strengths and weaknesses in this regard. In addition, they help in identifying candidates to be considered when an opening occurs.

Nonmanagerial Personnel. Personnel inventory systems are also invaluable in the current utilization and placement of nonmanagerial employees, particularly those who are represented by a union. In such cases, promotions, demotions, layoffs, recalls, and other employee transfers may be governed by specific agreements usually based on seniority and job ability. Such information should be used to prevent mistakes in the placement and utilization of operating personnel in order to avoid unnecessary complaints and grievances, and should be readily available.

Promotion Systems

In facing the future, a company must be assured of having sufficient depth of talent to meet new challenges in the face of a constantly changing business environment. This is particularly true of an industry where change is the rule rather than the exception; in this situation people must be available who can progress into higher levels in the organization as openings occur. There needs to be an ever-present reserve strength to enable the organization to accelerate its efforts on current programs and, at the same time, explore new business opportunities. Further, there should be a sound promotional procedure which enables the best-qualified and most deserving people to be considered for advancement throughout the organization.

Most companies have a policy of looking internally for promotable talent to fill openings, though occasionally it is necessary to look to outside sources for experienced people. The latter is particularly true when there are breakthroughs into new areas of technology or when the organization needs to reinforce current technical or managerial specialities. Most companies find it advisable to conduct an annual college recruitment program so that a sufficient supply of new talent is introduced into the organization.

By and large, however, organizations fill most openings through internal sources. There are several good reasons for this. A company's own people are tried and tested, and there should be little doubt concerning their ability and potential. In addition, it makes good economic sense to promote instead of hiring from the outside. Possibly of even greater importance, a good promotional program affords one of the strongest stimuli to job performance. Most people, to be motivated in their jobs, need to recognize that opportunity exists for them, that they are being fairly evaluated, and that they will be considered for future openings.

To reap the benefits which accrue from a strong promotional system, an organization must initiate and maintain a comprehensive personnel appraisal and development program. The promotional system can be only as good as the personnel who are in a position to move up the ladder. A department or section with strong backup through all levels (including hourly skills) tends to be people-centered. The supervisors in such groups spend time in evaluating subordinates, conducting on-the-job instruction, and encouraging people to grow and improve. Furthermore, they set a strong personal example for others to follow. As a result, staff members are better qualified to perform their jobs, possess a higher degree of morale, and are in a position to fill openings at higher levels.

INIT	LAST NAME	DEPT NO	BADGE NO	SOCIAL SECURITY NO	YRS IN IND	YRS IN AERO IND	PATENTS AWARDED	DIVISION	APPROVED BY:	DATE

A. EDUCATION

COL 1 HIGHEST LEVEL	COL 2 SUBJECT	COL 3 YR	COL 4 HRS	COL 5 COLLEGE

NOTE: WRITE IN OUTLINED BLOCKS ONLY

B. MILITARY INFORMATION

COL 1 SELECTIVE SERVICE CLASSIFICATION	COL 2 BRANCH OF SERVICE	COL 3 RANK	COL 4 YRS OF SERVICE	COL 5 DATE OF RETIREMENT

C. PROFESSIONAL ORGANIZATIONS

	COL 1 ORGANIZATION	COL 2 LEVEL OF PARTICIPATION
1		
2		
3		
4		

D. PROFESSIONAL LICENSE

COL 1 TITLE OF LICENSE

E. FOREIGN LANGUAGES

	COL 1 LANGUAGE	COL 2 PROFICIENCY
1		
2		
3		

CURRENT ASSIGNMENT

1 CATEGORY		
2 GROUP		
3 ASSIGNMENT		4 LENGTH TO DATE
5 FUNCTION		
6 PRODUCT AREA		7 PROGRAM

PROFESSIONAL INDEX QUESTIONNAIRE
(SEE INSTRUCTION GUIDE)

Front

F. EXPERIENCE SKILLS

		COL 1	COL 2	COL 3			COL 4				COL 5	COL 6	COL 7	COL 8	COL 9	COL 10
		CATEGORY	GROUP	ASSIGNMENT			FUNCTION				PRODUCT AREA	PROGRAM / TASK	COMPANY / AGENCY	LENGTH / ASSIGNMENT	DATE END OF ASSIGNMENT	TEACH/PUB
				WORD 1	WORD 2	WORD 3	WORD 1	WORD 2	WORD 3	WORD 4						
CURRENT ASSIGNMENT	1															
	2															
	3															
	4															
	5															
	6															
	7															
	8															
	9															
	10															

Reverse

Fig. 6-2. Typical "skill catalog" questionnaire.

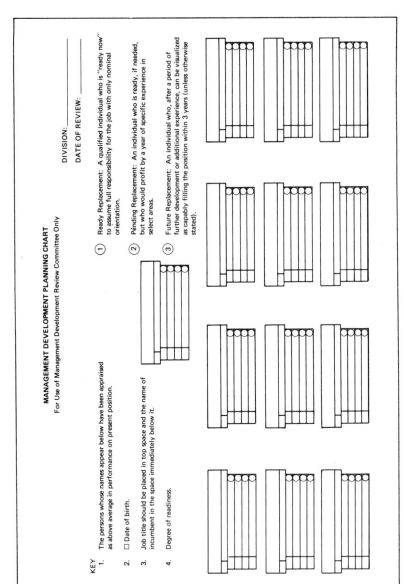

Fig. 6-3. Typical management development planning chart used to inventory management personnel and skills.

Promotional Criteria. The factors which determine individuals who are capable and deserving of promotion cannot be placed into a formula and fed into a computer. Instead, the best possible judgment must be used to match the characteristics of staff members with the characteristics of the job. Although this task does not lend itself to mathematical analysis, it is possible to establish criteria relative to such promotional selections.

Performance record. The best single criterion for promotion is the individual's performance in his present job. This is one reason why companies spend considerable effort in conducting various performance appraisal programs and measuring and recording such information on a formal basis.

Sometimes performance fails as a prediction criterion since there are individuals who succeed well at one level and yet cannot handle the increased responsibility at a higher level. In general, however, in selecting those for promotion, performance in present job is the best starting point.

Personal qualifications. Other factors to consider are personal qualifications. Some of these pertinent qualifications are included in the job specification sheet which accompanies the written job description. Such factors as education, experience, physical requirements, and necessity for travel are used in evaluating jobs, and these can be good guidelines in evaluating candidates. In addition to the qualifications in the job specification, others should be determined in order to match candidates most effectively against job standards. In regard to education, it is advisable to consider formal schooling if this is pertinent to the accomplishment of the job tasks. It is also good to consider the extent to which individuals maintain a program of continuing personal education. Particularly in evaluating people for key managerial and technical assignments, it is vital that successful candidates be those who keep themselves constantly aware of new developments in their field. This, of course, requires constant self-study, oftentimes on an informal basis. It is important, then, not to evaluate formal study only, but to consider those continuing efforts which people make to improve themselves.

Length of service. Length of company service, along with merit factors, should also be weighed in making promotions. Employees must realize that consideration will be given to consistently good performance extending over a period of time and that their willingness to invest their careers with their company is recognized. This is not to say that a company owes marginal or below-average performers with long service a permanent job with ever-increasing responsibility. It does mean that service should be one factor deserving of consideration when higher level openings occur. It should be considered along with the other criteria in making final determinations.

Test scores. Psychological test scores are sometimes used in reinforcing the other criteria in selecting people for promotion. Many jobs, particularly in management, administrative, and technical areas require that the successful individual have certain levels of intelligence, aptitude, and other characteristics vital to job success. For such jobs test results are particularly beneficial when used in conjunction with personnel appraisals. It goes without saying that test results should never be the sole criterion in making personnel decisions.

Promotion Boards. Careful deliberation is important in selecting and promoting managerial personnel from the first-line supervisor through higher levels of management. For this reason, many companies use promotion boards and set specific procedures to handle such upgradings. Through these methods, the most careful across-the-board consideration is given to all qualified and deserving candidates for supervisory positions within the organization.

Basically, the promotion boards consist of groups made up of key managers who review candidates for promotion or demotion within the supervisory ranks. If the supervisory change is taking place at lower levels, the meeting is generally held within the department; the department head might serve as chairman, and department managers may compose the remainder of the committee. Managers from other departments who know the candidates are also sometimes invited. A member of the personnel department may be included to furnish additional data on the candidates.

At higher levels, a board is usually comprised of executives who may look throughout an entire corporation for the best-qualified personnel for promotions in any of its divisions. When this is the case, it is important that a good executive inventory system be in existence at corporate headquarters containing all pertinent information relative to the competence and potential of its key personnel. One company uses the form shown in Fig. 6-4 to plan and record action taken in selecting and promoting managerial personnel.

The Attraction of New Skills

In the course of normal operations, it often becomes necessary to supplement existing skills with new personnel who can add strength and depth to an organization. Such needs arise as a result of several factors. Particularly during recent years as companies have extended their interests into new scientific and administrative fields, demands have grown for skills which previously were either not utilized or were actually nonexistent. Concurrent with demands for new types of skill

MANAGEMENT SELECTION
AND
DEVELOPMENT SUMMARY

| | Born Mo. Yr. | Serv. Date Mo. Yr. | Dept./Clock No. | Last Wage Mo. Yr. | Increase Amount | APPROVED ORGANIZATION CONTROL | DATE |

CANDIDATE'S NAME
LAST   FIRST   MIDDLE

	CLASSIFICATION	LG OR SG	RATE	APPROVED SECTION CHIEF
Present				
Proposed				APPROVED DEPARTMENT MANAGER

NAMES OF OTHER CANDIDATES

SUPERVISORY APPRAISAL COMMITTEE APPROVAL

PURPOSE OF CHANGE OR ADDITION:

TYPE WORK FOR WHICH PROPOSED:

DATE APPROVED   DATE REVIEWED

NUMBER OF EMPLOYEES SUPERVISED

	No.	LG/SG	CLASSIFICATION	NO.	LG/SG	CLASSIFICATION	NO.	LG/SG	CLASSIFICATION	NO.	LG/SG	CLASSIFICATION	NO.	LG/SG	CLASSIFICATION
Present															
Proposed															

HISTORY:

PERFORMANCE:

DEVELOPMENT:

EVALUATION:

PSYCHOLOGICAL

PROBATIONAL REVIEW

SATISFACTORY   QUESTIONABLE   UNSATISFACTORY
☐☐   ☐☐   ☐☐

PROBATIONAL SUPERVISOR.

REVIEW IN _____ DAYS

WHEN CANDIDATE IS BEING CONSIDERED FOR PROMOTION THE PERSONNEL EVALUATION SUMMARY IS PRESENTED TO AND DIS-
CUSSED BY THE SUPERVISORY APPRAISAL COMMITTEE.

WHEN THE CANDIDATE IS BEING CONSIDERED FOR DEMOTION THE SAC CONSIDERS ONLY PAST AND PRESENT JOB PERFORMANCE.

IF DEMOTION IS APPROVED BY THE COMMITTEE THE PERSONNEL EVALUATION SUMMARY MAY BE CONSIDERED FOR PURPOSES OF
PLACEMENT.

THE PERSONNEL EVALUATION SUMMARY IS ON FILE AND AVAILABLE FOR DISCUSSION.

Fig. 6-4. Management selection and development summary form used by one major company in selecting and promoting managerial personnel.

has been the expansion in certain areas utilizing existing skills. In addition, normal turnover develops needs for replenishment of talent.

Constant needs for new talent are apparent in any progressive organization. Such needs usually result in an initial search throughout the organization to determine if openings can be filled internally through promotion or transfer. When such people are not available, it becomes necessary to investigate sources outside the organization.

Generally, an overall employment program consists of three phases: (1) college recruitment (new graduates), (2) professional staffing (scientific, administrative, and managerial), and (3) general skills staffing (crafts, clerical, etc.).

College Recruiting. Good relations between business organizations and the colleges and universities can be of invaluable assistance to campus recruiting efforts, both with regard to securing undergraduate as well as graduate degree people. In addition, such relations, particularly with institutions in the vicinity, are productive in support of employee educational efforts.

Good relationships develop through interactions between business people and faculty members, business grants for scholarships, and other campus endeavors. Honest and aboveboard dealings with the institutions and the students being recruited is essential. In regard to the latter point, there are cases where businesses for one reason or another, have run afoul of the ethics committees of the college placement councils.

On the college campus, the placement director is the key to developing sound institutional relations. He counsels students regarding companies, arranges company interviewing dates, schedules students for interviews, and performs other tasks in helping student and company to get acquainted. Needless to say, his opinion of any company and its recruiting practices may directly affect his handling of that organization. Also; the placement director often communicates with faculty members regarding his opinion of different business concerns.

The placement director can also be valuable in establishing faculty contacts. He will set up faculty meetings with company representatives, arrange luncheon dates, and promote other contacts if he is so inclined. Also, in certain cases, the placement director may, at his discretion, make available to companies lists of graduating students at bachelor's and graduate levels.

In regard to graduate students, there is a growing trend for placement offices to establish special recruiting visits and encourage master's and doctoral candidates to schedule their interviews during this period.

Thus, it is in the best interests of any business to foster good relations with college placement offices at all institutions where it recruits. Failure to do this, or any short circuiting of these agencies, can jeopardize future recruiting.

Many companies are fortunate in having representatives who are members of the various college placement associations in areas where they recruit. These associations promote productive individual contacts and have allowed people to understand the kind of college relations program which will work best on each campus.

It is a fact that a standard program cannot be established that will fit each and every educational institution. Some universities feel that college visits by company personnel, outside of regular recruiting time, are greatly overdone and that professors and students are being bothered too much. Other institutions state that they do not see enough of company personnel.

Thus, if a program of college relations is to extend beyond the contacts with the placement office, it would make sense to find out if the institutions want this and, if so, what kind of program they feel is reasonable and, at the same time, helpful to them. Otherwise, instead of engendering improved relationships, the opposite may occur.

If there is one thing the company can bring to the campus, it is practical and applied knowledge. This can be accomplished in several ways which will enhance company prestige:

1) Much help can often be gained through company participation in graduate seminars, faculty meetings, student professional societies, and other similar gatherings. An analysis of company personnel should be made to determine those individuals who are capable, technically and personally, of participating in such an effort. A list of these people should be made; detailed personal background information is desirable as well as information concerning the person's areas of competency and specific subjects which he is prepared to discuss. This list can be forwarded to all of the institutions on the company's recruiting schedule.

Above all, participating company personnel must be briefed in advance and, possibly, have their presentations evaluated. They should take care to stick to their subjects and to avoid giving an advertising pitch. A desirable aspect of this type of approach is that it provides for the institution inviting the participant to the campus instead of having the company impose itself upon the institution.

2) Another productive approach is through prerecruiting to secure names of graduates, make initial contacts, talk to faculty to learn of promising people, etc. Here again, some institutions do

not favor this kind of effort so that extreme care must be taken not to disrupt past relationships. In other cases, clearance can be gained through the college placement office, and this office may even provide help.

3) Career days afford another opportunity to present information to students and faculty. Conducted at numerous institutions in recent years, these involve a display and participation of several employees to discuss various aspects of their companies.

4) Invitations are also extended to companies to furnish company displays in college libraries.

5) Requests can also be honored to supply materials and equipment for college laboratories.

6) Invitations for plant visits can be made by companies to college faculty members. Faculty members can also be offered summer employment. In this regard, the company should not get carried away and offer full-time employment to faculty people without clearing the matter with the institution.

7) Perhaps the most welcome approach which can be made to any institution is to offer teaching help on a part-time basis or to establish a full-time academic chair.

Campus interviews are usually twenty minutes to half an hour long. Elaborate brochures and other printed material are often made available to the student in advance of the interview. Needless to say, he should carefully study such information so that he will know as much as possible about his prospective employer. Also, in advance of the interview he should complete the application form provided by the company or, in some cases, the standard form prepared by the placement office.

During the relatively short interview, the recruiter really has two jobs. On the one hand, he is interested in learning as much as possible about the student. The application form is of great help in showing the individual's background, curriculum studies, grades, and interests. Additionally, the recruiter will also appraise factors such as personality and appearance, plus other qualities that may be necessary to perform properly in a particular job.

In addition to making a sound evaluation of the interviewee, the recruiter must explain significant factors about the company he represents. In general, he should describe the company products and types of jobs available, together with opportunities and challenges, wage-and-salary policies, and fringe benefits, and he can provide additional information that he knows the applicant will be interested in. Obviously, he himself must be very familiar with these things, and he has to know his company well in order to intelligently convey such information.

During the course of the interview, the recruiter forms an opinion regarding the applicant and tries to determine whether he meets the requirements of the job in question. Also, the student evaluates the company and the job opportunities described by the recruiter. If there is mutual interest, it is customary to extend an invitation to the applicant to visit the company.

During the visit to the company, the applicant will be provided with additional information and will be interviewed by one of the supervisors in the group where the job opening exists. It is also a good practice for the company to introduce the applicant to some of the younger employees from his college or university. In this way, he can get direct information on how these people like the company and the work they are doing. This will help him decide whether to accept a possible employment offer.

In-plant interviewing is coordinated by the employment department, which abides by the same good practices used in campus interviewing. The day should be planned to give the applicant as meaningful and pleasant a visit as possible.

Either during or following the in-plant interview, the college recruiting office and the operating department compare notes. If both are favorably inclined, a job offer will be communicated. This may be done verbally during the visit or later on by mail. The offer includes the starting date, job title, starting salary, and perhaps other details about future opportunities and benefits.

Normally, the applicant will interview a number of different concerns and may make several visits to different company locations. He will naturally evaluate the opportunities and compare many factors before making his final decision.

Recruiting Experienced Professional Personnel. Many of the approaches used in securing experienced professional personnel are similar to those employed in securing college graduates. The experienced person being sought, however, is seldom actively seeking employment as is the college graduate, unless his company has met with some setback such as the loss of a major contract. Instead, he is likely to be happily engaged as a highly productive employee in a reputable firm. He is more mature, perhaps active in community affairs, and is highly regarded by his company and professional associates. He is rewarded financially in line with his existing capabilities. He is not a marginal performer who is likely to be in a surplus category or in danger of being laid off by his present employer.

The extreme difficulty of attracting and hiring such experienced personnel can be readily recognized. To reach objectives in hiring qualified people within realistic time schedules at reasonable cost, an aggressive recruiting program is necessary. Employment personnel and line management must work closely in applying the best techniques for establishing bona fide requirements, arranging search efforts, conducting out-of-town and in-plant interviews, and administering a prompt and sound hiring program.

A program for employing experienced professionals has several phases:

1) Planning of the program in line with predetermined requirements and qualitative standards
2) Determination of sources of outside manpower and cultivation of effective relationship with these sources
3) Recruiting
4) Follow-up.

Determining how many new experienced employees are needed is usually the responsibility of either the line department or a separate manpower planning organization. In many companies the instrument for initiating the hiring process is an employment requisition properly and completely filled out and approved by a designated management level. Qualitative standards for types of personnel needed are defined on the requisition form (degree, years of experience, skill specialty, classification, department, type of experience needed, etc.).

Sources of manpower are then located and evaluated by employment personnel. Skill sources may be developed through analyzing applicant files, through recommendations of company personnel, advertising, private employment agency referrals, technical societies, professional search consultants, state departments of employment, university alumni files, and others.

These sources must be continually cultivated and kept up to date by:

1) Requesting new employees to provide names of former associates who might be qualified for employment
2) Requesting same information from current company employees
3) Utilizing magazine and newspaper advertising to take advantage of local situations or recruiting trips to particular areas
4) Cultivating relationships with effective employment agencies and search organizations
5) Attendance at technical society meetings where recruiting is acceptable and likely to be successful
6) Maintaining good applicant files with retrieval capability.

Once prime sources for talent are determined, an aggressive recruiting campaign is in order. This requires an out-of-town "expedition" in most cases to the location where the talent exists. Often a newspaper, mail, or telephone advance campaign will be used to line up interested applicants. In this phase of the effort particular experience in employment recruiting is essential. There must be enough publicity given to the program to attract desirable people for interview; at the same time, an overly aggressive campaign can lead to repercussions.

Employment people usually do out-of-town recruiting alone with the prime objective of qualifying talent against requirements. Obvious misfits are quickly rejected; resumes of possible candidates are sent to the plant for further review; persons who appear highly qualified may be invited to the plant for interview by line people.

Out-of-town recruiting trips may require the assistance of line managers when large numbers of requirements exist and on-the-spot hiring is to be accomplished. In this case, the recruiter and technical person unite, using a team approach which has proved very successful.

The employment office serves as the clearing house for receiving resumes and applications, routing them to appropriate departments, and receiving them in return with recommendations for action. It then approves and extends invitations for in-plant interviews, arranges hotel reservations, notifies the line organization of interview dates, and pays travel expenses.

Employment conducts preliminary in-plant interviews, rolls out the "welcome mat," draws out pertinent information not contained in resumes, analyzes personality characteristics of applicants, and assures the exposure of the applicant to maximum interviewing time in the interested department. The department then conducts the technical in-plant interview. This should be done in a professional and personal fashion, with a thorough explanation of the organization, the general work area, and the work requirements and challenges. The department should evaluate the applicant technically, discuss conclusions with the employment representative, and recommend that an offer be made if he meets the qualifications. The employment office then officially extends the offer to the applicant in accordance with the line department's recommendations, or tells him that an offer will not be made.

Follow-up requires a continuously aggressive attitude by both employment and line departments to keep negotiation time spans to a minimum. Employment should personally follow up with the department for decisions on applicants who have been in the plant for interviewing. Employment should also follow up applicants for decisions on offers that have been extended, and should provide written or verbal information to the line departments as soon as an offer is made or when the applicant rejects or accepts an offer. When start dates are established, the line department should be informed.

Executive and Managerial Employment. A modification of normal practice is required in securing executive and top scientific personnel. Procedures in analyzing sources, arranging interviews, and gaining acceptances are quite similar to those already mentioned. The prime difference lies in the manner of contacting and dealing with the individuals involved.

Obviously, hiring one select individual is not the same as attracting a number of lower level professional people to fill normal requirements. All efforts must be pinpointed to the individual, interviews arranged to suit his particular needs, and more overall attention accorded him than would normally be the case. In other words, an employment effort must be tailored directly to the prospective employee on an individual basis.

General Skills Employment. Just as care must be taken in the employment of professional personnel, so must careful attention be directed to the hiring of technicians, craftsmen, and clerical personnel. Some companies have literally hundreds of job classifications which fit in this category, and keeping them filled with competent people is a never-ending task.

Many of the same services can be used as in the case of other forms of hiring. Most such hiring is done within the general vicinity of the company's facilities, a factor that makes it important for the company to be known as a "good place to work." Here a sound community relations program pays off. Residents of the community will naturally be drawn to a company which is known to treat its people well, offers steady employment, and is a "good neighbor." Also, the extent to which the company offers training and opportunity for individual growth and advancement exerts a powerful influence in inducing people to visit its employment offices.

It is particularly important in the case of general skills hiring to maintain good applicant files. Many candidates for employment are "walk-ins," that is, they are not responding to any specific advertisements or other inducements. Sometimes, by chance, a walk-in may appear at just the right moment to fill an existing opening. This is not the usual case, however. Typically, the applicant finds that either there are no openings available at the moment or that his skills do not match current requirements. It is important at this point to determine whether he does possess skills which might be used in case openings should develop and, if so, to have him complete an application form. Filed by skill specialty, such forms serve as a valuable bank of talent from which to fill future openings.

Local advertising is usually productive in attracting skilled personnel. Also, state departments of employment, as well as certain private agencies, do a good job in this respect. Vocational and technical high schools are also good sources. And no company should fail to establish close contact with community colleges whose two-year programs are increasingly turning out excellent technicians in many fields.

Evaluating the Applicant. Whatever form of employment hiring is being conducted, success often hinges on the accurate evaluation of applicants. Here, several sources of information can be used, including the referral source, the application form, the actual interview, and personal or business references.

Referral source. Experience with sources of talent soon shows which are competent in referring people to meet specific organizational needs and which are deficient. For instance, one source may do a consistently good job in referring personnel to fill clerical slots. It could be a private agency or a state employment office which tests and screens applicants in accordance with agreed-upon standards. On the other hand, an organization may have had extremely good luck with a certain executive search firm in attracting high-level personnel. An organization which evaluates its sources of talent usually knows where good applicants come from and conversely which sources are less productive. An applicant cannot be judged fully on this basis, but it does provide one indication of his worth.

Application form. The application form is a tool which should be reviewed fully and intelligently. First must be the assurance that the form elicits the information from the applicant which is needed in evaluating his background. Many companies use different forms for professional and nonprofessional personnel and place different emphases in accordance with the level of personnel being recruited. For example, if a scientist or manager is being sought, it is essential to require detailed information regarding education, offices held, professional society participation, papers published, and awards received in addition to specific work experience. Perhaps extensive travel and knowledge of a foreign language may also be prerequisites. At any rate, the form used should fit the jobs to be filled and provide enough data to screen applicants effectively prior to the personal interview. Naturally, care must be taken not to make inquiries which violate federal and state laws.

Personal interview. The interview is usually the first personal contact between the applicant and the employer. Customarily, the first interview takes place in the employment office. In the case of walk-ins, and persons who are responding to advertising or who have been referred by an employment agency, the employment interviewer talks to the individual, and if he appears qualified, arranges for him to be interviewed by a manager in the department with the opening.

Many interviews, particularly those involving key applicants, are prescheduled with arrangements made in advance. An application form has already been reviewed by the requesting department with instructions forwarded to the employment office to invite the individual in for a detailed discussion. Oftentimes, out-of-town applicants are asked to travel some distance; it is customary to pay travel expenses plus room and board for such visits, and to make hotel and transportation arrangements.

During the formal interview, there are three functions which the manager must perform: (1) complete the evaluation process, (2) give the applicant detailed information about the job and the organization, and (3) begin establishing a sound relationship between himself and the applicant, who may in a short while become a key employee.

In conducting the interview, the following points should be considered:

1) The interview should be planned. Determine in advance what information is needed from the applicant and what questions should be asked. It might be well to put this in writing. Planning also involves allotting sufficient time free from interruptions. In the case of high-level applicants, an entire day or more may be needed. The applicant should be exposed to other key personnel, and he should see the company's facilities; if he is from out of town, he will need time to evaluate housing and schools.

2) Have a suitable place to conduct the interview. It is not necessary to usurp the president's office, but comfortable surroundings with adequate privacy are required.

3) Know the job requirements in detail so they can be communicated to the applicant. The job description may be helpful here, but do not just cover the basic duties. In addition, discuss job objectives and challenges as well as future opportunities and the relationship of the job to the total organization.

4) Put the applicant at ease. An interview is not an inquisition. A friendly greeting will help get things off to a good start and prepare both interviewer and interviewee for the discussion which is to commence.

5) A good interview is in reality a give-and-take session with participation on both sides. The applicant should be permitted to express himself as fully as time will allow. At the same time, the interviewer should keep control of the session in order to elicit all

the information needed to reinforce the data included on the application form.

6) No matter what opinion he has gained of the applicant, the interviewer should close the session in a friendly fashion. If he has made a definite decision, he may decide to communicate it immediately to the applicant. In case of a "yes" answer, he will want to cite the job challenges and opportunities and mention how well the applicant will fit into the organization. In case of a "no" answer, he will explain why the applicant does not meet requirements and will wish him well. As is often the case, it may be impossible to make an immediate decision, and in this case the applicant is told to expect an answer in the near future.

7) Follow-up to assure that proper action is taken is next in order. For example, the employment office needs to be told whether to make a formal offer to the applicant.

Psychological testing. As a part of the interview process, many companies use psychological testing. This was discussed earlier in connection with the promotion process.

Personal references. Reference checking is another vital phase of the evaluation process. Many application forms provide spaces for the applicant to include character references; such references are of limited value, however, since the applicant generally provides names of persons whom he knows will respond positively. Previous employers and supervisors are a good source of information, but the applicant's present employer should never be contacted without specific permission. Also, former colleges and universities can be checked to substantiate educational information. The telephone is increasingly popular for obtaining reference checks since individuals are frequently more frank than they would be in written communications.

PERSONNEL DEVELOPMENT

The training and development of personnel at all levels is vital to the success of any organization. Maintaining a competitive edge in any business is dependent upon a number of factors, but the most important of these lies in individual talents and potential. The extent to which human resources are kept productive and up to date determines the fate of the entire enterprise. More than ever, today's changing technology in administrative as well as scientific realms creates a need for continued emphasis on personal growth and development. From craftsmen to chief executive, the emphasis is on acceleration of learning and improvement of performance. Many systems and approaches are being used from company schools to train the new hire in the elements of his first duties to executive programs sponsored by graduate schools of business. Table VI-1 indicates the range of training and education activity in one large corporation.

The "knowledge explosion" of recent years has created business educational needs which never existed in the past. This section of the chapter will look at the various aspects of personnel development in which business is involved today and will deal with some of the challenges of the future.

New Employee Orientation

Good orientation of new employees is one of the most basic supervisory responsibilities. In most companies, hiring is a continuous activity. At any given time, new people are being absorbed—from all walks of life—either as replacements to take care of normal turnover or to fill new jobs caused by expansion and addition of new projects.

The quality of the initial orientation directly affects the extent to which new employees succeed as members of their work groups. Few people ever forget their early days on a new job. All of us can look back and recall the manner in which we were received by our original supervisor and fellow employees. Some may recall the warmth of the introductions made to them and the help and encouragement they received. Others may have had a very negative experience and can remember the feeling of insecurity and dissatisfaction which resulted.

A correct induction and orientation procedure probably is the best available tool for eliminating turnover. Industry-wide figures show that the greatest turnover takes place during the first six months of employment. This indicates strongly that opinions formed during the person's first days on a new job are important and lasting. The new employee decides very early whether his new company is the type of organization in which he desires to invest his future or whether he will grasp the first opportunity to move elsewhere. Most of his opinion results from the manner in which he is accepted and made to feel "at home" by his supervisor and fellow employees.

Before a new person can be successfully developed to his peak performance, his supervisor must first create the right attitude on his part so that he is prepared to learn and grow. Most new employees are nervous and unsure of themselves in new surroundings. The new man has a strong desire to be accepted and to gain self-confidence. Obviously, if we fail to put him at ease, gain his interest, and offer encouragement, we establish a barrier which prevents his gaining the vital skills he needs.

Our goal in dealing with the new employee is to stimulate him to

Table VI-1. Training and Education.

Company Objective	Executive Development	Management Education	Management Appraisal	Engineering and Science Education	Technical Skill Training
Purpose	To build depth in executive talent	To improve skills in management	To appraise management performance and potential	To promote advanced knowledge in areas of new scientific discovery	To develop job skills and familiarize employees with new products

Specific programs in support of objectives	1. Appraisal of executive potential
	2. Developing individual growth plans
	3. Providing development in:
	  a. Business skills
	  b. Interpersonal relations
	  c. Industry in American society
	
	4. Executive counseling
		1. Presupervisory training
		2. Supervisory discussion program
		3. Evening school of management
		4. Special departmental programs and seminars
		5. Understudy development:
		  a. Coaching
		  b. Counseling
		  c. Delegation
		6. Outside sources:
		  a. Seminars
		  b. Colleges and universities
		7. Management library
			1. Maintain management records
			2. Evaluate management performance
			3. Identify potential
			4. Inventory management capabilities
			5. Recommend management personnel for promotion
			6. Counsel supervisors
			7. Determine management training needs
				1. Career planning and counseling
				2. Engineering orientation programs
				3. Evening school scientific study
				4. In-plant master of science programs
				5. Doctoral fellowship program
				6. Outside institutions:
				  a. Undergraduate
				  b. Graduate
				7. In-plant seminars
					1. Planned on-the-job training
					2. Vestibule programs:
					  a. Machine shop
					  b. Sheet metal
					  c. Electronics
					  d. Tooling
					  e. Assembly
					  f. Welding, etc.
					3. Evening company programs
					4. Cooperative programs with city and county schools

peak efficiency in the shortest time. The degree to which we succeed depends to a great extent on the job we do right at the start.

New employees are usually interviewed, screened, and hired through an employment office. On the morning when new people report for work, they are often given a formal induction talk by a member of the personnel department. A discussion of company products is given, company benefits are explained, and company rules, safety, pay procedure, and other subjects are described.

The new employee is then escorted to his department. At this point one manufacturing organization follows the following simple orientation program:

1) *Third-level supervisor* (general foreman or equivalent).

   Greets new people; gives general description of work performed; explains its importance; attempts to make employees feel at ease; gives brief descriptions of departmental policies and procedures; introduces people to second-level supervisor.

2) *Second-level supervisor* (foreman or equivalent).

   Greets people; outlines organization of group; shows new employee how he fits in; stresses that employee will receive the help and guidance he needs to get off to a good start; explains what is expected from employees such as safety, good housekeeping, and quality, etc., with a few words on each subject; introduces new employee to first-level supervisor.

3) *First-level supervisor* (assistant foreman or equivalent).

   Greets each person and tells him he appreciates having him working in his group; states he is present to help; explains functioning of group and importance of each worker and his job; physically orients new people to cafeterias, restrooms, tool cribs, etc., and explains any procedures they need to know; introduces new employee to certain fellow employees; checks to see if there are any questions; gives word of encouragement and commences job instruction using standardized techniques; follows up orientation according to person's needs. Utilizes top-skilled employees as necessary to assist him.

General Training

The twentieth century, with its advanced mechanization, has intensified the critical need for craftsmen who can handle the technical problems of production. With production becoming less dependent upon physical effort and more upon intelligent application of skill, many types of training programs have been refined or newly devised.

Industrial managers are for the most part well acquainted with the apprenticeship form of training—a tradition dating back to 2100 B.C.

under the Babylonian Code of Hammurabi. At that time, the instructor was the father and the student the son; today it is the supervisor or company trainer and the employee.

As is generally known, an apprentice is a worker who learns, according to a written agreement, a recognized skilled trade requiring two or more years of work experience on the job supplemented by appropriate related trade instruction. Apprentice work schedules must contain enough work activities or operations to guarantee all-around competence in the trade, and supplementary classroom training provides knowledge of required theory. State and city departments of education often will assist in providing such programs as a part of their adult curricula. The Bureau of Apprenticeship of the U.S. Department of Labor can also provide valuable assistance in initiating apprenticeship programs.

Many companies which do not conduct formal apprenticeship programs still sponsor educational activities designed to develop skills in the new worker or upgrade the skills of older employees. Some of these programs are conducted during working hours in company classrooms; others may be offered on a voluntary basis after hours in company evening schools. Here subjects such as blueprint reading, shop mathematics, electronics, tool planning and design, and cost estimating are taught. In addition, textbooks and self-teaching materials such as programed learning courses may be made available. Some shop managers establish departmental libraries where employees can check out training literature. Notices of courses offered by nearby schools are often displayed, and program catalogs may be made available.

Such attention to formal education benefits the worker as well as the organization. It should not be forgotten, however, that the basic source of personal growth is the job situation itself. Supervisors, particularly those at the first level, must realize that one of their prime responsibilities is the development of their work force. Not only must enough people be qualified to perform their current task, but also there must be assurance that future skill demands are understood and developmental action taken in advance.

The time and attention given by the supervisor to personnel development provides assurance that his operation is prepared for future requirements. Also, it does much to enhance his relationships with his people. Probably nothing does more to promote trust and confidence than the interest taken by a manager, at any level, in the well-being and future of his people. Also, the influence on employee motivation is readily understandable since needs for growth and achievement are inherent in everyone.

To obtain results, the supervisor must be concerned with the effective planning of training within his operation, as well as the actual conduct of the training process. Successful planning of employee training involves an analysis of personnel strengths and weaknesses, plus a sound knowledge of present and future demands which are and will be placed upon the operation. The needs of the new employee are usually evident. A good appraisal system is helpful in understanding the training needs of older employees and in pointing out developmental actions which should be taken, particularly if it is oriented toward evaluation of results rather than traits. Specific evidences of good and poor workmanship as recorded in the appraisal can be put to good use as a basis for determining individual needs.

Problems which arise such as increased scrap and rework rates, poor housekeeping, failure to meet quantity or schedule standards, and increased accident rates indicate a need for immediate action. Perhaps the best method of evaluating needs is the day-by-day observation of employee performance. The supervisor who is close enough to his people and their operations can readily detect personnel who need assistance.

The Training Timetable. A training timetable is also a very helpful device (see the sample shown in Fig. 6-5). Such timetables indicate the present proficiency of each employee, the number of people required to perform the departmental operations, and the employees who need specific training. Further, they serve as a method of planning needed training.

To build a timetable like the one shown, first record in the left margin the names of all employees in a given job classification. In our example we are considering the classification of aircraft assembler. Next, write in the various jobs or operations which are required to be performed in the job classification. Use the diagonal space for this purpose.

At this point, write next to the operations the number of people needed to perform each one. Allowances should be made for contingency factors such as absenteeism, shifting work loads, accelerated schedules, vacations, and so on. Next, a symbol is needed to indicate each individual's proficiency in performing the various operations. Some symbols are shown on the sample timetable; however, any supervisor can generate his own to fit his particular needs.

Once symbols are established, the supervisor merely applies them in the timetable to reflect the proficiency status of his people. It will be apparent where individual training attention is needed. Also, the supervisor can schedule dates when he plans to have people trained. If enough people are not being trained in line with requirements, the fact becomes known immediately.

To make a training timetable work well, the supervisor needs to

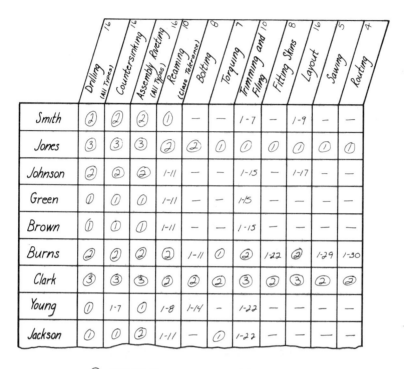

① MEANS WORKER CAN DO THE JOB BUT NEEDS CONSIDERABLE FOLLOW-UP

② MEANS WORKER CAN MEET REQUIREMENTS OF JOB, IS DEPENDABLE, BUT NEEDS SOME FOLLOW-UP

③ MEANS HE IS OUTSTANDING IN HIS SPECIALTY, REQUIRING LITTLE OR NO FOLLOW-UP

– MEANS HE DOESN'T NEED TO KNOW THE JOB OR OPERATION

1-14 } INDICATES THE DATES SUPERVISOR HAS SET FOR HIMSELF
1-22 } WHEN HE PLANS TO HAVE UNTRAINED MEN PREPARED TO DO
      } JOB IN ACCORDANCE WITH SPECIFICATIONS NOTED IN ①

Fig. 6–5. Part of a general training timetable for an assembly job.

know the magnitude and complexity of not only the department's present, but also its future work load. He should keep abreast of changes in technology, processes, equipment, tools, and all the other factors which influence his operation. Just as the physician and scientist must constantly update their knowledge, so must people in management ranks, from foreman to top executive. The necessary information can be gained through internal company communication, and through exposure to outside sources such as books, periodicals, seminars, conferences, and academic courses.

The supervisor who relies on these sources can readily assess the impact of the future upon his department's operations and personnel.

He will comprehend what his people will need to know and will understand what skills they should possess to cope with tomorrow's challenges. Thus he can plan his training program in accordance with these needs of the future.

The Job Instruction Process

Four steps must be taken during the job instruction process. These four steps apply whether a new man is being taught his first job or a present employee a new job.

The four steps should be taken regardless of the kind of job. They apply to every instruction task. These steps are:

1) *Prepare* the learner
2) *Present* the operation
3) *Try out* performance
4) *Follow up.*

Step One: Prepare the Learner. Before an employee can benefit from instruction, he must be properly prepared to learn. He should be put at ease, his interest aroused, and his self-confidence developed. Finally, the instructor should determine how much the employee already knows.

Put the learner at ease. Before teaching can begin successfully, the instructor must put the learner at ease. A nervous, jumpy employee is in no mental condition to receive or absorb new ideas. Nothing will do more to ease the learner's mind than to have the instructor adopt a friendly, helpful, interested attitude. If the instructing process is approached as if it were a disagreeable chore, the learner will find it practically impossible to relax.

The instructor must appear unhurried, no matter how much pressure he may be under from other duties. If the learner feels he is to be rushed, his overanxiety to absorb instruction quickly will render his mind less receptive.

Arouse interest. Until the learner's interest is aroused, instructional ideas are likely to "go in one ear and out of the other." The desire to learn comes only after interest is stimulated.

A few introductory words about the interesting features of the new job, the opportunities it presents for the man who is qualified, or references to the success of others on the same job will help to whet the learner's appetite for knowledge about the job.

Build up learner's self-confidence. A job always looks more difficult to a learner at the beginning. Every difficulty seems magnified. It is natural that he may have some misgivings concerning his ability to master the job. It is therefore of utmost importance that something be done to build up the learner's self-confidence.

Young workers being trained for their first job are likely to be over-impressed with its complications and difficulties. Older workers may feel convinced that "an old dog can't learn new tricks." Self-confidence must be built up in both young and old workers before they are taught a new job.

At the beginning, do not overemphasize the difficulties of the new job. Assure the learner that he will be given plenty of time and oppor-tunity to master the job thoroughly. Assure him that he will have ample opportunity to ask questions and clear up any details before he is left to handle the job on his own.

Check what learner already knows. It will help to bring the learn-er's mind right up to the point of receiving instruction if the instructor can refer to points of similarity between the new job and jobs or exper-iences which the learner has had previously. This will give him a feel-ing of "at homeness" in approaching the new job.

The new duties will not seem nearly so difficult to master if the learner is made to feel that certain knowledge, dexterity, or skills developed in the past can be applied to the new job.

Step Two: Present the Operation. In presenting the informa-tion and the operations involved, mere *telling* alone will not suffice. Mere *showing* may not put the "know-how" over to the learner. Only a combination of *telling, showing, illustrating,* and *questioning,* properly used, will make instruction 100 percent effective.

How to tell. In the "telling" part of your instruction, bear in mind the following points:

1) Make your telling very simple.
2) Go slowly and do not tell too much at once.
3) Make use of questions so that the employee will "tell himself," thus making him think and sharpen his interest.
4) Be sure that you do not use any terms, words, or expressions whose meaning may not be clear.
5) Use illustrations related to things he already knows.
6) Tell him over and over again if necessary, giving him time to absorb each item.
7) In checking to make sure that the employee understands, do not simply ask him, "Now, do you understand?" He can answer such a question by saying "Yes," whether he understands or not. It is better to ask him to explain to you what you have just told him.

How to show. Merely telling a person something is not enough. One remembers things that are *seen* much better than things that are only *heard.* Therefore, a demonstration before the employee's eyes is a very necessary part of the instruction. In "showing him how," observe the following points:

1) Demonstrate each operation of the job step by step, thus reinforcing in his mind what you have told him about doing the job.
2) Position him so that he sees the demonstration from the same angle as yourself.
3) Go through the motions at a rate sufficiently slow for him to see each operation clearly. Remember that the hand may be quicker than the eye.
4) Be sure to show him the simplest, easiest, shortest, and most efficient way to perform each operation, explaining as you go along.
5) Point out the danger points in doing the job.
6) Encourage him to ask questions as you proceed with your demonstration.
7) Repeat the demonstration several times if necessary, until he thoroughly understands.

Step Three: Try Out Performance. Before the learner is put "on his own," he should first be tried out in the actual performance of the task. Give particular regard to the following points:

1) The performance tryout consists of having the man go through the operations of the job under your watchful eye to make sure that he thoroughly understands each operation.
2) Performance tryout also consists of asking the man questions to check his understanding of all the facts about the job upon which his judgment and decisions concerning the job must be based. Ask questions beginning with *why, what, how, when, who,* or *where.*
3) During the tryout step, take the opportunity to correct the worker's mistakes calmly, patiently, and thoroughly. Above all, do not excite him.
4) After sufficient performance tryout has assured you that the learner has a good grasp of the job, he should be given a word of encouragement and told to proceed with the work on his own.
5) In leaving him to himself on the new job, advise him to bring his questions and problems to you if and when any arise.

Step Four: Follow-up. After you have finished the preparation, presentation, and performance tryout steps, there still remains the important follow-up step in instruction. Observe these points:

1) Follow up closely to be sure that the newly instructed man is carrying out instructions to the letter.
2) Be careful to follow up in such a way that the man does not get the impression that you are merely critical. Make your follow-up patient and helpful.
3) During the follow-up period, come back to the man at his work-place at frequent intervals where this is possible. Observe his work, give him an opportunity to ask further questions, and add to the instruction already given by informing him of the finer points and short cuts of the job.
4) Emphasize safety factors in the follow-up.
5) Encourage him and try to build up his confidence.

The follow-up step in the instruction may be considered at an end when the newly instructed man is able to do his job with the same amount of supervision normally given to qualified workers.

Management Development

Identifying and developing management talent, from first-line supervisors to top executives, is a concern of any business. This concern demands that emphasis be directed at improvement of current management performance as well as the creation of suitable depth in management reserves at all levels.

Managers do not just happen; they do not grow by chance. Management potential must be sought and nurtured. This involves maintaining a proper growth climate in which learning is stimulated. Further, management development requires the active participation of each management level in applying sound development methods in grooming subordinate managerial personnel plus those beneath the first level of supervision who have management potential. While responsibility for development rests in the line organization, staff support is usually beneficial; indeed many companies have training or education departments with experienced management instructors who assist in the process. Consultants are also called upon to lead programs of various types. Many different approaches and techniques are being used in industry today to develop managerial talent.

Inventorying Management Skills. As mentioned previously, most organizations maintain some management inventory system to help in determining managerial strengths and weaknesses and depth of talent. This information is vital in planning developmental efforts as well as in identifying managerial personnel for promotion.

Managerial Coaching and Counseling. Coaching involves the constant effort which any level of management employs in helping subordinate managers grow and develop. It assumes that every contact provides an opportunity for the supervisor to add to the subordinate's knowledge and experience. It is closely akin to coaching in sports. The coach assigns tasks to the team member, observes his performance, and makes necessary corrections. He also reinforces desirable performance by pointing out aspects of good behavior as well as correcting mistakes. The prime requisite to coaching is to delegate meaningful and challenging work to the subordinate along with responsibility for results. Coaching involves learning by doing and is probably the best single development method.

Counseling is a more formal development process and usually follows the personnel appraisal involving communication of evaluation results to the subordinate. Counseling, however, should not be restricted to the post-appraisal interview. In reality, it is a summary discussion of results achieved, strengths and weaknesses, and other aspects of performance. It enables the supervisor to work with the subordinate in evolving career plans, setting goals and objectives, and defining individual development needs. While coaching is a constant process, counseling is done intermittently as the need requires. The steps involved in the counseling process were discussed earlier. Handled correctly, counseling is a powerful stimulant in improving both performance and potential of subordinate supervision.

Some companies have staff counselors in their personnel departments who can offer added assistance to line management. Such people are particularly knowledgeable in assisting managers and other employees in career planning and can help in defining and planning the kind of learning experiences which will enable the individual to meet his personal goals.

Formal Management Education. While the core of management development is centered on the supervisor-subordinate relationship, formalized management education is vital in reinforcing coaching and counseling efforts. Of the factors contributing to management success, there are many which can be improved through lecture, conference, and similar methods.

Some companies maintain a full curriculum of courses and use a combination of employee-instructors as well as consultants, usually faculty members from nearby institutions. Subjects range all the way from basic fundamentals of management to the socio-politico-economic environment. Many organizations, large and small, conduct periodical internal management seminars to discuss quality, safety, maintenance, production schedules, and other subjects, and staff experts are often used to lead the discussions. Other organizations subscribe to management literature and disseminate it to management personnel.

Management clubs have sprung up in many companies. Some are

social in nature, but most have an educational objective. One thing that many of these clubs have done is to invite outside speakers to address members on topics of interest to management.

Organizations such as the American Management Association offer seminars covering topics which span the entire management spectrum. Also, credit courses in business are offered on almost every college campus and are usually available on an after-working-hours basis. Indeed, complete undergraduate and graduate degree programs may be pursued through evening study on the campuses of many major universities.

Of particular interest to higher level managers are the executive programs available at many leading universities, ranging from one-week short courses to the full-year MIT Sloan Program.

The manager, while concerned with keeping up to date on new aspects of business knowledge, also must keep abreast of the new and changing technologies which he supervises. This is particularly true of engineering or research and development managers, who have real problems keeping up with the state of the art while at the same time carrying heavy administrative work loads.

Job Climate. Good management development can be stimulated only when a good job climate exists. The environment surrounding the manager can either be a stifling influence which prevents growth, or it can be a very dynamic factor in stimulating constant development.

Much of what we call "climate" is dependent upon the organization of the supervisory function and the degree of real status and authority which supervisors possess. To some extent this must be "built" into the supervisory job. A poor climate is one where little real authority exists and the supervisor himself becomes merely a "go-between," linking subordinate levels with those who actually make decisions. A good climate is one where as much authority as possible is delegated down the line, providing supervisors with an opportunity to exercise their management skills and capabilities.

Pre-Supervisory Training. Many organizations have found that they cannot successfully give a skilled craftsman or technician supervisory responsibilities without prior development and training. The selection and training of new supervisors is a challenging task.

One company has successfully used an initial selection process involving nominations and approvals. The first three levels of management who are familiar with the people involved refer applicants to the company's education department, using a form similar to the one shown in Fig. 6-6. The applicants are tested and given personal interviews to explain the program for which they are being considered and

PRE-SUPERVISORY RECOMMENDATION

(Note to Foreman or Supervisor)

To insure that we have sufficient qualified people available for positions in first line management, it is necessary that we carefully choose and train a nucleus of outstanding employees as potential supervisors. We request your help in identifying those people under your supervision who have the leadership potential needed for success in management. Please analyze your people carefully and consider those you propose in light of the characteristics as presented below. Please route the form up the line to your superintendent who will forward it to the Education Department.

Name of Candidate _____ Badge Number _____

Present Assignment _____ Shift _____

Please check the statements which best describe this individual.

_____ He demonstrates a high degree of dependability and takes pride in the type of job he performs.

_____ He has a good knowledge of technical job requirements and can adapt quickly to new assignments and changing conditions.

_____ He is well respected by his supervisor and fellow employees and has indicated the ability to inspire confidence in a work group.

_____ He has strong personal drive and ambition with potential to develop a similar feeling of enthusiasm in others.

_____ He has demonstrated a high degree of initiative; he likes to accept a challenge and carry it through with a minimum of follow-up.

_____ He communicates well, absorbs information readily and expresses himself clearly to others.

_____ He has demonstrated a high degree of loyalty to his group, his supervisor and the company as a whole.

_____ He has attained a good degree of maturity, appears to have a personal goal and has been preparing to reach it.

_____ He is the type of person you would like as a subordinate supervisor.

Has the candidate been delegated any leadership responsibility be his immediate supervisor in the past? If so, what functions and how would you evaluate his performance?

What other qualities does this man possess which lead you to recommend him as top potential for supervision? (Use other side of sheet if necessary.)

Signature of Evaluator _____

Reviewed by _____

Fig. 6-6.   Form used to nominate individuals for pre-supervisory training.

to determine their level of interest in accepting managerial responsibility.

Once the candidate is admitted to the program, he is assigned to a supervisor in his department who will serve as his coach. The potential supervisor is given progressively more important work assignments to help him understand the functions of supervision. He may lead small task groups or actually take over the supervisor's job during periods of absence.

In addition to on-the-job training, the trainee supervisors receive formal instruction from experienced management trainers. This instruction covers basic supervision subjects, including leadership and human relations, communications, job planning, labor relations, safety, and quality control. Each trainee is periodically evaluated, and those who succeed in the program form a pool of future supervisory talent.

Smaller companies which do not have management training personnel can enlist the support of a nearby college or university to line up instructors for the formal phase of such a program.

Understudy Identification and Development. The extent to which people are ready for higher level management positions is a measure of real company strength and flexibility. It determines the confidence with which the organization can look to the future and accept new challenges.

By definition, an understudy is a person trained to assume all the responsibilities of the job ahead. Strong emphasis in such development is placed on learning by doing. People gain needed understanding only through experience in handling responsibilities in the higher classification coupled with constant coaching and counseling.

Understudy development should evolve as a normal management procedure. Each manager should be evaluated on his ability to train someone to take his own job, and his own promotion can be made contingent upon his having trained a suitable replacement for himself.

Understudy selection should be based upon the normal appraisal process. At least at the higher levels, it should be formalized to the extent that the company's corporate-level executives examine individual appraisal data and approve the selections.

Actual development of understudies may take several forms, but on the whole is based on delegation—with the manager at one level breaking off pieces of his own job and progressively assigning them to the subordinate. Gradually, as the subordinate gains experience and confidence, his readiness should increase to the point where he can successfully make the transition from old job to new.

Understudy assignments vary considerably. In come cases, the individual may retain his current classification while in an understudy role. Or, he may be named as an assistant *to* his superior, in which case he can receive delegated assignments on a full-time basis. In some instances the understudy is designated as a full-fledged assistant, and he may manage several operations in addition to the one for which he was previously responsible.

On the whole, understudy assignments depend on a number of factors, including the structure of the organization, the depth which already exists, or the need for assistant managers or directors to help shoulder the management load. Before action is taken, these and other factors should be considered.

Above all, good understudy training must exist from top to bottom with an identifiable "pool" of talent developed beneath each management level. Furthermore, there must be an understanding that this kind of program merely presents the candidate with the opportunity to learn; it is no guarantee of promotion.

Professional Nonmanagerial Development. Many organizations contain large numbers of professional personnel who perform nonmanagerial functions. These include engineers, scientists, accountants, and planners. Some of these may be new graduates who have just joined the business. Others are more experienced people who may or may not have the potential or aspiration to move into a managerial position.

Development of these individuals can be just as vital as the development of managers. Oftentimes they are the resource which keeps the organization viable and competitive through generating new ideas and concepts, making technological breakthroughs, and generally conducting the requisite technical aspects of the company's business. If obsolescence is allowed to develop in such individuals, if they are applying outmoded knowledge to new problems, the competitive edge is lost.

Progressive corporations spend much time and money in keeping professional personnel conversant with their respective specialities. In general, the same methods are employed as in other types of development, with both internal and external resources being used. On-the-job training, coaching, counseling and career planning, formal study, company libraries, seminars and symposiums are all part of the overall program. In addition, management can encourage employees to participate actively in professional societies, secure professional licenses, write papers, make presentations, and serve as part-time instructors in nearby colleges and universities. Some companies make special awards in recognition of outstanding contributions made by employees in their respective fields.

Special attention should be given to the professional personnel who are concerned with planning, research, and business concepts. These conceptually oriented individuals are usually the personnel upon whom real progress is dependent. They generate the new ideas and otherwise take the lead in the creative efforts needed to obtain new business, either in existing or new product areas. Any organization needs a core of talented professionals who are more oriented to the future than the present. Sometimes such people are assigned to the research and development department, but they may be found anywhere in an organization. They often work together as a technical and administrative team to explore new business opportunities and lead the proposal effort along with the sales organization. Such individuals must be kept up to date in their respective fields of activity, and efforts should be made to keep them well motivated.

Special attention has to be devoted to the marginal performer. Often such people can be motivated to overcome their deficiencies through updating their skills and knowledge. If this is impossible, other steps may have to be taken such as reassignment or, if necessary, eventual separation.

STAFFING, DEVELOPMENT, AND EQUAL OPPORTUNITY

It is important in staffing and development actions to understand the various federal and state laws and regulations which pertain to an organization.

The Civil Rights Act of 1964 (Title VII) and other federal regulations prohibits employment discrimination based on race, color, religion, sex, or national origin. In 1968 an additional law became effective prohibiting discrimination based on age.

Failure to comply with the provisions of equal opportunity legislation can lead to legal action against the company and against specific individuals. The aggrieved person may file his complaint with his State Civil Rights Commission or with his regional Equal Opportunity Commission if there is not a state commission. Those who feel discriminated against because of age may file a complaint with the Wage and Hour and Public Contracts divisions of the U.S. Department of Labor.

An investigation is then conducted, records examined, and affected persons interviewed until all available facts are disclosed. A decision is then rendered by the agency either favoring the complainant or closing the case. If the decision is in favor of the complainant, various mediation and conciliation efforts are conducted between the agency and the company in an effort to reach an amicable settlement. Should such efforts fail, the agency may recommend that the case be adjudicated in state or federal courts.

Some forward-looking business organizations today are going far beyond mere compliance with equal opportunity regulations. They are establishing special programs for disadvantaged people, in some cases with federal financial aid. The latest program, JOBS (Job Opportunities in the Business Sector), sponsored by the National Alliance of Businessmen in conjunction with the Department of Labor, provides industry with federal funds to hire and train the hard-core unemployed.[1]

There are other means by which an organization can take "affirmative action" in regard to equal opportunity. One, of course, is to actively seek qualified minority applicants. Here the assistance of organizations such as the Urban League, National Association for the Advancement of Colored People, Bureau of Indian Affairs, Latin American Research and Service Agency, state employment offices, and neighborhood action centers may be secured. Many of these organizations run job placement offices and pre-screen candidates for employment before referring them.

Assistance can also be provided to predominantly minority secondary schools and colleges. Counselors, faculty, and students can be invited to tour industries and gain firsthand knowledge of jobs available and preparation required. Often surplus equipment and material can be provided and speaking engagements arranged. In the Denver, Colorado, area, for example, a youth motivation program has been established whereby successful minority people in various occupations go to the schools and help counsel with students. Other companies have arranged for special in-plant counselors to assist minority employees in career planning and guidance.

SUMMARY

This chapter deals with the human element as it relates to sound organization. It is concerned with the attraction, development, and motivation of personnel at all levels. As is expressed in the U.S. Navy text *Navy Leadership:*

> Good men will produce results with medieval or even poor organization; the human factor will triumph even well-nigh insuperable difficulties, but good men will produce better results with good organization. Good men and poor ships are better than poor men and good ships. The ideal is good men with good ships.

The chapter begins with the problem of proper manpower planning, taking into consideration qualitative as well as quantitative aspects. It

---

[1] For further information, write JOBS, 726 Jackson Place, N.W., Washington, D.C. 20506.

then stresses the importance of proper job classification and manpower appraisal. Considerable attention is given to the promotional process as well as the acquisition of new personnel. Next, it deals with making "good men" even better—through sound programs of training and development. Finally, the subject of equal employment opportunity is discussed with attention devoted to legal as well as affirmative action aspects.

chapter 7

communication

Organizations are composed of persons who, by combining their specialties, can achieve a desired goal which would be unattainable to them as individuals. For cooperation to exist, a process of interaction among persons must be developed. Since organizations consist of people, the interaction process required for cooperation to take place is necessarily that of communication. Any manufacturing enterprise, corporation, or business, or for that matter any human organization, contains a communication system. Through the process of communication, the organization works to achieve its goals.

Any communication if it is to serve its intended purpose should satisfy at least four criteria:

1) It must be understood
2) The individual receiving the communication should view it as compatible with the purpose of the organization
3) The communication should be compatible with the individual's personal interest
4) The individual should be mentally and physically able to implement the communication.

In this chapter an operational definition of the word "communications" will be presented. In addition, the development of a quantitative understanding of the word "information" will facilitate a better understanding of the elements of a communications system. Examples of communications effectiveness among elements of a manufacturing enterprise will be presented and discussed. Also, sections are devoted to the development of communications systems for special project and manufacturing R&D activities. Finally general guidelines are provided for written and oral communications.

COMMUNICATION THEORY

The theory to be developed depends upon the initial acceptance and understanding of an operational definition of the word "communications." Communication can be thought of as a mechanical process by which one mechanism affects another. As a working definition it has been proposed that, "Communication is the discriminatory response of an organism (object or mechanism) to a stimulus."[1] These definitions indicate that a communication is initiated only to effect some predetermined result and that it has failed if the desired result is not achieved. Thus a message that evokes no response, or the wrong response, is not a communication.

Human-to-Machine Communication

In the industrial system, a high percentage of the communications are human to machine. When a production scheduler writes a work order for work center #10 to turn 100 shafts on a given day, he is attempting to communicate with the machine. The departmental foreman and the machine operators are links in the chain between scheduler and machine. If the machine produces 98 parts instead of the desired 100 shafts, the communication received by the machine and transmitted to the raw material was 2 percent in error. The original message called for 100 successful machine operations, but only 98 operations got through. Out of the original 100-part message, two parts were in some manner lost in transmission. Once the concept of human-to-machine communication is accepted, machine-to-machine communication appears logical, and it then follows that in some portions of our industrial communication system, machines will be directing humans.

Systems Evaluation

The terms "information theory" and "communication theory" are frequently used together and are often thought of as synonymous. Modern information theory has developed as an outgrowth of electrical and mechanical communication system studies. To develop quantitative theories for information-handling communication channels, it was first necessary to define and measure information. This was accomplished by a statistical definition. Information is defined statistically not so much in terms of what is said as what could be said. Information is a measure of one's freedom of choice in selecting a message.

---

[1] S. S. Stevens, "Introduction: A Definition of Communication," *Journal of the Acoustical Society of America,* Vol. 22, No. 6 (1950), 689.

The power of information-communication theory can be properly evaluated by considering the nature and scope of the mathematical problem that is presented and solved for the simplified communication system. Dr. Claude Shannon is generally credited with the development of the following formula for information transmission in a communication system:[2]

$$I = TW \log (1 + P/N)$$

Where: I = Information content
        T = Message transmission time
        W = Band width of information channel
        P = Signal strength
        N = Noise strength

The terms of this equation can be compared by analogy to an industrial organization's communication network. The evaluation of a communications system normally progresses from an initial qualitative system analysis to the determination of the mathematical form of the system processes; finally a mathematical model may be developed and a set of operational hypotheses selected. Since it is often not possible to state immediately whether or not the postulates correspond with reality, a testing program is necessary to check the computed performance of the model against the known responses of similar real organizations. In this manner a measure can be made of the validity of the original assumed hypotheses. When the model and the actual situation do not fit, the model postulates are repeatedly adjusted and retested until the model predicts with the desired degree of accuracy the general real system performance. This degree of accuracy varies with individual situations; for some systems a model giving only a good qualitative understanding of a process is a major achievement.

The Communications Model

Because organizations operate by information transfer and control themselves with respect to goals, models of the communication system have often been suggested as a device for measuring organizational efficiency. Such communication models are concerned with the internal structure of the organization and are presently used in a qualitative sense to point out weak areas in the organization and its communication system. Used properly, communication models are capable of supplying information regarding:

---

[2] Claude E. Shannon and Warren Weaver, *The Mathematical Theory of Communication* (Urbana: University of Illinois Press, 1949); see also *Communication and Culture,* Alfred G. Smith, ed. (New York: Holt, Rinehart, and Winston, 1967), 38.

1) The communication network which exists at a given time
2) The control processes within the network
3) Changes in the communication network and control processes.

In the industrial organization, we are normally concerned with the movement of discrete products through a manufacturing system with a finite capacity. Both the information and the products moving through the industrial system are exposed to varying amounts of noise and consequently are always subject to some finite error probability.

The basic elements of an industrial communication system are shown in Fig. 7-1. The information source is the device, person, etc., which in order to produce a desired change in the state of the destination, selects a desired message from a set of possible messages. The transmitter changes the message into a signal which can be conveniently transmitted by the channel. We say that the transmitter encodes the message for transmission. The channel is the machine over which the signals representing the message are transmitted to the receiver. The receiver decodes the signals into a message meaningful to the recipient.

The simplest organizational communication channel exists between two people. A transmission and reception mechanism exists at each end point. These simple channels can be linked together in various ways to form an organizational communication network. Channels can be connected in series or in parallel or any combination of these two. The transmission of a message through a channel is slowed by the number of receptions and transmissions of the message before the message reaches the final reception point. Transmission time increases when the message passes through reception-transmission points, and distortion may be intoduced at these points. This distortion and increase of message transmission time is analogous to noise in information theory. Noise is essentially any deviation from the original source intent, and consequently noise might well be called "error."

The information content of a message is roughly proportional to the number of words within the message. Also, as shown in Shannon's model, the time of transmission in information theory is directly analogous to the time a message requires to arrive at the desired reception point. An analog for the signal power of the message is difficult to find, however. Since the signal power occurs only in the signal-noise ratio, a quantitative analog is not necessary. The mere fact that the message, or signal, is sent is reason to give this quantity a value. It is believed that this value would be best represented by a constant. Further, as the noise factor shows promise of being measured quantitatively, the signal-noise ratio can then have different values, depending on the interference, or noise, characteristics of the channel.

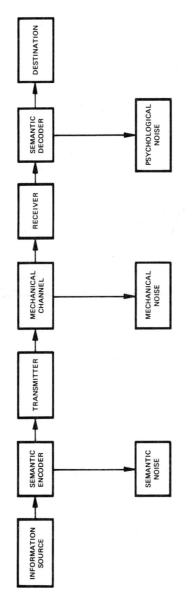

Fig. 7-1. Elements of a generalized communications model.

Clearly, it is the responsibility of industrial management to develop the most efficient, rapid, and accurate system possible for the transmission of the customer's order from the sales department through the plant to the shipping department. The industrial organization may be thought of as a complicated communication system which enables the customer to communicate with the shipping clerk. The organization exists to convert the input command into the desired output.

Theoretically a human machine's ultimate transfer characteristics are expressible in terms of his purely electromechanical characteristics. Suppose in such an industrial communication model the human components are replaced by equivalent electromechanical components with identical physiological characteristics. The model would then predict the best possible performance achievable from that industrial system. Since the electromechanical substitutes are endowed with all the human capabilities including memory, but excluding all emotions, the model would predict a performance unimpaired by the noise introduced into the real communication system by emotional conflicts. Human emotions thus add to the real industrial organization an additional degree of unpredictability, with a resultant probability of increased system error.

For example, the engineer may receive the problem in the form of a set of specifications that must be satisfied, or he may be confronted with the physical situation itself. In any event, a major concern is the translation of some real situation into a suitable model or representation that can be studied and manipulated. This translation can be effected by means of words, pictures, sketches, graphs, equations, and such audio-visual means as motion pictures, television, and scale models.

Substantial blocks of technical information are stored in men's minds. In addition to these living information storage areas, engineers and managers have found that information can be stored as well as transmitted by pictures, sketches, written reports, etc. In recent years engineers have greatly extended man's ability to collect, store, and organize information through the use of computers and their magnetic memory drums, tapes, and cores.

The Application of Communication Theory

Communication theory can be applied industrially on both a microscopic and macroscopic basis. Microscopically, communication theory data and techniques are available to give quantitative answers to a wide variety of problems involving the individual human machine. Macroscopically, communication theory enables the engineer and manufacturing manager to assume the proper perspective in evaluating the overall communication system. They are able to translate the requirements of good humanistic-mechanistic communications into engineering terms and properly evaluate qualitatively, if not quantitatively, the relative effects of each factor.

Because on a microscopic level the analysis of the information capacity of the mechanical machine has been formalized, only the problem of the human machine will be considered. Even in the most menial tasks, the human machine is employed only in situations where the operations require some decision making. In ordinary time-and-motion analysis, the industrial engineer wishes to minimize the time required for a combination of physical movement time and decision time. Decision time is the lag between stimulus and response.

Time-and-motion analysis may be considered a study in human information generation and transmission. Man's information transmission capacity is limited by the fixed constraints of the human motor system and by the kind of coding required for individual tasks. Maximum human information handling capacity requires the selection of both an optimum stimulus code and an optimum response code, and finally the matching of the two coding schemes.

An interesting application of the concepts of communication theory involved the manager of a substantial manufacturing operation who was being overwhelmed by a flood of paperwork. The consultant given the task of organizing the information flow to the executive decided to apply communication theory rules to the situation. The manager stated that the primary function of his position was to make decisions regarding the allocation of men and resources to meet the requirements of the division. These requirements were brought to him in the form of reports from his subordinates. In studying the contents of the paper flow across the desk of the executive, the consultant shortly realized that the signal-to-noise ratio of the letters and reports was low. It was obvious that the executive had the channel capacity (experience, ability, and time) to produce the required decisions, but that a more efficient coding procedure was required. The papers to be handled were found to fall into two general classifications: (1) reports on work in progress, and (2) statements of problems requiring an ultimate decision.

To better utilize the executive's capacity, a coding procedure was instituted. Each communication was classified as either a progress report or a request for a decision. Staff members writing reports which offered information feedback on existing projects were instructed to attach a short statement regarding the anticipated progress so that actual and anticipated results could be compared. Communiques involving new problems were required to state clearly the alternative decisions available, the recommended solution, and the manpower and resources required to effect this solution. Problems were not to be presented without a recommended solution. When recommended solutions were not possible, an outline of the possible alternatives was submitted.

Although the logic of this procedure was elementary, it gave the executive a finite channel capacity and permitted the accurate transmission of information at a maximum rate. By way of explanation, the amount of information involved in each decision is a function of the number of alternatives available. Thus a decision involving a large number of alternatives would require more time to clear a fixed capacity channel than a decision with few alternatives. Since the coding procedure permitted a reduction in the amount of information connected with each decision, it resulted in a corresponding increase in the rate at which decisions could be reached.

As an example of downward communications, another plant found that its production rate was very low and its rejection rates unusually high. The company was manufacturing short runs of fairly complex electronic computer assemblies. An investigation of the problem revealed that the engineers on the project were preparing detailed blueprints which the female employees on the wiring and assembly lines had difficulty in reading. The production impasse which had developed was resolved when the engineers presented the same information by means of a set of simple pictorial sketches.

COMMUNICATION IN THE MANUFACTURING CYCLE

This section discusses the effective use of communication within the manufacturing organization to achieve management goals. Special attention is given the functions of forecasting and production control. Before discussing these two functions, it will be useful to categorize the most common manufacturing operations and discuss their similarities and differences.

Basic Types of Manufacturing Operations

The three basic types of manufacturing operations, classified according to length of production run, are: job-shop operations, continuous production, and short-run manufacturing.

Job-Shop Operations. The job shop typically fabricates a number of products over relatively short intervals of time. Departments or work centers are organized around various types of multi-purpose machines operated by a skilled labor force, often with piece rate incentives. Individual work centers may be used for operations such as turning, drilling, milling, and tapping. Often, partly because of the profusion of centers, control of work in process becomes critical. Frequent machine setups are necessary, and work scheduling or "shop loading" becomes an important matter.

Job shops perform relatively little assembly work because they are usually producing single parts from raw stock for larger companies. In-process and finished goods inventory is minimal since items are produced in small lots, often to fill immediate customer needs.

Continuous Production. Continuous or mass production industries typically produce highly standardized items over long periods of time. Working on very large lots, and often producing for inventory, the continuous manufacturing process employs highly specialized machines and a relatively unskilled labor force. Although the labor force is not highly skilled, the man-machine production output ratio is characteristically high and piece rate incentives are not usually provided.

Materials to be fabricated are fed directly into a line of machines, and the process is continuous—each successive operation proceeds in a predetermined, generally inflexible sequence. A uniform flow of parts occurs within the plant, and the process is sensitive to interruption from breakdown or other disruption. Automobiles, consumer durables, and electronic components are examples of products manufactured in continuous production plants.

Short-Run Manufacturing. Short-run manufacturing, the median between continuous production and job-shop operations, contains certain elements of both. Short-run manufacturing is characterized by relatively short production runs of any one part or product and the scheduling of production to customer demand or even customer orders. The labor force is often a mix between skilled and semi-skilled employees, and both multi-purpose and single-purpose machinery may be used.

The aerospace industry provides good examples of this type of manufacturing. Aerospace fabrication operations contain many of the elements of the job shop (intermittent manufacture and small lots). Although the assembly operations resemble those in continuous manufacturing operations, they lack the high volume, highly automated assembly lines of the latter.

The Forecasting Function

Job shop, continuous production, and short-run manufacturing organizations have differing communication requirements. Another way to say this is that the three types of industries require different models to describe their communication needs.

One manufacturing communication need is met by the forecasting function. Forecasting is performed differently and serves varying purposes in each of the three types of industry. For any manufacturing activity, however, the forecast is a projection indicating the kinds and amounts of units to be produced over a future time period. Sales orders, markets trends, stock requirements, and long-term corporate goals serve as inputs to the forecast. Operating reports and information for decision making are related to the major elements of the manufacturing activity through the information system.

Forecasting Methods and Inputs. While forecasting methods in the manufacturing area may not need to be as sophisticated as those employed in other corporate areas, a number of well-refined techniques have been developed to assist manufacturing in matching output with production needs.

Operations research models, for example, are available to accommodate various data patterns. Constant, trend, and cyclical or seasonal data functions can all be successfully modeled. Through regression analysis the model can be selected which best fits the existent data. It should be noted, however, that the accuracy of a "least squares" technique such as regression analysis depends upon the amount and the accuracy of the available historical data. In addition to operations research models, other forecasting techniques can be used. Two of these are exponential smoothing and the moving average.

As may be gathered from the foregoing discussion, most manufacturing forecasting methods are of the projection type, that is, the forecast merely projects into the future those events that have occurred in the past. For this reason greatest reliance is placed upon factors such as sales history rather than upon current economic conditions or expected product developments.

One of the major data inputs for manufacturing forecasts is supplied by the marketing department. Marketing studies past sales and predicts future sales levels, and the estimated future sales figure then becomes the production goal. The manufacturing department uses the sales forecast for shop loading and to establish material and manpower requirements.

For example, given a short-range forecast, the labor requirements can be projected based on standard hours. Whether or not standard hours agree with actual estimates depends on how well the quantity is estimated and/or negotiated. In attempts to improve labor requirements forecasting, some large manufacturers have instituted complex labor reporting schemes.

As stated, the forecast is also used to develop material requirements. A bill of materials is prepared, and it becomes the input to other functions such as inventory control, purchasing, and manufacturing control. It also serves as a control on materials usage. The parts list and the exploded view are used to trace the required parts or subassemblies needed to produce a final assembly. Production of such a list is a complicated task because nomenclature is often not standard, engineering changes occur, and additions and deletions are common. **Forecasting for Job Shops.** The job shop is basically a collection of various labor skills and machinery which markets its availability, and it fabricates a wide range of dissimilar products. These factors, plus the fact that the shop receives a variety of orders at fluctuating volumes, are at the center of its forecasting problem. The solution to the problem requires flexibility in the assignment of men and machines, approximation of an "ideal" product mix, and future determinations with respect to these factors. Proper assignment of employees and equipment and the other demands of a varied product mix flow usually require short interval scheduling. Determination of the future shop load is based upon current order loads, labor force, machine inventory situations, etc. It is helpful to break out production ceilings for major product lines in the manner shown in Fig. 7-2.

PRODUCT (SCHEDULES) CEILINGS
DECEMBER 1, 1969

	1969 DEC. (21)	1970 JAN. (22)	FEB. (20)	MAR. (21)	APR. (21)	MAY (21)	JUNE (21)	JULY (13)*	AUG. (20)	SEPT. (21)	OCT. (23)	NOV. (19)
SEMI-AUTOMATIC SEAM WELDERS												
RBX	125	125	125	125	23	---	---	60 ‖	125	125	125	125
Mark I	135	135	100	100	100	90	90	45	90	90 ‖	90	90
Mark II	2	2	5	5	5 ‖	---	---	---	---	---	---	---
Mark III	51	90	65	70	100	100	125	75	125	100 ‖	100	100
CKTB	---	---	---	---	---	---	---	2	2	2	2	2 ‖
RSDT	100	150	200	250	250	300	300 ‖	150	300	300	300	300
B-88	140	135	150	135	140	140	140	70	140	140 ‖	140	140
B-8 TL	23	30	30	36	50	50	50	25	50 ‖	50	50	50
	576	667	675	721	668	680	705	427	832	807	807	807
N/C WELDERS												
R-500 (Body)	---	---	---	1	2	2	2	2	2	2	2	2 ‖
Sleevers	---	---	---	1	1	1	1	1	1	1	1	1 ‖
S	---	---	---	---	---	---	---	---	1	1	1	1 ‖
Monk (Imp)	---	---	---	1 ‖	---	---	---	---	---	---	---	---
Monk (TMW)	---	---	---	---	---	---	---	---	---	---	---	---
2 Bar (Mod.BI)	5	---	7	8	5	5	5	5	5	5	5 ‖	5
3 Bar	5	8	1	---	3	3	3	3	3	3	3 ‖	5
"C" (Heads)	76	48	84	84	84	144	144	72	144 ‖	144	144	144
Gilboss	---	24 ‖	---	---	---	---	---	---	---	---	---	---
Butoforge	---	2	2	1	2	2	2	2	2 ‖	2	2	2
Hi-Sp. Decks	---	6	12	18	20 ‖	---	---	18	18	18	18	18

* Two weeks vacation   ‖ Covered by ceilings

Fig. 7-2. Forecast of product production ceilings for major product lines.

Job shop forecasting begins as a communications flow initiated by customer orders. Through the use of customer orders as input data, a bill of materials is developed and exploded to produce inventory requirements. The workload is then forecast by applying standard times for direct labor and setup. To these standards a waiting line factor is applied to determine the approximate job completion time. Each job is scheduled independently of all others on a finite capacity basis.

A typical document output from the central information system would be the weekly projection of manpower requirements. This projection can be based upon a two- to three-week forecast with orders on hand serving as the starting point. One of the major problems in attaining accuracy is the labor standard relied upon. The amount of variance applied against the standard will affect the accuracy of the forecast, and for this reason an elaborate labor data collection system is required to produce accurate and timely labor variance reports and updating. Manpower requirements can be summarized for planning as shown in Fig. 7-3.

Forecasting for Short-Run Manufacturing. As mentioned, examples of fabrication industries combining elements of job shop and assembly line operations occur in the aerospace industry. In these hybrid configurations, production and job costs are highly critical, and thus their projection, recording, and analysis are of great importance. In addition, the wide variety of components used in any one job makes their forecasting a necessity. Electronic data processing has made possible the presentation of timely information for decision making and operating documents.

Forecasting for Continuous Production. Continuous manufacturing operations involve different forecasting and communications requirements. The continuous assembly firm often schedules production for months in advance on the basis of forecasts. The type of forecast most critical to the mass production plant is based upon market analysis rather than production considerations as in the job shop. Forecasts control the fabrication of parts and the production of subassemblies. It is generally in the final assembly that the specific order is treated. In consumer product industries, where relatively little custom work is done, the entire production line, including the assembly areas, is forecast controlled. To ensure proper functioning of the forecasting system, a data bank should be created; it should contain as much useful information as practical and should be designed for easy access on a daily basis. Procedures should be set up so that users can obtain their own data with a minimum of effort and with little need for understanding how the system actually works. Once the forecast is made, a manufacturing plan is established which is based upon the expected product demand. As indicated in Fig. 7-4, depicting certain elements in the manufacturing cycle, forecast information from the central information system is available to process engineering, industrial engineering, and process control groups. Some common formats and uses for this data are the following: (1) support of cost reduction programs, (2) evaluation of new equipment requirements, and (3) summarization of projected manpower requirements by product, process, and operational group.

Thus, the problem of efficient communications is a common need throughout all of the functional relationships discussed. Detailed

MANPOWER REQUIREMENTS SUMMARY

DEPARTMENT	January 19, 1970			January 26, 1970			February 2, 1970			February 9, 1970			February 16, 1970		
	4 Wks	8 Wks	12 Wks	4 Wks	8 Wks	12 Wks	4 Wks	8 Wks	12 Wks	4 Wks	8 Wks	12 Wks	4 Wks	8 Wks	12 Wks
1	187	112	67												
2	71	20	(3)												
3	40	10	(6)												
4	35	34	22												
5	222	133	71												
6	9	3	1												
7	29	16	7												
8	(3)	(33)	(40)												
17	200	117	73												
48	78	52	32												
49	(26)	25	16												
51	36	18	9												
54	39	7	(10)												
56	(3)	(4)	(4)												
58	40	29	26												
68	13	9	4												
70	5	2	(1)												
Total Needed	1004	587	328												
Total Excess	32	37	64												
Net Result	972	550	264												

( ) Excess

Fig. 7-3. Forecast of manpower requirements by department. This document is generated by the Management Information Department based on current orders and Marketing Department projections.

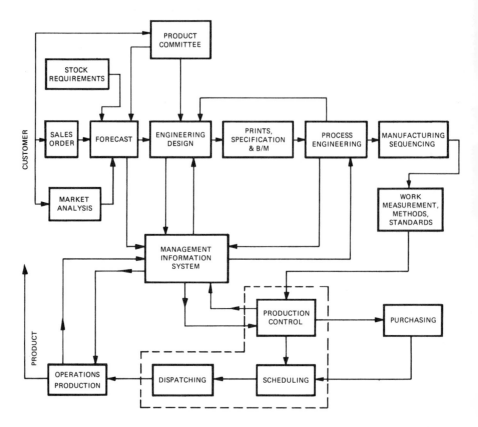

Fig. 7-4. Elements of the manufacturing cycle.

model development is unique for each plant configuration. However, certain basic concepts of communications theory can be universally applied. For example, the format of the documents and their intent can be analyzed with respect to channel capacity, semantic clarity, and other similar criteria. At a higher level, the communications network and its support of the organization goal can be analyzed by repetitive application of the basic principles of communication theory and by performing summations along various paths. If desired, the introduction of statistical functions will result in solutions stated in probabilistic terms.

Production Control

The function of production control is an additional area of consideration. The term "production control" covers several control activities including scheduling, dispatching, production follow-up, and shipping.

Broadly stated objectives for the production coordination function include knowledge of the completion date for a job, at what stage it will be at any given time, what penalties have been exacted to meet a given schedule (and what costs have been generated), while at the same time providing for conflicting and changing priorities. A listing of some variables which enter into production communications would include: schedules, lead/lag factors, priorities, product dimensions and weight, and customer parameters. In an ideal situation, a manufacturing system under complete control will be able to provide information on the arrival times for specific jobs at specific work centers. Additionally, the influence of disruption of a schedule can be determined along with the best remedial sequence and job mix.

Job Shops. Certain elements of production control in a job shop environment will be considered with respect to the employment of electronic data processing and the generation of communication documents for operating and managerial personnel. Among the necessary prerequisites for production planning are the following: predetermined manufacturing steps for a given product, machine setup standards, and operating standards. The time between operations—including the time completed parts wait to be picked up, the time it takes to move from one center or machine to another—and the waiting line time for the next operation must also be known. Calculations for transit time are usually based upon experience and can be adjusted as conditions change. In Fig. 7-4, the relationships of process and industrial engineering functions, as providers of this information, can be seen. Additionally, in coordinating job shop production, a data collection system is an important requirement. The data must be collected often enough so that the schedule may be recalculated to reflect current shop conditions.

Scheduling involves both the planning and execution of production work. In the planning phase, orders from the planning function are related to available machines and manpower. In the execution phase the actual order is directed to the shop, based upon the plan developed. In the average job shop, machines and the labor force have capacity constraints; therefore, planned orders must be scheduled in a logical sequence to take advantage of the available process functions. These planning and execution phases consist of several stages; the first is the scheduling within the dates at which each process or each part or lot shall be started or finished. The second stage is the scheduling of the order in relation to other orders. This will depend on the delivery date of the order, inventory of raw materials, and relative dates of completion of other components. The sequence in which each order or lot should be assigned to machines is determined in this manner.

The final stage is machine loading. Starting with a required completion date, starting dates of each process are determined. Reference to machine load reports will then yield the nearest available date for starting. When all processes on all parts or lots have been assigned to machines, the scheduled plan of manufacturing is considered complete. Fig. 7-4 shows that this completed plan is passed along to the dispatching function. The input from the information system to dispatching is one of designating the release date of this manufacturing plan. The dispatching function releases the finished plan of manufacturing to the operations or production function as indicated in the cycle of manufacturing schematic. The output of a production control system in the job shop consists of several reports, the purposes of which are to relate actual progress to previously established plans and schedules, give notice of incipient delays, and provide facts for analysis and prompt executive action.

Short-Run Manufacturing. In the case of the short-run manufacturer, many attempts have been made to solve the problem of scheduling. The technique used is often a reflection of how critical the problem is to the particular company. Since companies in this type of manufacturing frequently produce to custom order, scheduling often becomes a compromise between the time at which a job should be done and the time at which it can be performed in view of previous commitments.

An approach adopted by some companies who operate in this environment has been a method starting with the required completion dates of jobs on order. From this, a weekly schedule is made. By using this date as a starting point, and then working backwards, determination of peaks and valleys can be made. Using the computer, a schedule is built up on an iterative basis, seeking a more accurate solution with each iteration. In a fairly stable situation, this technique can be used, but it is not appropriate for a situation in which priorities are changing.

Figs. 7-5 and 7-6 illustrate the kinds of schedules used to maintain proper job priorities.

Continuous Production. Production coordination in continuous manufacturing is simpler than in either the job shop or hybrid assembly operation because production is almost always to inventory. However, the scheduling of production almost to maximum plant capacity brings about many problems in terms of inventory control and control of investment.

In conclusion, it should be noted that efforts to create an optimal solution to production scheduling, using mathematical simulations and computers, have not as yet been successful. The reports produced are

01/20/70 DEPT 1 MACHINE GROUP 0610 D SS FLOOR ALLEN 2 DR PR PAGE 12

PART NUMBER	S.O.	OPERN.	ID	REMARKS	CHANGES	PRIORITY	HRS	HRS 787	HRS 788
T1 6528	541974	30–0	0			510			1
H1 22 403	557995	32–0	3			512		17	
E1 31268	531421	10–0	0	NO MATERIAL		513			2
E1 44572	528125	20–0	3			514		4	
HK 1 28	552401	42–0	4			517	R	3	
755 676 4	562589	10–0	1			522	R	2	
HK 50 19 2	506204	20–0	0			525	R		2
HK 50 19 2	506204	30–0	0			525	R		2
T1 1541	541982	25–0	0			526	R		1
C 3286	512156	30–0	0			534			1
HK 1 15 2	552396	10–0	0	NO MATERIAL		569	R		11
H1 21 419	552946	81–0	0			569	R		3
Y1 90052	503733	31–0	4			583		3	
H1 19 402	552917	11–0	1			601	R	101	
HK 13 30	558957	31–0	0	NO MATERIAL		601	R		5
H1 19 446	552935	30–0	0			616	R		9
HK 3 508 10	552451	10–0	0	NO MATERIAL		618	R		2

Fig. 7-5. Computer-generated schedule indicating the work load for a specific work center. The item to be machined is identified by part and operation number. Special remarks and load hours are also listed.

PAGE 130   01/14/70

S O	PART NUMBER	DEPT	MG	OPERN	HOURS	TSD	WTD	PRIORITY	ID	CARDS
544597	C1 5004 Y	48	0935	21–0	51	801	820	710	0	
		52	0000	25–0	4	806			0	
		5	1521	30–0	47	809			0	
		5	1570	40–0	20	813			0	
		5	1570	50–0	16	814			0	
		INSPECTION								
544598	C1 5004 Y	48	0935	21–0	51	820	839	818	0	
		52	0000	25–0	4	825			0	
		5	1521	30–0	47	828			0	
		5	1570	40–0	20	832			0	
		5	1570	50–0	16	833			0	
		INSPECTION								
544599	C1 5006	2	1310	12–0	58	784	839	612	0	ISD
		48	0830	23–0	37	790			0	ISD
		48	0830	24–0	19	792			0	ISD
		2	1350	25–0	19	795			0	
		17	0200	33–0	25	798			0	
		1	0662	40–0	31	802			0	
		5	1440	50–0	12	805			0	
		65	2810	60–0	21	808			0	
		21	3126	65–0	2	813			0	

Fig. 7-6. Scheduling document listing remaining operations on a series of parts. Priorities (to meet delivery dates) and standard times to complete each operation are listed.

used as guides for plant managers, foremen, and the workers themselves. But these people must make on-the-spot modifications based upon actual floor conditions. As a result the shop schedules are often suboptimal documents.

COMMUNICATION IN SPECIAL PROJECTS AND MANUFACTURING R&D ACTIVITIES

Removed from the mainstream of the manufacturing cycle, but nevertheless an important factor in the total communications structure of an industrial organization, is the information exchange in special project and R&D activities. One of the problems of project communications in a complex technological environment is that of translating information. Masses of technical data must be abstracted or translated into pertinent form in order to be meaningful to upper management. The problem of translation has particular impact because there is often no staff group possessing technical project knowledge as well as an awareness of the broad and sometimes subtle middle and upper management needs for information. The translation aspect of communication is a two-way street, however; the receiver as well as the sender must be explicit concerning the quality of information to be supplied and the format to be used in its presentation.

An effective communications scheme for special project and research and development operations will contain several important phases. These may be identified as: (1) generation of objectives, (2) forecast implementation, (3) measurement of progress, (4) program review, and (5) performance appraisal.

Generation of Objectives

In a typical traditionally evolved system objectives may be generated by means of external input from groups such as technical marketing sections, production or product planning, product engineering groups, and advance systems planning. Such input may be initiated by the project leader through written inquiry and/or review meetings with the appropriate groups. This approach offers good program control and definition, and in the case of manufacturing R&D activities, offers a broad exposure of research technology to those groups that can apply new technology to advance product needs.

There are pitfalls in generating objectives. For example, caution must be taken not to overorganize objectives to the extent that the communicative document generated creates a restricted, inflexible program which can tolerate no slippage. Clarification of objectives is one significant advantage to be derived from the direct contact of project personnel with those areas of the larger organization which use the project group's technological output. In addition, some objectives are generated by project personnel in consultation with their immediate supervisors. Once a consensus has been achieved, the completed document may be reviewed with the project staff, and the full copies of the document can be circulated to pertinent groups throughout the corporation for additional comment.

Although external input usually plays a more important role in the generation of short-term objectives than does internal input, internal technological contributions become of paramount importance in the generation of long-term objectives. As a rule, long-term objectives are established on a yearly basis to cover the subsequent five-year period. The first two or three years of the five-year forecast are often reasonably well defined, but the last two years are usually limited to broad technological trends with fewer specifics. The importance of a five-year, or long-range, forecast is not limited to its value in establishing program or technology direction. The long-range forecast can also play a vital role in establishing the proper climate for project personnel—a climate in which responsibility is recognized and in which productivity requirements can be met. A further advantage of formalized forecasting lies in the cementing of a communications link with upper management relative to new technology and budget planning. In too many cases top management fails to authorize good programs because of R&D middle management's failure to communicate effectively the story that needs to be told. Long-term forecasts enable managers at all decision-making levels to become conditioned to a program of technology. With proper orientation these managers can more quickly grasp the need for continuity of effort and for continued budget support. Figs. 7-7, 7-8, and 7-9 show typical documents used for determining and communicating the analysis and costs associated with the development of a specific project.

Forecast Implementation

The second step in project communication involves implementation of the short- and long-term forecasts through preparation and issuance of program proposals. A program proposal is a formal document intended to communicate all relevant aspects of the recommended program for management approval. It can include the following sections: abstract, technical discussion, phasing diagram, manpower assignment, and budget required (both capital and operating). See Fig. 7-9.

A proposal can cover a broad technological area and treat in some detail the specific projects to be initiated in that area. A total of five program proposals might detail the plans for twenty specific projects

---

Form No. _____

ENGINEERING PROJECT AUTHORIZATION

Project Title: _____ Project No. _____

_____

Requested By:_____ Date _____

PROJECT OBJECTIVE:

BASIC JUSTIFICATION:

GENERAL SPECIFICATIONS:

COMPETITION:

MARKETING COMMENTS:

Projected Cost   _____

Projected Time   _____

Projected Completion Date   _____

Submitted by: _____

Approval by Eng. Mgr.   _____   Date _____

Approval by Eng. Group Mgr. _____   Date _____

Approval by V.P. Eng.   _____   Date _____

Fig. 7-7. Engineering project authorization.

TIME AND COST ESTIMATE

	TIME	COST
I. FEASIBILITY STUDY	____ man hrs. @____ /hr. =	_____
II. PROJECT DEVELOPMENT		
A. Engineering Prototype		
1. Design & Calculations	____ man hrs. @____ /hr. =	_____
2. Manufacturing & Assembly	____ man hrs. @____ /hr. =	_____
3. Test & Evaluation	____ man hrs. @____ /hr. =	_____
4. First Engineering Estimate	____ man hrs. @____ /hr. =	_____
5. Material		_____
Sub-Totals	____	_____
B. Manufacturing Prototype		
1. Design & Layout	____ man hrs. @____ /hr. =	_____
2. Detail	____ man hrs. @____ /hr. =	_____
3. Manufacturing & Assembly	____ man hrs. @____ /hr. =	_____
4. Test & Debug	____ man hrs. @____ /hr. =	_____
5. Material		_____
Sub-Totals	____	_____
C. Engineering Test Pilot Lot		
1. Redesign	____ man hrs. @____ /hr. =	_____
2. Detail	____ man hrs. @____ /hr. =	_____
3. Manufacturing & Assembly	____ man hrs. @____ /hr. =	_____
4. Lab & Field Test	____ man hrs. @____ /hr. =	_____
5. Second Engineering Estimate	____ man hrs. @____ /hr. =	_____
6. Material		_____
Sub-Totals	____	_____
D. Release	____ man hrs. @____ /hr. =	_____
TOTAL DEVELOPMENT TIME & COST	____	_____

Fig. 7-8.   Time and cost estimate for engineering project administration.

DATE _____

PROJECT ANALYSIS

PROJECT TITLE: _____

OBJECTIVE _____

_____

_____

_____

_____

AV. POTENTIAL SALES UNITS PER MO. _____ PER YR. _____

LIFE OF PRODUCT IN YRS. _____ TOTAL NUMBER OF UNITS _____

AV. SALES PRICE PER UNIT $ _____ TOTAL SALES VALUE $ _____ (ITEM A)

EST. AV. DIRECT COST PER UNIT $ _____ TOTAL DIRECT COST $ _____

    TOTAL CONTRIBUTION OVER LIFE OF PRODUCT $ _____

EXPENSES OVER LIFE OF PRODUCT

MANUFACTURING PERIOD EXPENSES (_____ X D. C.) _____

SELLING EXPENSES _____

CONTINUING ENGINEERING _____

GENERAL ADMINISTRATION _____

PROMOTIONAL EXPENSES _____

_____

    TOTAL EXPENSES OVER LIFE OF PRODUCT $ _____

GROSS PROFIT OVER LIFE OF PRODUCT BEFORE TAXES (ITEM B) $ _____

REQUIRED INVESTMENT

*DEVELOPMENT COST (ITEM C) _____

  TOOLING _____

OTHER _____ _____

    TOTAL INVESTMENT $ _____

NET PROFIT OVER LIFE OF THE PRODUCT BEFORE TAXES $ _____

TECHNICAL LEVERAGE

$$\text{SALES} = \frac{\text{TOTAL SALES (ITEM A)}}{\text{DEVELOPMENT COST (ITEM C)}} = \boxed{}$$

$$\text{PROFIT} = \frac{\text{GROSS PROFITS (ITEM B)}}{\text{DEVELOPMENT COST (ITEM C)}} = \boxed{}$$

ASSUMED STARTING DATE OF PROJECT _____

RELEASE DATE FOR FIELD TEST PROTOTYPE _____

START OF FIELD TESTING _____

RELEASE DATE FOR PRODUCTION TOOLING _____

DELIVERY DATE OF FIRST MACHINES _____

DEVELOPMENT COST AND MANPOWER REQUIREMENTS

DEVELOPMENT LABOR AND MATERIAL COST _____

_____ ENGINEERS AND DESIGNERS FOR _____ MOS. @ $ _____ / MAN MO. $ _____

_____ DRAFTSMEN AND DETAILERS FOR _____ MOS. @ $ _____ / MAN MO. $ _____

_____ LABORATORY PERSONNEL FOR _____ MOS. @ $ _____ / MAN MO. $ _____

    *DEVELOPMENT COST (ITEM C)

ADDITIONAL MANPOWER REQUIRED _____

CHANCE OF TECHNICAL SUCCESS [_____]   CHANCE OF COMMERCIAL SUCCESS [_____]

Fig. 7-9. Project analysis form used to determine the economic potential of proposed projects.

within the department. Many large companies suggest that the document be prepared in its entirety by the responsible project personnel. The proposal is based upon internal or external ideas and production and product needs. Further, it is most often the responsibility of the section head (first-line supervisor) to obtain confirmation of the need for the program from related internal or external groups. The completed program proposals are assembled into a single document for distribution to upper management, and copies of individual proposals are given to each member of the appropriate project group.

Proposals demand a high degree of commitment on the part of each contributor. Personnel submitting proposals normally establish the target dates and/or decision dates, and they must realize the importance of fulfilling these commitments. The meeting of target dates is important owing to the interrelationship of each project with other projects within the total system. The target date–decision date format also forces upon all those involved in the total project a realization that regular progress must be measured either in finite or general judgment terms. Project personnel must understand that once having failed to meet a milepost, they must take realistic steps to establish and meet a new set of goals. It is difficult, but extremely important, to create an environment in which failures can be readily discussed and the project reviewed without hesitancy, pretense, or blame.

Fig. 7-10 shows a typical project schedule used to monitor the achievement of objectives on a periodic basis. Each milestone is associated with a scheduled completion date and area of responsibility.

In addition to providing a yardstick for the measurement of progress, the program proposal concept also supplies a basis for upper management approval of particular programs. Through this vehicle, continuity of reporting as well as familiarity with the program can be maintained easily since the original program proposal remains as the base point for subsequent oral and written reports. A monthly progress report, which is prepared by middle management for distribution to upper management, can also be used to reflect the phasing and target dates continued in the pertinent program proposal.

Measurement of Progress

The third phase of communications system synthesis relates to techniques for measuring progress. This area is perhaps the most difficult of all because self-rating is indirectly involved, and the ability and willingness to frankly recognize failure or delay is a prerequisite. Another measurement difficulty exists because of the controversy frequently created by attaching quantitative values to project mileposts.

Nonmathematical expressions best characterize advances, and it is here that middle management must provide a communications link in the form of a translation bridge for upper management. It should be realized that many managers have conditioned themselves to extract a great deal of data from summary and graphical presentations. Two typical examples of summary reporting techniques are shown in Figs. 7-11 and 7-12.

Over the above monthly review meetings and monthly written progress reports to management, a system of semi-annual and annual departmental reports can be structured to improve the measurement of progress over a longer period of time. Such reports can also improve departmental effectiveness in establishing, as well as fulfilling, goals. One desirable practice for the communication of major program objectives in the semi-annual report involves the placement of a limitation of about three pages to each major program. The first page might contain a synopsis of program status, while the second page repeats the objective, elaborates on status in some depth, and reviews current and future approaches to problem areas. The third and subsequent pages contain samples and/or photographs to illustrate the progress previously described. The document is structured so that a manager can read one section to get a thumbnail sketch, or read the entire report to obtain an in-depth status report. The introductory page to each program report is stamped as "on schedule," "off schedule," or "ahead of schedule" to clearly indicate overall status.

One of the purposes of this reporting technique is to continue the emphasis upon personal involvement and commitment, for laboratory progress is predicated upon each professional making a conscientious commitment to achieve. A prerequisite to achievement after commitment is the willingness to report progress honestly, that is, by cutting through verbiage and frankly citing the stumbling blocks.

The annual report, though it covers all programs conducted during the year, should be structured much like the semi-annual report. This report can be supplemented by a letter from the department manager outlining the major accomplishments as well as the major program deficiencies for the year. Both the semi-annual and annual report are distributed to key management members in R&D, laboratory personnel, and selected members across the total corporate structure.

Thus far, the value of progress measurement has been stressed from the standpoint of its usefulness to project personnel and middle management. Progress reporting has a prime value internal to the laboratory or project group, but of almost equal importance is the link which a concise, well-written progress report can provide to upper management whether technically or business oriented. This is particularly true

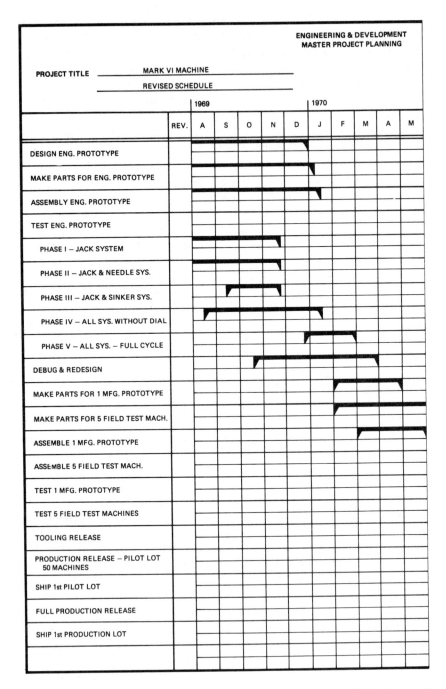

Fig. 7-10. Schedule showing project objectives on a time scale. Each milestone is

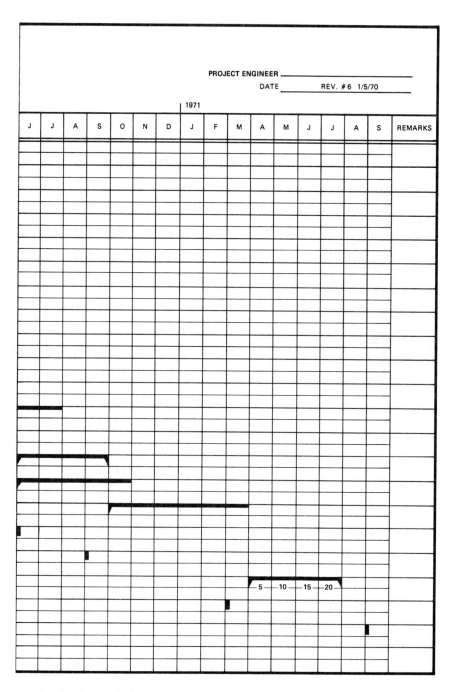

associated with a scheduled completion date and area of responsibility.

PROJECTS BEHIND SCHEDULE				DATE:
PRODUCT	PROJECT TITLE	PROJECT LEADER	PROJECT MANAGER	REASON FOR DELAY

Fig. 7-11. Summary reporting form used to communicate projects behind schedule.

with a semi-annual or annual document where impact is carried by the reporting of progress over a relatively long period of time during which advances are easily perceptible. Monthly reports are valuable to middle management, but they lose some of their impact with upper management because month-to-month progress often is not dramatic and clearly distinguishable.

Program Review

Program reviews form the fourth link in the communications network. The review of technical projects by various levels of management and technical peers serves three worthwhile purposes. First, such a review provides technical guidance and input from supervisory personnel. Second, a forum is provided for personnel to present individual projects. Third, program review provides a means for management to let the professional know that his work and his contributions are valued and important.

The format used for these reviews varies and ultimately is designed to fit the function of the research or special project group. The basic review document, however, regardless of discussion format, is the program proposal previously described. A variety of communication aids can be utilized, but the principal medium is visual. There are several commercially available techniques to produce 8-1/2 × 11 inch projection transparencies. These are easy to prepare and convenient to transport. This method of presentation is invaluable in retaining group attention, permitting group discussion leadership, and enabling a relatively large group to view data or diagrams simultaneously. Only perti-

ENGINEERING & DEVELOPMENT
PROJECT COST ANALYSIS
SUMMARY SHEET

PROJECT TITLE ____________________ PROJECT ENGINEER ____________________

COMPONENTS OR FUNCTIONS	DATE			DATE			DATE			DATE			DATE			DATE		
	TARGET COST			1st ENGINEERING ESTIMATE			2nd ENGINEERING ESTIMATE			MANUFACTURING ESTIMATE			ESTIMATE AFTER ENG. & MFG. REVIEW			FINAL ESTIMATE		
	REMARKS			REMARKS			REMARKS			REMARKS			REMARKS			REMARKS		
	PARTS COST	ASSY. COST	TOTAL COST	PARTS COST	ASSY. COST	TOTAL COST	PARTS COST	ASSY. COST	TOTAL COST	PARTS COST	ASSY. COST	TOTAL COST	PARTS COST	ASSY. COST	TOTAL COST	PARTS COST	ASSY. COST	TOTAL COST

Fig. 7–12. Summary reporting form used to communicate progressively refined cost estimates for projects under way.

nent material should be presented at meetings of this type. The material is often problem oriented and therefore, technically stimulating. Lengthy speeches or presentations should be kept to a minimum in order to retain the interest of the group.

Performance Appraisal

Performance appraisal is the fifth phase of the effective project communication system. The complete communications system requires performance evaluation or appraisal as the final element in closing the communications loop. Personnel performance on pre-established program goals serves as a constructive nucleus for a mutually profitable performance appraisal. The effectiveness of a communications system has a very simple yardstick of success—that is, the efficiency and dispatch with which research and special projects can be utilized commercially. Once the technical validity of a program is established, communications between and among project personnel can aid greatly in achieving early commercialization of the development.

Fig. 7-13 shows one format that can be used in reporting the status and degree of success in completing a specific project.

We have suggested that effective personnel are informed personnel whether in top management or staff positions. The key area of emphasis for today's project middle manager is communications, or the translation of information, in order that higher management and project staff members can understand what needs to be accomplished.

Communications tools must efficiently convey a large quantity of information. For this reason, the various formal documents used for project initiation and control should be concise in format and pertinent in content. Caution has to be exercised to avoid over communication, or excessive detailing of a program plan document to the extent that it reflects a restricted, inflexible plan that can tolerate no slippage. In addition, a communications system cannot substitute for lack of technical or planning expertise, since sound planning strategy and technical competence are prerequisites to, rather than a result of, effective communication. An important aspect of the network is the interpersonal communication of results, accomplishments, and future goals developed through performance appraisal.

Finally, it must be emphasized that a successful communications program demands persistent and progressive effort on a day-to-day basis. Continuity of effort in communications is as important as the information content of the program itself.

PRODUCT LINE A

PROJECT TITLE: Adaptations to Meet New Market Conditions

OBJECTIVE:

Maintain capability leadership of machines in their respective classifications.

EXAMPLES:

Methods for handling synthetic polymer materials on all models.

1. Special binders
2. Combination compressed air and suction tensioning attachments

Methods for multiplying selection capability for special purposes.

General adaptation to special manufacture

    Accumulators; stitch quality, graduation, etc.

CURRENT STATUS AND EFFECT ON SALES:

One-third of the total development completed during May, 1970; hardware developed included in all current sales and at least in part responsible for support of such sales.

ENGINEERING & DEVELOPMENT COSTS (TO DATE):

    1970 $35,000

ASSESSMENT OF SUCCESS:

    Technical   80%
    Commercial   50%

Fig. 7-13. Form used for reporting the status and degree of success in completing a specific project.

ORAL AND WRITTEN COMMUNICATIONS

Written communications present a special challenge. With feedback one can reevaluate channel capacity, modify the coding system, and correct semantic mismatches, but a writer has no feedback channel. In written communications, the writer himself must determine what type of channel will best suit a given reader and then select a code that will match the code characteristics of the channel. Before the writer can decide what message to transmit and consider the effect the message will have on the reader, he should perform three tasks:

1) Analyze the information gathered
2) Identify the primary and secondary readers
3) Synthesize and edit the information.

A human report writer might be described as an integrated communication system. For example, the information source, an essential part of a complete communication system, is the mind of the writer (assisted by external memory devices such as notes and data sheets). Acting as the information source, the writer mentally selects the message to be transmitted and determines the intent. The report writer's mind is also a semantic encoder because the writer must select the channel to be used and encode the information into appropriate symbols (words, numbers, mathematical symbols, etc.). The transmitter performs the physical act of recording the symbols as signals; the writer can perform this function by writing the report out in longhand, by typing it, or by dictating it to a secretary or onto electronic equipment.

The written report is the mechanical channel. The eventual reader of the report performs the function of receiver in reading the signals as symbols. The semantic decoder translates the symbols into message. The destination is the mind of the reader, which serves as a decision center to be influenced by the message.

Semantic noise occurs in the form of faulty word choices, improper sentence structure, inadequate detail, and poor organization. Mechanical noise includes errors and inconsistencies in typography, poor physical layout of illustrations, overcrowding of text, poor reproduction qualities, and even such items as a binding that prevents the reader from keeping the report open at a given page. Psychological noise is any emotional reaction on the part of the reader that decreases his channel capacity, thus distorting the message. Doubt, disagreement, boredom, and even anger are the common negative reactions of technical readers. The source of psychological noise may be the message itself, semantic or mechanical noise in the message, or some external stimulus.

Each receiver may be classifed according to his importance as a reader. Whenever a report is to form the basis of a decision or whenever action of any sort needs to be taken on the information the report carries, the person or group who will make the decision or take the action is the primary reader. Others who may receive the report for information only are the secondary readers.

It is important to make this distinction in rank among readers because the writer should always consider first the needs of the primary reader. This is the best way to guarantee a wise selection of information, channel, and code for transmitting a message to those who "need to know." When authorization for action is requested or given, it is particularly important to convey the message so clearly that it cannot be misunderstood. To accomplish this the writer should take into account the backgrounds of all his various readers. It is important also, as stated before, to convey to the reader the purpose of the desired action so that he may make his best contribution to its success. This applies to instructions sent down the organizational line as well as to requests for authorization sent up the line.

Once the writer has met his responsibilities to the primary reader, he should try to satisfy at least some of the needs of the secondary reader. One technique to achieve this objective is to include material of interest to the secondary reader, but relegate it to an appendix. Another way of dealing with the secondary reader is to present background material with which the primary reader is familiar in a letter of transmittal or a foreword addressed specifically to the secondary reader.

All readers, whether primary or secondary, have certain channel capacity characteristics in common. They also have special channel characteristics, some of which are psychological, that differ greatly. By placing himself in the reader's place, the writer can see the reader's basic needs. First, the reader must be able to understand the intended message clearly and without unnecessary work. Secondly, he wants to be able to read the communication rapidly. Scientific and engineering writing is read at work, in the laboratory, in the office, in places where the pressure and pace of activity force a rapid reading. The well-paced report will allow the reader to move through it rapidly; he must if he is ever to finish the pile of papers on his desk. Finally, all readers want to be able, if necessary, to read discontinuously. A reader is often interrupted during the reading of a report. The careful writer, realizing this, will provide convenient stopping and starting places.

Several suggestions can be made to assist in the preparation of an effective report:

1) *Organize the material to be presented.* The basic framework of a written communication can be compiled in outline form and reviewed or revised before the complete text is prepared. This step is particularly important in the preparation of dictated material.

2) *Make the title meaningful and, if possible, brief.* Single-word titles are satisfactory only for a piece of writing that covers a broad or general topic. In the title, the reader needs an accurate statement of what the writing covers. This increases the reader's channel capacity for it immediately eliminates many of the pseudo possibilities and directs the reader toward the true subject material.

3) *Summarize the high points.* One of the best ways to bring the important points of an investigation to the attention of a reader is to use an informative summary or abstract. This captures the reader's attention immediately by placing the main conclusion up front. Keep the abstract short, but do not hesitate to be quantitative. This again increases the reader's channel capacity by eliminating false possibilities.

4) *Provide sufficient background material.* The amount of background material in any report should be directly related to the intended reader's knowledge of the investigation. On the other hand, if the report is addressed to a reader who is not familiar with the project, the writer must take particular care to fill that reader in on the "why" of the investigation. The informed readers can always skip over what they already know. This step is taken to reduce the semantic noise in the message.

5) *Associate the unfamiliar with the familiar.* The accuracy of a transmission is improved if semantic noise is reduced by defining new terms or old terms applied in new or unusual ways. Use familiar words and use technical jargon or engineering slang with caution. If your reader is a specialist who understands it, such shoptalk may be economical; if he is not, you are leaving him in the dark. For instance, the expression "TLP" is suitable only if your reader knows that it means "total liquid product." If specialized language is necessary for precision or convenience, it should be defined the first time it is used. Something obvious to you, however, may be a complete mystery to your reader. Another aid to your reader's understanding is the use of concrete, picture words and active verbs. This is especially important for engineers, who of all writers should be practical and

definite. Consider the statement, "Inefficient operation of the manufacturing process is caused by inadequate sizing of the intermediate unit relative to the others." A more concrete and active version might be: "The polymerizing kettle is too small for the rest of the plant. This limits the output of resin." Abstract words are sometimes the refuge of the man who does not want to admit that he is short of facts. The effective writer presents facts in vivid, lively words. Armed with the facts, one could say in the example just cited: "The polymerizing kettle has half the capacity of the rest of the plant. Doubling kettle capacity would raise resin output from the present 10 tons to 20 tons per day."

6) *Describe the whole before the parts.* Just as the reader needs a picture of the whole problem in the introduction, so he needs similar guides throughout the presentation of evidence. In order for him to understand a new concept, a new machine, or a new method, he must first have a clear idea of the essence, function, and purpose of the concept, machine, or method. He needs an overall framework into which he can fit the parts as they are described.

7) *Develop a sound structure.* Once the reader has some conception of the whole, the parts should be presented to him in a sequence consistent with the nature of the subject matter. This sequence could be chronological, or some other logical sequence such as order of importance or cause and effect might be used. Usually, one method is better than another for a particular situation. Selection and emphasis are among the most important tools of the manager or engineer. Scientific accuracy may sometimes call for the inclusion of everything related to the subject, but engineering judgment places facts in perspective. This perspective is most important when you are writing for those not in a position to evaluate for themselves. If alternative courses of action must be offered, state which you favor and why. Ultimately in the line of communication a single course of action must be taken; the pyramid of evaluation, with a broad base of fact, comes at the top to an apex of decision.

8) *Emphasize the primary ideas.* All the details that go into a description will not be of equal importance. Sometimes, however, the reader attaches undue weight to a statement simply because the writer was not careful in separating and labeling his primary and secondary evidence. If a certain piece of secondary information contains so many details or qualifications that it requires a large amount of text, it should be summarized and relegated to an appendix. Descriptions of procedure often fall into this category, as do development of equations and discus-

sions of test equipment. Organize your writing with unity, emphasis, and order. Every part of your writing should serve the reader by contributing to your main theme. Emphasize the important and subordinate or drop the less important to avoid burdening him. Lead him by a straight path of logical presentation. All of these aims are served by outlining in the manner discussed above. If the subject is complex, single-topic cards make it easy to select, group, and arrange ideas.

9) *Separate fact and opinion.* Since the pronoun "I" has been outlawed from many areas of technical writing, the author's personal views are frequently mistaken for those of accepted authorities in the field. Such common expressions as "It is believed that . . ." and "It is concluded that . . ." are cases in point. Two important communication principles are involved. If the reader is misled into accepting opinion for fact, then the accuracy of the communication has been decreased and more noise introduced. On the other hand, the reader may lose channel capacity if he has to guess continually whether the material is fact or opinion.

10) *Code the report for fast reading.* Use descriptive headings and subheadings freely. Descriptive headings and subheadings act as an internal table of contents, quickly directing and orienting the reader to the various topics covered in the report and permitting him to read selectively. Also, headings help the reader find his place quickly after being interrupted. Place topic sentences at the beginning of paragraphs. Placing the topic sentence at or near the beginning of a paragraph allows your reader to skim through the report. This form of controlled redundancy greatly improves the accuracy of the transmission.

11) *Use simple sentence structure when the thought is complex.* Whenever the thought is involved or otherwise difficult to describe, the sentence structure should be uncomplicated. Much has been heard from the readability experts about the need to write simply. They say to use short words and sentences; be concise; avoid unnecessary words. You should do this for your reader so that he can follow you with the least effort. Sometimes the long word expresses your meaning more precisely, but don't use it just to impress. Here a dictionary of synonyms is useful, especially if it compares meanings. Too many chemical engineers *agitate* rather than *stir, ameliorate* rather than *improve, attempt* rather than *try, discontinue* rather than *stop, inaugurate* rather than *begin,* and *utilize* rather than *use.* What is more, many of the long words used are abstract enough to leave a little loophole in meaning. Using words loosely not merely confuses

but cheats the reader. Long, complicated sentences are even worse. At best they tend to confuse the reader, requiring him to go back and figure out what the writer really said. At worst they are traps for the unwary writer, making him say what he does not mean.

12) *Make full use of graphic aids.* Curves and tables that summarize detailed results are a valuable redundancy. Most readers have trained themselves to extract the information they need, at a glance. Ideally, graphic aids would be placed immediately following their reference in text.

13) *Avoid footnoting secondary or reference material.* If secondary or reference material bears directly on the topic under discussion, try to work this information parenthetically into the text. Footnoting forces the reader to drop his eyes from the text to the footnote and back to the text again—a tiring process that badly hinders rapid reading.

THE IMPACT OF ELECTRONIC DATA PROCESSING

In the previous discussion of the manufacturing cycle the concepts of data storage areas and a centralized data bank were mentioned. In considering the transition of certain manufacturing functions to computer augmented systems, it is easily seen that certain attributes of digital computers are well suited. The storage of large amounts of data and the rapid systematic recall of this data are readily performed tasks. In addition the rapid performance of a series of computing tasks using a human designed algorithm can be readily adapted to an existing manufacturing cycle.

Consider the transformation of a manually performed communications task to a computer-generated output. Beginning with an explicit statement of some computational task in terms of certain words or equations, a programer can write a program. In the most general case, this program will take the form of a compiler which will cause the computer to examine the statement and then write a program which will cause the computer to perform the task in question. When the program is fed to the computer, the computer will carry out the required task.

Writing programs is a lengthy and uncongenial task. An engineer or manager who has a suitable compiler available can specify what he desires to be done using a compact sequence of allowed words and equations. By means of the compiler, he can cause the computer to translate his statement of the problem into the long, detailed, and obscure (to a human being) sequence of computer instructions.

The best-known compiler is Fortran, which is used to convert instructions written in a symbolism closely resembling standard mathematical notation into computer programs. Compilers are very useful to programers in instructing computers to carry out a wide variety of complicated tasks. The binary digits stored in the memory of a computer can be used to specify numbers, but they can also specify or encode words, musical notes, or logical operations. Thus, besides their use in performing complicated mathematical calculations, computers have been used to make a concordance of the Revised Standard Bible, to simulate the operation of a telephone switching system to recognize spoken digits from 0 to 9, to play checkers and to learn to improve their game, to play chess, to prove theorems in geometry and symbolic logic, to create unusual musical sounds, and to compose music according to the rules of first species counterpoint.

Such uses of computers have stimulated thought concerning the nature of the recognition of human words, the structure of various languages, the strategy of winning at games, and the structure of music. When new knowledge so arrived at is put to use in programing the larger and faster computers of the future, it is difficult to foresee what their limitations may be.

A computer manufacturer envisions a large centralized data bank similar to that illustrated in Fig. 7-4. In addition to the added precision and accuracy which will accompany the computerized management and manipulation of manufacturing data (e.g., bills of material, specification references, inventory level, work center scheduling, etc.), there will be an important impact on manufacturing communications. As previously discussed, the frequency with which a document is translated at a node point will be reduced. Thus, the number of inaccuracies introduced will be decreased; since the encoding function will be more responsive to the ultimate receiver, semantic noise will be reduced. For example, let us consider the case where cost information on a particular product line is required by the marketing group. Since cost data are available directly from the central data bank, the semantic problems of encoding an accounting document are eliminated. If the information required concerned a marginal cost per unit, the problem of extracting this from a variance costing system would be eliminated.

As optimistic as these statements seem, there are additional factors to be considered. There is a potential for a large volume of data to be generated by the computer center. If attention is not given to principles of communication, channel capacity, and quantity of information to be communicated, inefficiencies can result. The computer output to be used should be analyzed in the same terms as any document presented for analysis and decision.

SUMMARY

The problems of communication have been reviewed from three standpoints:

1) The communicator who wishes to effect some specific result and consequently must code his message in such a way as to overcome the mechanical noise of the transmission system plus the semantic and psychological noise of the receiver.
2) The receiver who must first determine what information the message was supposed to convey and next what course of action to follow as a consequence. Information theory, of course, applies to what was said; decision theory, on the other hand, concerns itself with what to do.
3) The designer of a communication system who through the use of information theory can resolve problems concerning channel capacity, coding, and redundancy.

Communication in the manufacturing cycle has been discussed in terms of its effective use within the organization to achieve the goals of management. The discussion included the problems of job-shop operation, short-run manufacturing, and continuous production. It was concluded that the efforts to date to produce optimal production schedules by means of computer simulation had not been successful in any of these areas.

The problems of communication in special projects and manufacturing research and development were considered. Considerations of the necessity of reviewing the contributions of individuals in these activities were discussed. The importance of oral and written communication is stressed, and the impact of electronic data processing upon this field is treated.

chapter 8

organizational change

AN ORGANIZATION MAY BE VIEWED as a system that requires inputs in the form of materials, personnel, equipment, funds, and so on. The organization likewise is dependent upon its outside environment for the disposal of its outputs, which take the form of finished products, professional services, waste materials, etc. Thus the viable manufacturing organization is described most simply as a system capable of converting inputs into outputs of sufficient greater value to permit the accrual of profit.

When its environment or technology changes, an organization must adapt to meet that change. On the input side, an organization may have to realign itself in accordance with changes in its sources of raw material and other supplies. Alternatively, the organization may have to effect a new organizational structure in order to attract trained personnel needed to operate the new technology. On the output side, the organization may face new competing product lines. Internal reorganization may be the best way to reduce product costs and thus remain competitive.

In regard to changes in technology, when methods of manufacture are changed, realignments are often necessary. The change may be simple—perhaps only one machine operator is required for a new milling machine instead of two. Other changes may be more far-reaching, however, as will be shown in a subsequent case study.

Change is a natural part of the life of an organization, and few organizations exist which have not experienced changes in internal structure at one time or another. Changes are more apt to occur during periods of rapid organizational growth or during periods of decline. They may take the form of frequent minor adjustments or infrequent major alterations with far-reaching effects on the organization and its members. Generally, an organization makes changes only when its management is under substantial pressure.

Certain organizations seem to adapt more readily to change than others. As a rule, larger corporations have the greater human and financial resources required to accomplish change. On the other hand, a small company may have a degree of flexibility that many large firms lack. Change is more easily brought about in organizations where it is not uncommon and thus is not feared.

Some organizations are highly resistant to change, both in organizational structure and other respects. These organizations do not attempt to adapt themselves to changes in their environment and often pass out of existence. Closed-system organizations, such as those typically found in government, and other monolithic institutions have the least capacity for change. This is partly because one of the primary (though unstated) objectives of such an organization is to protect and preserve its internal structure and traditional ways of operating irrespective of changes in its environment or core technology.

Irrespective of the level at which management operates, there is a responsibility to build an effective working organization which is capable of carrying out its objectives. Inevitably these objectives change, and the organizations must change with them.

One technique of adaptation is a change in the structure of the organization. Often, a rearrangement of structure and functions is necessary in order to increase the effectiveness of the organization in dealing with a changing environment or a new set of competitive conditions. Frequently, such organizational shifts are accompanied by changes in personnel or systems.

Unfortunately, organizational theorists have not devoted a great deal of attention to the processes involved in organizational change. Thus the conceptual basis of organizational change is not clearly understood.[1] Nevertheless practicing managers must recognize the need for change and take steps to see that appropriate changes are implemented.

This chapter is not concerned with the theoretical aspects of organizational innovation but rather addresses itself to the practicalities of change. We accept the fact that organizations are dynamic; change occurs constantly whether sought or not. The outside environment is also dynamic, thus forcing the organization to change in order to sur-

---

[1] For a good orientation in the theoretical aspects of organizational change, see James Q. Wilson, "Innovation in Organization: Notes Toward a Theory" in James D. Thompson, ed., *Approaches to Organizational Design* (Pittsburgh, Pa.: University of Pittsburgh Press, 1966), 193–218. Wilson sees organizational innovation as occurring in three stages: (1) the conception of the change, (2) the proposal for the change, and (3) the adoption and implementation of the change. Cf. the approach taken in this chapter.

vive. An organization, even the most bureaucratic, cannot become a completely closed system because it is dependent upon inputs from outside; likewise its output must be disposed of.

We shall point out some of the reasons why change is necessary, and discuss ways whereby the need for change may be recognized. Planning and implementing change, the operational part of the manager's responsibility for change, is considered, and some dysfunctional or undesirable elements connected with organizational change are examined. Finally, this chapter discusses management's overall responsibility for organizational change.

The main emphasis is on changes in the so-called formal organization as defined by organization charts, position descriptions, and approved systems of internal operations. It is recognized that in almost every situation an informal organization also exists which either complements or conflicts with the formal structure. A basic responsibility of management is to establish an effective formal organization. It is also important to assure that the informal organization provides support to, rather than works at cross purposes with the formal structure.

ORGANIZATIONAL CHANGE: CASE STUDIES AND RATIONALE

Organizational change takes place when some alteration is made in the form or structure of the organization, or when its basic functions are altered. As a result the responsibilities of certain operating or staff departments are changed, or there is a shift in the reporting relationships between units. Organization change occurs when new departments, subsidiaries, or operating units are created, or existing ones are combined, split up, or disposed of.

In commercial enterprises, the change is often likely to take the form of shifts between structures based on functions, products, processes, or regions. Major organizational change takes place when a firm decentralizes its operating units, or shifts from a loose affiliation of dispersed units to a strong central control from a corporate headquarters. On the other hand, some organizational changes can be relatively minor in scope and importance. An example might be the consolidation of two small, related departments into one department.

Two case studies in organizational change are presented below. The first describes a major corporate reshuffling, affecting the entire company from top management on down. The second case study illustrates the creation of a new organizational unit for numerical control (N/C) operations made necessary by technological changes in the production processes of a medium-size manufacturer.

Case Study 1: Change from a Functional to a Product Organization

Fig. 8-1 illustrates a change in the organizational structure of a metalworking company. The company has two products, A and B. A is an old line product, and the company was originally structured around its manufacture and sale. Product B has been developed by the company's engineering group, and over a period of years this product achieved a strong sales growth in market areas somewhat different from Product A markets. Except for the limited use of some common production equipment, the two products are manufactured by different processes. The growth of Product B, and management's intention to

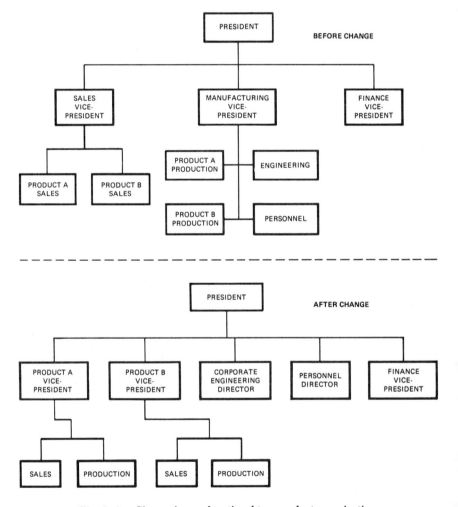

Fig. 8-1. Change from a functional to a product organization.

continue that growth and search for new product lines, suggested the need for a major change in organization.

An organizational structure based on product lines has been established with Products A and B being assigned separate sales and production functions. Corporate staff functions of engineering and personnel were also established. It was necessary to make significant changes in the responsibilities of certain management personnel. Transitional problems were encountered, but the change from functional to product line organization strengthened the company and gave it the flexibility it required for continued growth.

Case Study 2: Creation of a New Organizational Unit

Fig. 8-2 illustrates an organizational change involving the consolidation of functions for N/C equipment operations. Before the change, N/C equipment was operated by the Manufacturing Department, with parts programing in the Manufacturing Engineering Department. Top management felt that the established manufacturing and engineering organizations were not placing the proper emphasis on the development and use of N/C equipment. There were additional problems in relating N/C operators to other workers. To deal with the problems more effectively, an N/C Operations Department was created by transferring selected functions to this new department from the existing Manufacturing Department and Manufacturing Engineering Department. A small engineering staff group was set up in the N/C Operations Department. The Production and Inventory Control Department was assigned additional responsibilities for evaluation and determination of new N/C applications.[2]

Rationale

As the examples point out, organizational change can have different purposes, and can take different forms. It depends on the needs of the company. Existing units can be divided, consolidated, or eliminated; new units can be formed. With no change in basic structure, the organization can be effectively altered by changing the responsibilities of existing units. The short cases above described situations in which management made its decisions to change the organization based on present needs and future requirements. Unfortunately, there are many firms in which organizational structure is no more than the accidental by-product of random actions and decisions made by management over a period of time. This approach results in an unplanned and often illogical organization, which may or may not do the job.

---

[2] For more information on planning for N/C operations, see Raymond E. Howe, ed., *Introduction to Numerical Control in Manufacturing* (Dearborn, Mich.: Society of Manufacturing Engineers, 1969).

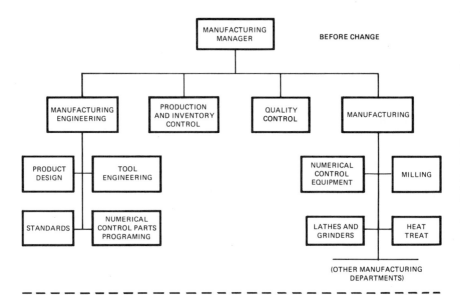

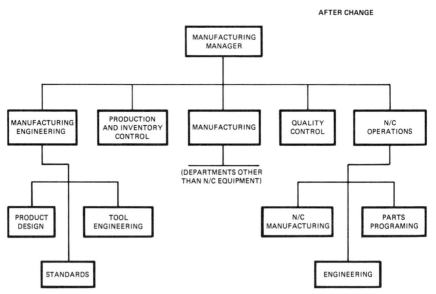

Fig. 8-2. Creation of a new organization unit.

Organizational change should be purposeful; change should not be implemented except to improve the operation of the organization or one of its subunits. Certain factors act more strongly than others to bring about organizational change. Generally, change occurs as a result of basic changes in ways of doing business. The primary reasons for organizational change are:

1) Changes in manufacturing methods
2) New products or services
3) Geographic shifts in markets
4) Growth in size of the organization
5) Changes in internal systems or methods of operations
6) Declining profit margins.

In recent times, these factors in combination have resulted in frequent organizational changes of the following types:

1) Companies with expanding international operations have found it necessary to realign both domestic and foreign organizations to support the growth of overseas subsidiaries.
2) Companies with widely diverse operations and product lines have reorganized to combine similar lines and have appointed group vice-presidents to gain better control and coordination between lines.
3) Companies with several divisions manufacturing the same products have consolidated duplicate operations as an economy move.
4) Companies with new, rapidly growing product lines have undertaken major rearrangements of marketing functions in order to broaden their marketing efforts and maximize new product growth.

Alert management can bring about effective organizational change. Skill is required to evaluate the need for change and the kind of restructuring which will improve organizational performance. Unfortunately, changes in organization have proved to be disappointing for many companies; the expected results simply have not materialized. Frequently, management has restructured their organization when what was really needed was an improved system, or better qualified personnel. When poorly planned organizational changes are implemented, lowered organizational performance usually results, along with stress and confusion not apparent before the change.

On the other hand, managements sometimes avoid organizational restructuring, even when this is the proper solution to the problem.

Often change is avoided because management is not sure how to bring it about, or how to deal with the resistance which may accompany it.

RECOGNIZING THE NEED FOR CHANGE

The need for organizational change can be recognized either in advance or after the need for change has become pressing. Ideally, management should be able to anticipate today the kind of organization it will need tomorrow. When this is true change can be planned for: people can be found and trained, facilities can be acquired, and systems and procedures can be developed to assure the proper operation of the new organization. Unfortunately, this set of conditions does not always occur in the real world. A new technological development, a new competitive product, a sudden change in markets, costs, or prices, or the unexpected departure of a key executive—any one of these occurrences can result in a rapid shift in needs. The probability of the unexpected, of course, does not relieve management of its duty to try to recognize the need for change, and to plan for and develop an organizational structure adapted to the needs and objectives of the firm.

Factors Requiring Change

To recognize the necessity for organizational change to meet future needs, management must have some capability for forecasting the basic conditions within which the firm is likely to find itself operating in the future. A broad range of considerations may enter into long-range organizational planning, including the recognition and evaluation of such factors as the following:

1) Marketing factors, including geographic patterns, distribution channels, promotional objectives, product variety, size and location of major customers, competitive products, and rate of technological advance in industry.
2) Production and procurement factors, including cost and complexity of productive processes, quality requirements, integration of production stages, plant location, and technical development in processes.[3]
3) Personnel factors, such as skill requirements, availability and cost of labor, and relations with unions.
4) Management factors, such as need for close coordination between organizational units, plans for growth, profit objectives, use of

---

[3] On this last point, see especially James R. Bright, ed., *Technological Forecasting for Industry and Government: Methods and Applications* (Englewood Cliffs, N.J.: Prentice-Hall, 1968).

computer-supported systems, and management's philosophy of control.

5) Financial factors, including importance of new financing, and sources of funds.

6) Regulatory factors, such as government legislation on products, processes, or acquisitions or disposal of organizational units.

The list above is not exhaustive but is intended to convey the idea that long-range organizational planning, is, like long-range planning for other purposes, based on broad considerations relating to the firm and basic trends within its industry and markets. This kind of planning is not simple, and requires a great deal of management's attention. One difficulty facing managers is the lack of time to devote to such planning. It is nevertheless true that the manager who correctly anticipates his future organizational problems, and recognizes the need for adaptive change, is in the best position to plan for and carry out improved organizational restructuring. He will contribute greatly to the success and effectiveness of his organization.

Distress Signals

All too often organizations suffer from the fact that they should have been changed long ago. There are a number of distress signals which such organizations display. These signals may indicate a need for organizational change, or may be symptomatic of a need for changes in personnel, systems, or basic business policy. It is not difficult for an observant manager to perceive the signs of distress; it is more difficult to determine the kinds of corrective action which may be needed.

The indications most frequently displayed where change is overdue are the following:

1) There is confusion over who is responsible for what.

2) Management is more interested in evaluation and analysis of past performances than in planning for the future.

3) There is continued argument over the present usefulness of old systems and methods.

4) There is greater allegiance to departmental than to company goals.

5) The organization is made up primarily of older employees, and seems to have difficulty in attracting younger people.

6) There is a history of rejecting new ideas or approaches to solving problems, and an inability to handle new problems or challenges.

7) There is continuing poor performance, compared with reasonable standards.
8) A service department is unable to provide the services required.
9) There is poor morale, as evidenced by high turnover, frequent absences, and many grievances.
10) There are complaints from managers that they are constantly dealing with problems which should be handled by their subordinates.
11) There are overlapping or duplicate functions.
12) There are frequent meetings to clear up misunderstandings.
13) There is a virtual absence of communication or interaction with the rest of the organization. This is particularly true of staff groups.

The organizational unit in trouble can generally be recognized by these symptoms. It should be pointed out, however, that these symptoms may indicate difficulties in addition to those associated with poor organizational structure. Other problems may also exist, such as inadequate training, unqualified personnel, poor systems or procedures, bad physical location, misunderstanding of duties, or inadequate supervision. The manager's job is to determine the causes of poor organizational performance and to plan for and make corrective changes.

PLANNING AND IMPLEMENTING CHANGE

Decisions on organizational change should not be made until management achieves a thorough understanding of the existing organization and its functions. This understanding is best obtained by conducting a study to identify problems and develop and evaluate alternative solutions. The reasons for problems must be accurately identified before a solution can be found, whether the final solution is an organizational rearrangement or other improvement. The following series of steps is suggested as an approach to planning and implementing organizational change:

1) Study the existing organization and its functions
2) Identify problems and opportunities for improvement
3) Formulate a tentative solution and discuss it with the managers affected by the change
4) Prepare a recommended plan of organization, and obtain approval by management
5) Implement the new organizational structure
6) At a later date, audit the results and make further changes if necessary.

Study of Existing Organization

A thorough understanding of the organization is necessary before problems can be properly defined and solutions determined. This understanding is best gained by analyzing the organization to obtain an accurate conception of the functions being performed. The actual operations of the unit may be different from those indicated by existing organizational charts or written procedures. Even supervisors are often not fully aware of all the kinds of work being done by their units.

First, the study must have the endorsement of the manager of the unit. Without his backing, little will be accomplished. The manager should have a clear notion of the purpose of the study and the approach to be taken.

The purpose of the study should not be announced as that of changing the organization. There are two reasons for this. First, it cannot be determined in advance that organizational change is actually necessary. Second, if the manager feels that the decision has already been made to change his unit, he is more likely to resist the study. It is generally preferable to state that the objective of the study is to look for opportunities for improvement in such things as systems, external communications, or relations with other departments. Few unit heads will offer much resistance to an objective search for improvement opportunities.

Personnel for the Study. The selection of personnel to conduct the study is often a problem. There are basically three sources available, as follows:

1) Company management or line personnel, working on a part-time or special project basis
2) Company staff personnel, as from the internal audit or procedures staff
3) Outside consultants or advisers, such as the management services staff of the company's public accounting firm or an independent management consulting firm.

Each of these approaches has its own advantages and problems. The selection of study personnel will depend on the complexity of the problem and the talent and availability of people and cost.

The amount of manpower necessary to conduct an organizational study will depend on the size and complexity of the organizational unit to be studied. For studies involving only a survey and analysis of organizational functions, one or two staff members are usually sufficient. If the study also involves an extensive review and analysis of detailed systems and procedures, the manpower needs will double or triple.

The Three-Phase Approach. Once the persons to be responsible for the study have been selected, a plan should be prepared. Such a plan should be brief, and in outline form. It should include the objectives of the sutdy, the major steps, and an estimated time schedule. The study plan will prove useful as a progress guide, and will be helpful in keeping the study on the right track.

The study of an organizational unit should include three phases: orientation, fact-finding, and analysis. The purpose of the *orientation* phase is to explain the study to those who would be affected by it. This can be done in an informal meeting, which should include a question-and-answer session. The orientation meeting should emphasize the constructive purpose of the study, such as the need to improve control over quality, or reduce order processing time. The meeting should not be used as a forum for criticism of the existing organization or its performance. People below the supervisory level are usually not included.

The orientation phase is important and should not be sidestepped in the interest of getting the study off to a fast start. Without the understanding gained in the orientation phase, people affected by the study may resist it strongly.

Next comes the *fact-finding* phase. The purpose of this phase is to obtain sufficient information about the organizational unit under study to permit the development of sound, objective conclusions about the kind of organization needed. The significant facts about the organizational unit should be gathered in the following ways:

1) Interview the managers, supervisors, and other key employees of the organizational unit, as well as those in other related units. The interviews are an extremely important source of both factual data and views on opportunities for improvement. Much of the interview data will be in the form of opinions of the interviewees. Well-thought-out opinions, coming from persons familiar with the organization and its problems, can and should be given considerable weight in the study. It is necessary that the person doing the fact-finding have good interviewing skills. It is particularly important that the interviewer be objective and without apparent bias.

2) Obtain available organizational charts, position descriptions, and other documentation of responsibilities of the organizational unit. The documentation should be updated so as to show the current state of affairs.

3) Review work flows of all significant processes in the organizational unit. Flow charts should be obtained to indicate the principal steps in the processing of work, and the flow of information both within the unit under study and between it and other organizational units.
4) Determine the significant information needed for decision making, its source, and the way it is used in the organization.

It is important to involve both supervisory and management personnel in the study. They should be asked to provide information and personal views about functions of their unit, and to make suggestions for improvement. While the knowledge of any one supervisor may appear limited to his own field, the accumulated knowledge of all supervisors and managers in a group is usually great.

During the fact-finding phase, the person conducting the study should take careful notes and build a well-documented file of information. This collection of data becomes a raw material for use in the next phase of the study.

The third phase of the study is the *analysis of information* obtained about the organization. There should be a review of the strengths and deficiencies of the organization, its structure, responsibilities, and functions, the flow of information and work, and relationships with other operating and staff units. The purpose of this analytical review is to enable the person doing the study to develop sound conclusions about major organizational problems and opportunities for improvement. This phase, like the fact-gathering stage, requires skill, time, and objectivity.

Identification of Problems and Opportunities for Improvements

This step follows naturally from the first step, and is based on the conclusions resulting from the facts and opinions gathered. Problems and opportunities should be clearly spelled out, and should be supported by the facts obtained in the study. As a general rule, it is easy to define an organization's major problems. These usually become obvious during the study as a result of interviews with management personnel and the review of functions and performance. Problems will normally relate to either an unacceptable level of performance, or excessive costs to achieve the necessary performance level.

During this part of the study, it should be determined which of the problems identified can be solved by rearranging the organization. Often, in the course of such studies, it is found that problems result from other causes. Many times apparently hopeless organizational units can be set straight by redesigned systems, improved flow of information, or upgrading of personnel.

In looking at the organizational functions and identifying its problems, it should be recognized that the basic purpose of organizations is to accomplish work, solve problems, and make decisions. The relative weights of these different purposes will vary for different organizations. Therefore, it is important to identify the kinds of work done, the problems that must be solved, and the decisions that must be made. Understanding these basic requirements will often point the way to the most logical and effective organizational structure.

Formulation and Discussion of Tentative Solutions

Once it is determined that there is a need for a change in organizational structure, a tentative solution should be developed which best meets the needs and objectives of the business. The tentative solution should include a clearly defined organizational chart with all major functions assigned to appropriate units of the organization. The solution need not be a highly detailed one, but should be conceptually sound and should meet all major requirements. It is often practical to develop an alternative solution which will permit an evaluation of different approaches to solving the problem.

In formulating a proposed change in organizational structure, the most important factor to consider is the critical outputs which the organization must provide in order to succeed in its purpose. For example, if the organizational unit is an inventory and production planning department in a small-order job shop, the critical outputs may be daily updating of production and delivery schedules, accurate information on location and status of orders, and correct scrap reporting. In this situation, the organizational unit is a service department whose output is information needed by other operating units.

As another example, the organizational unit under study might be a regional warehouse. In this case, the critical outputs could be same-day shipments of goods, immediate billing, back-order notification to customers, and accurate weekly replenishment orders to the manufacturing source. In this situation, the critical outputs of the organizational unit are determined by competitive factors. In both the situations described, the organization must produce the critical outputs or fail in its purpose. For this reason, any organizational change must be designed to assure the ability of the organization to deliver the critical outputs. Each business or department has its own unique problems and requirements for success, and organizational structure must be tailored to meet those demands. At times, it may appear that any one of several arrangements would enable an organization to perform its critical output requirements. The selection of the best structure then depends on other factors, such as future plans and objectives, internal systems and communication needs, cost, or personnel limitations.

The tentative organizational solution should consider any known future plans or objectives which may affect the organizational unit. For example, a proposed rearrangement of a manufacturing department should reflect future plans to acquire additional production facilities. A determination of future plans and objectives will permit the development of an organization which can make a smoother transition and will be better able to implement those objectives when the time comes.

Another important consideration is the effect of a proposed organizational change on systems and communications, both within the organizational unit and between it and other units. It is almost impossible to change an organizational structure without disturbing old lines of communication and systems and procedures. Unfortunately some otherwise sound organizational changes go awry after it is discovered that under the new arrangement there is a breakdown of communications. People within the organization no longer get the information they need; other organizational units fail to receive the information they want. The result is confusion, and a frequent judgment is that the "new organization just doesn't work." This condemnation might have been avoided had the communications and systems requirements of the organization been considered, and the organization structured accordingly.

The organizational form to be proposed should be attainable. In order to be so, it should represent the kind of organization that can be established and made operative within the time, cost, and personnel limitations which exist in the business. There is little to be gained from suggesting an organizational arrangement which requires personnel skills or work methods that are beyond the reach of the company.

Ordinarily, the tentative organizational solution should not violate the basic general principles of organizational theory. Once formulated, the proposed plan should be checked against established principles, and deviations from principles should be noted. Where deviations exist, they should be corrected, so long as organizational performance is not adversely affected. As a practical matter, the organization does not have to conform to all the traditional principles of organizational theory in order to be workable. (This matter was discussed in Chapter 2.) The most important criteria is the capacity of the organization to perform its essential functions and to deliver its critical outputs at reasonable cost.

After the tentative organizational solution has been developed, it should be discussed with the management personnel who are affected by the proposed change. This would include executive personnel, managers of closely related units, and the managers of the unit under study. This review is an important step because it permits management to see what kind of organizational plan is being developed, and to make comments and suggestions for improvements. The review also helps in identifying potential problems which the organizational change might cause. In addition, it often serves to stimulate thinking which helps to ease the implementation of the new organizational structure.

Preparation of a Recommended Plan of Organization and Obtaining the Approval of Management

After the tentative organizational proposal has been discussed with those to be affected by it, it should be amended as necessary. Next a detailed recommended plan should be prepared and presented for review and approval by top management. The recommendation should include the following elements:

1) A brief statement of the problems of the existing organizational structure, the opportunities for improvement through restructuring, and the objectives of the new arrangement. Objectives should be stated in quantified terms, if possible (orders processed per day, backlog levels, etc.).

2) Organization charts, showing both the existing and proposed organizational structure. A useful chart format is one which shows major functions by organizational subunit. An example is shown in Fig. 8-3.

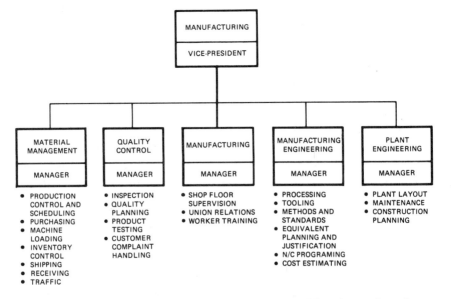

Fig. 8-3. Recommended manufacturing organization and functions performed.

3) Position descriptions for all key managers and supervisors in the recommended organization. The descriptions need not be detailed, but should clearly show the repsonsibilities of each position.

4) Flow charts of each of the major systems and work flows of the organization.

5) A plan of action for bringing about the change. The plan should indicate the major phases or steps required, the responsibility for each step, and time schedule. A sample plan of action format is shown in Fig. 8-4.

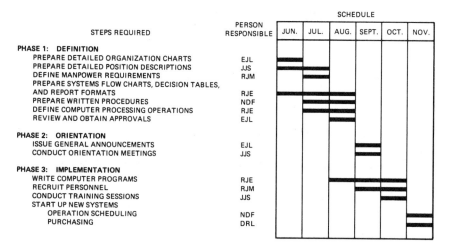

Fig. 8–4. Materials management department. Above is shown a sample general plan of action for organizational change.

6) Statement of requirements in terms of personnel and cost. The need for new or better-qualified personnel should be identified, and any added costs associated with the organizational change should be estimated. Again, there is no need for great detail; however, management should be informed of the personnel and dollar resources needed to support the recommended change.

Management's job is to review the recommended plan, modify it as required, and approve or reject it based on its merits. Once approved, the planned change must have the active support of top management.

Implementation of the New Organizational Structure

Implementation of the new organization may follow any of several paths, depending on the complexity of the structure, the number of organizational subunits affected, and the degree of change involved.

There are several requirements which are common to almost all reorganizations. These requirements, outlined below, are basic responsibilities of management:

1) Make a general announcement to all employees of the change to take place, indicating its objectives, advantages, and the general plan for making the change.
2) Indoctrinate personnel in the departments directly affected, making sure they understand their responsibilities and are fully informed of what the organizational change means to them individually.
3) Hire and train new or additional people required.
4) Provide adequate authority to any new organizational units or positions to assure that they can perform the functions for which they are responsible.
5) Allow sufficient time for the new organization to develop.
6) Keep management informed of progress, using the recommended plan of action as the guide.

During the process of implementing a new organizational structure, managers should be alert to any problems which may develop and should take action to correct them. The managers and supervisors involved in a reorganization should keep one another advised of needs and difficulties encountered; the need for frequent communication during the early stages cannot be over-emphasized.

Auditing the Results and Making Corrective Changes

After a new organizational structure has been in effect for a period of time, management should take a look at the capacity of the unit to meet its objectives, and should make corrective changes if necessary. One advantage of new organizational arrangements is that old methods and systems can be disposed of and new techniques developed, sometimes in rapid succession. This situation can create additional demands for improved systems or better qualified personnel. The restructured organization sometimes exerts positive new demands on other organizational units, and top management should recognize this effect. In the rapidly growing company organizations may need to be in a constant state of controlled change and development. Frequent review and evaluation by top management are required to assure the continued viability of the organizational structure.

HAZARDS AND UNEXPECTED OUTCOMES

There are several hazards which often accompany an organizational change. They vary in degree but are nearly always negative in nature.

Under the best of circumstances, a rearrangement of the organization will create some temporary resistance or confusion, which may be quickly dispelled by an alert management. On the other hand, a poorly planned or illogical organizational change may fail or cause serious disruptions due to active employee resistance or massive confusion.

Management which is considering a change in organizational structure should be aware of the potential pitfalls. During the course of making a change, managers at all levels should be alert to the problems which may come up, and should take early action to deal with them. Fortunately, the positive aspects of the well-planned organizational change usually offset the negative, and such changes can be made smoothly. The fact that there are pitfalls and occasionally negative by-products should not be used as an excuse to avoid a needed organizational change. What managers should understand is that certain side effects are almost inevitable; however, they can be minimized if anticipated and dealt with carefully.

Resistance to Change

The most common by-product of organizational change is resistance to it. Resistance may come from subordinates or managers at any level in the organizational unit involved, or may even develop in other closely related organizational units. Resistance can take many forms, ranging from grumbling and gossiping, to loud protests, strong opposition, work slowdowns, or even employee walkouts. Obviously the greater the resistance to the change, the less likely the change is to succeed.

The basic source of resistance is the informal organization. Usually loosely structured and based on personal relations, the informal organization serves as an internal communications network and social system within the working group and relates members one to another in distinct ways. The informal organization, however it may be formed, is almost always resistant to change. The more well established the informal structure, and the stronger the personalities of its key members, the greater the resistance is likely to be. By understanding the informal organization, management will be better able to bring about change in the formal organization. (The great advantage of the informal organization is that it ensures that the work will get done. It is a major error to attempt to suppress it.)

By studying organizational changes, behavioral scientists have been able to discover some of the characteristics of resistance to change:

1) Resistance will be greater if employees feel that the organizational change is—in effect—a management plot against them, as

evidenced by lack of communication from management or lack of involvement on the part of employees.

2) Resistance will be greater if the change requires individuals to deviate from the standards of the group with which they identify themselves. For example, resistance could be expected from a production planning supervisor if a change in systems or responsibilities tended to downgrade his position.

3) Resistance will increase if there is no channel provided for the airing of employee dissatisfaction with a planned organizational change.

4) Resistance is less when the data or findings pointing to the need for change are gathered by those who will be affected.

5) Resistance is less if a change is supported by the high-prestige members of the working unit. The high-prestige members are those whose opinions and judgments are respected and followed by their fellow-workers, irrespective of their organizational titles or positions.

6) Resistance will be less if there is advance knowledge of the change.

7) Resistance generally will be lowest among high-level management people and highest among lower-level managers and employees.

8) Resistance will be less if those affected by the change can participate in determining the methods and plans for implementing it.

Certain types of organizations and people seem to have a greater resistance to change than others. Functional-type organizations often breed resistance to change because the people in such organizations may develop a narrow or rigid point of view. The exceptionally intelligent employees are often a source of resistance because they can devise the most convincing reasons for not changing.

The fear of change is often more disruptive than change itself. When some kind of change is expected, but employees do not know why, when, or how it will occur, trouble is almost certain to occur. When resistance to change does develop, management should try to find out why and deal with the problem quickly. Normally most forms of resistance can be handled if management communicates fully to the employees the reasons for and advantages of the change. The employees should be aware that management is determined in its aim to bring about improvements through organizational change. At the same time, employees should be made to feel that managers will be sympathetic to their grievances.

Other Pitfalls

Although resistance, in varying degrees, is probably the most universal problem related to organizational change, there are also other pitfalls which are occasionally encountered. Some of these hazards are summarized below:

1) When an organizational structure is altered, there will inevitably be changes required in the systems and procedures used in the organizational unit. Sometimes other organizations are also affected. The effect of organizational change on systems and procedures must be determined to assure that operating routines are compatible with the revised organizational structure.

2) Staff people assigned to assist in directing an organizational change may become so preoccupied with the technical aspects of the project that they forget the effect of the change on people. This can lead to suspicion or rejection by employees.

3) Sometimes a change is made to take advantage of a powerful individual or to protect a weak one. An otherwise nonsensical organizational form is created, with one man's personality in mind. This approach has its obvious dangers, particularly for line operating positions. It is more feasible for temporary or staff type positions. It seldom works for long.

4) Sometimes new positions do not have clearly spelled out duties or well-defined reporting relationships. The result is stress, misunderstanding, and political maneuvering within the organization. This only expends organizational efforts unproductively.

5) Management occasionally attacks the problem of change with initial enthusiasm and then loses interest, allowing the new organizational structure to drift, or evolve on its own. This may work out, providing the head of the organization is a strong manager. Otherwise the new organization may become less effective than the one it replaced.

6) Top management frequently expects too much too fast, and loses patience when the restructured organization does not yield expected results quickly. It takes time for any organization to develop to its fullest potential.

7) As a solution to an organizational problem, a strong manager may be assigned to take over a division or department, based on the assumption that he has all the management skill required to bring about needed improvements on his own. This quick and unthinking approach may present a good manager with an overwhelming set of problems, without sufficient resources to deal with them. He may become an unnecessary sacrifice of corporate talent. Top management has a responsibility to gain a reasonably clear understanding of the extent of the organization's problems before assigning new people to solve them.

8) Sometimes the management and the operating personnel of a department are assigned the task of reorganizing their own

department. This usually fails, especially in the departments with a heavy load of daily routines. There is something akin to a Gresham's law for organizations[4] which says that daily routines drive out planning activities. The department whose primary function is routine processing will seldom be able to do the planning and research necessary to bring about a successful rearrangement to improve its own organization and functions.

MANAGEMENT RESPONSIBILITY

The development, growth, and change of the organization is a responsibility of management. In carrying out this duty management's job is to plan for, direct, support, and control needed organizational change. Managers need to be able to recognize when organizational change is needed, and should take the action necessary to bring it about. Companies should avoid the situation where an obsolete and ineffective organizational structure is permitted to continue, based on the vague hope that "things will get better."

The responsibility for organization belongs to top management. The president, division general manager, or other chief executive officer should establish the objectives for the organization as a whole and for its subunits. He should see that organizational planning is done, and that needed change is carried out in order to assure best overall performance of the organization for which he is responsible. Unfortunately top management often leaves the task of organizational change to lower echelons of management. Ideally top management establishes the firm's overall objectives and these objectives are finalized through the establishment of lower-level objectives. All members of management should participate in decisions on changes to meet these objectives.

Organizational change is best made within the framework of an organizational planning function carried on at a top management level. Some of the larger companies make use of separate staff departments for organizational planning and development. For example, one large international corporation maintains a two-man planning department at the corporate level. This department is responsible for organizational planning throughout the corporation, including foreign operations.

Smaller companies may not have the need or the resources to support an organizational planning group and instead must rely on the talents of their executive officers. Whichever approach is used, the planning function is a vital ingredient in developing and maintaining a

---

[4] According to Gresham's law, "When two coins are equal in debt-paying value but unequal in intrinsic value, the one having the lesser intrinsic value tends to remain in circulation and the other to be hoarded or exported as bullion."—*Webster's Seventh New Collegiate Dictionary*.

dynamic organization. Through the planning effort, company objectives and goals are determined, and the success criteria of the business are defined. Decisions about organization can then be made in order to assure the compatibility of the organizational structure with the objectives of the company.

Resource Inputs

An attempted organizational change has slim chance of success if it fails to receive enough support from managment. In deciding to realign an organizational structure, management should back the effort with a commitment of the resources needed for success. The resources needed are principally personnel and time.

Personnel. Qualified personnel are the key to any smooth-running organization. The structure of the organization, after all, only serves to permit people to work together more easily and efficiently. No organizational structure, however cleverly devised, can be expected to be effective unless there are capable people to do the work. The selection, hiring, training, and development of people is one of management's most challenging responsibilities. Attention to these personnel functions is doubly important in the organization that is undergoing change. Management must assure that competent people are made available to the organizational unit, and that unsatisfactory people are not placed in the organization where they can adversely affect its performance.

In selecting people for new positions or functions which are created as a result of organizational change, it is well to consider the personalities of individuals. A new job or function, which may not be fully developed or defined, is likely to require an aggressive or innovative person. Even so, he should be at ease in what may be a somewhat unstructured situation; he should have the ability to establish clearly the requirements of the new job. On the other hand, a person who is selected to fill a well-defined existing job may not need as much initiative in order to perform well. His job will be one of maintaining an existing function.

Financial Resources. In addition to qualified personnel, the change in organization will require financial resources. The cost of training people may be considerable, depending on the extent and complexity of the change. There may also be costs of retraining people displaced by the change. These requirements should not be overlooked.

Information Inputs

New organizations often require additional information from other departments in order to function smoothly. This is more likely to be the case where the normal output of the new organizational unit consists of routine decisions or operating plans, such as would be the case with a production planning department. When the purpose of organizational realignment is to improve the quality or timeliness of planning or decision making, the need for data and management information may increase sharply. The additional requirement for information should be spelled out in the study which precedes the organizational change. Top management should give its support by assuring that the needed systems for information flow are established and that other departments cooperate in providing data required for the success of the new organizational unit.

Support of Middle Management

The management people who hold the key executive posts in a realigned organizational structure need to have the backing and support of their superiors and peers elsewhere in the organization. The new executive group must be delegated any new authorities it requires to do its job, and these authorities should be clearly recognized and accepted. All too often, logically structured organizations have faltered partially because they are new, and partially because top management has been hesitant to grant the managers involved the authority needed to execute their responsibilities.

SUMMARY

Organizations exist in changing environments, and for this reason they must be dynamic in order to remain effective. Change in organization is an adaptive process; management, by planning, directing, and supporting changes in organizational structure can help to assure that the organization will be able to meet its objectives. As a part of its responsibility, management should recognize the need for organizational change and should take steps to bring it about.

Organizational changes can be made to yield many varieties and forms of structure of internal functions and relationships. The correct organizational change is one that increases the capacity of the organization as a whole to improve its performance, and is within the financial and time constraints of the company. New organizational arrangements should be designed to assure that the critical output requirements of the unit are delivered efficiently.

The fundamental need in bringing about organizational change is a broad knowledge of the organization itself. Its functions, processes, and procedures should be carefully reviewed and analyzed to identify problems and develop tentative solutions. A final recommended organizational plan should be proposed after the tentative solution has been discussed with the management personnel who will be affected by the change. The new organization should be implemented with strong support from upper management. Of great importance is the selection and training of qualified people to fill the key management and supervisory slots in the rearranged organization.

There are pitfalls and by-products which typically go hand in hand with change in organizations. Managers should recognize them in order to take the steps necessary to overcome them. Generally, most of the problems of change can be dispelled by good communication of management's purposes and fair consideration of the people affected by the change.

The responsibility for organizational change rests with top management, which should administer the process of organizational planning and direct organizational change. Furthermore, top management should provide the support needed to assure the success of new organizational structures.

George Strauss
University of California

afterword

manufacturing organization for the future

THE CRYSTAL GAZER'S ART has always been somewhat disreputable, and for good reason.[1] Not only is it impossible to check on his accuracy until long after his prognostication, but—if he wants to be read—he is strongly motivated to predict the sensational.

I have neither the courage nor the imagination of a Jules Verne. All I can be sure of is that the future, though different from the past, will be built upon it. Thus my predictions will consist merely of extrapolations of existing trends.[2]

The last decade has been one of rapid change. From our perspective this change seems to be occurring at an accelerating rate; however, we may be too close to judge accurately. For example, let us compare the two forty-year periods, 1890–1930 and 1930–70. As far as manufacturing is concerned, a respectable (if not ironclad) case may be made that organizational change occurred more dramatically during the first period than during the second. Thus we need a sense of balance. By the year 2000 the structure of most companies will be radically different from any we know now. But many organizations may be practically unchanged.

My discussion will proceed as follows: First I will deal with five developments which are bound to affect the future: (1) changes in the people who work in industry, (2) the impact of society, (3) the computer, (4) the process of change itself, and (5) changes in manufacturing technology. And then I will discuss how these changes will affect professionalism, functionalism, and decentralization.

---

[1] I wish to thank Peter Feuille, Roger Lamm, and Joseph Robinson for helpful criticisms.

[2] Such an approach naturally gives my predictions a conservative cast, since statistically we know that many developments are likely to occur which are presently unpredictable. Thus my "future" is not too far in the distance. Also my predictions are hardly original, as will be seen.

THE IMPACT OF PEOPLE

Youth seems to be in revolt today; not only through campus riots, but through their dress, hairgrooming, and mores. They seem to flaunt their rejection of their elders' values. To what extent will business suffer from this revolt?

It seems quite clear that there will be some impact, but the extent can easily be exaggerated. In the first place, the most active participants probably never intended to enter business in any event. In many cases they are the children of professionals who will eventually follow in their fathers' footsteps. Confrontations have been confined mainly to small numbers of students in elite universities. Few MBAs or engineers have been active militants.

However, the spirit of revolt has affected more than the actual participants. MBAs and engineers are asking that the jobs they take somehow be "relevant." At least in class, they are questioning some of the basic values of the "system" which they are being prepared to serve. Rightly or wrongly, many believe that large companies will treat them impersonally and stifle their creativity. Small wonder that many of the brightest look for employment in small businesses and consulting firms in the hopes that there they will be able to demonstrate their creativity.

To further complicate this problem, our business schools seem to be turning out MBAs faster than our businesses have learned how to use them. Some companies "stockpile" MBAs (and frequently engineers as well) and either place them on "make-work" jobs designed primarily for indoctrination or observation—or assign them to routine quasi-clerical positions which, until ten to fifteen years ago, were handled by high school graduates. There seems to be a great deal of unrest (and even alienation) among MBAs during the first five years of their company experience.

It is less clear how the youth revolt has affected the high schools, junior colleges, and state colleges from which business draws most of its supervisors and blue-collar workers. Of course hippie-type music and clothing are widespread throughout young America, but the pervasive acceptance of these may indicate merely that young people, as always, are more conformist and more accepting of fads than their elders. Like their parents before them, they may well exchange one form of conformity for another once faced with the responsibility of supporting a family.

Thus, the impact of campus revolt may be considerably dampened by the time it hits industry. Nevertheless its impact should not be ignored. There will be greater demands for jobs which are meaningful and challenging and which permit involvement and participation.

Hopefully, this demand will not exceed the ability of industry to handle it, particularly since the future may see work becoming increasingly challenging, *on the average,* with fewer and fewer "make-work" jobs. Perhaps equally important, human relations has been with us for many years, and several generations of business school graduates have been exposed to its teachings. As a consequence, the techniques of participation, job enrichment, communications, and so forth have been well legitimated. Though research suggests that many managers still look upon such techniques primarily as means of manipulating subordinates, they are unlikely to make an issue in *principle* of human relations in *practice.*

Fortunately, technology, personal expectations, and managerial values are all changing in the same direction, and the net impact of this will be felt in the way subordinates are treated. The changes will go beyond the simple reforms of early human relations, such as downward communications, appeals and grievance procedures, management interest in employee's personal problems, good fringe benefits, and the like; all these merely make the work environment more congenial. The changes in the future may well involve redesigning jobs and methods of compensation and control. To some extent individual job assignments will be broader and/or work will be done by small, largely self-governing teams whose members are free to divide up work as they wish. (On the other hand, some may gravitate to highly specialized prestigious positions in which they operate as individual contributors.) Compensation systems may be redesigned to reward outstanding performance or successful risk taking rather than seniority or merely adequate performance. Certainly opportunities for challenge should be provided at every stage in the manager's career, but particularly for the new MBA.

A word of warning, however. The changes mentioned above are not likely to become universal. Though the percentage of employees who expect a high degree of challenge from the job may be on the increase, not everyone will want challenge; further, for years to come there will be boring, nonchallenging jobs which could be redesigned to become more exciting only at prohibitive expense.

THE IMPACT OF SOCIETY

It has become customary to think of a business as an economic entity operating in an economic environment. Yet society is increasingly placing social as well as economic constraints on the businessman—he is expected to operate not only efficiently (i.e., profitably) but also in a socially responsible fashion. And what is "socially responsible" is being determined not simply by his conscience or by the teachings of his church, but also by active pressure groups and by increasingly detailed governmental regulations. Public relations have grown to involve much more than building a company image, while governmental relations means more than landing good contracts and abiding by written laws. The businessman is expected to be knowledgeable about, or at least acquainted with, consumer rights, ecology, urban blight, pollution, race relations, and even international affairs.

Thus the job of even top management has become more and more that of responding to pressures, or operating within constraints, rather than simply initiating action. (No wonder, for some, government employment is viewed as the place "where the action is.")

THE IMPACT OF THE COMPUTER

Though we are now at least one decade into the computer era, it is still too early to make an accurate forecast of its eventual impact on organizational structure. Certainly the computer will make a profound difference, but it is reasonably clear that the change is occurring slower than some have forecast.

In 1958 the *Harvard Business Review* published an article by Leavitt and Whistler, later widely reprinted, which made three major predictions: [3]

1) Business firms will centralize (or recentralize) because of increased information available to top management.
2) "A radical reorganization of middle-management levels should occur, with certain classes of middle-management jobs moving downward in status and compensation (because they will require less autonomy and skill), while other classes move upward into the top-management group." The line between middle and top management will be drawn more sharply than ever before.
3) Top management will evolve into a football-shaped, collegial form—in which all top managers have roughly equal status—concerned primarily with innovating and long-run planning.

In 1960 a fourth prediction came from Herbert Simon, writing in a book entitled *Management and Corporations 1985:* Heuristic problem solving and other information technology advances will cause rapid organization change, culminating in the *technical* capacity by 1985 to manage corporations by machine. [4]

[3] Harold J. Leavitt and Thomas L. Whistler, "Management in the 1980's," *Harvard Business Review*, Vol. 36. No. 6 (November, 1958), 41–48.
[4] Herbert A. Simon, "The Corporation: Will It Be Managed by Machine?" in *Management and the Corporation, 1985*, Melvin Asher and George L. Bach, eds. (New York: McGraw-Hill, 1960).

Since 1970 approximately marks the half-way point between 1958 and 1985, it is appropriate to examine the extent to which these changes are occurring.

There have been a number of studies made with far from unanimous agreement among them, but a few trends seem fairly clear. In the first place, despite costly start-up problems the computer is now widely used for bookkeeping operations connected with billings, payrolls, inventory controls, and the like. A number of clerical jobs have been eliminated and the character of many more has changed substantially. Particularly in banks and utilities job locations have moved from branch offices to central computer installations. Nevertheless, during the 1960s employment in clerical operations in the country increased faster than employment generally and faster than any other major occupational group except the professions. However, these changes had little to do with manufacturing.

How about centralization? The decentralization of the postwar period was largely negatively caused: operations in many companies had gotten too large and complex for efficient central control. Managers were overburdened with decisions; further, information was slow in moving through the chain of command, and it was often distorted in the process. In theory computers can help overcome these problems. The computer increases the amount of information available to top management, and aids in the decision process itself. Thus the computer can be used by top management to make decisions and to check up on subordinate compliance with these decisions. It can also be used to evaluate decisions made by subordinates at lower levels. On the other hand, the same information which can be transmitted to the top hierarchy can also be transmitted to the bottom. For this reason, the computer permits decentralization as well as centralization.

What has happened in practice? While there are several cases of the computer being used to permit more decentralized decision making, the balance of the research indicates a definite movement toward centralization. Some of the changes are reflected in revised organizational charts; others have taken the form of subtle, de facto changes in relative influence. The actual impact has varied greatly from company to company.

It may well be that in the short run the question is decided not so much by the technical capabilities of the information system as by the prevailing philosophy of management. Some top managers have taken advantage of the computer to manage their organization more closely; others seem to prefer to allow their subordinates greater discretion. My own opinion is that in the long run the extent of centralization in a given company will be determined not by management philosophy but by technical constraints, such as the necessity for close coordination and uniform procedures.

How about middle management: How far has it moved down the prophesied road to extinction? Middle management in computerized firms seems to have been vitally affected by the new technology, but not exactly as predicted. While some middle management jobs have been eliminated or drastically downgraded, others have been made more demanding. On balance, the computer has changed the nature of the middle manager's job more than the number of such jobs. Middle managers have been freed from routine tasks and now have more time for tasks which are less well structured. (On the other hand, the computer permits top management to keep closer tabs on them, and to establish much tighter deadlines.[5] All this tends to increase the tension under which middle management operates.)

There is little evidence to date of collegial top management or of "running" companies by computer. Computers perform routine computations and make some simple decisions, but most top managements make decisions the way they did ten to fifteen years ago (but with more up-to-date information). Judgment and intuition are still prime requirements for top management. This picture may change if there is a major breakthrough in heuristic programing and as managers trained to make use of such technology reach the top ranks. "Feasibility" and "cost-benefit" studies of the type impossible twenty years ago are now being utilized by the top management of some companies, and the number of these may well grow.

On the other hand, some of the most difficult problems faced by management (as well as society generally) in the last decade have turned out to be social rather than technical. Such problems as race relations and pollution are not easily handled by computer analysis. These may become increasingly aggravating and take up much of the spare time which the computer will presumably create. Furthermore, computers are most valuable for decision making in relatively stable environments; in the highly unstable situation which characterizes some industries computer programs may be quickly out of date.

We are still very much in the transitional stage. Again and again companies have learned that the introduction of computers was more painful than expected, but that eventually the bugs were worked out. As yet few organizations know how to make optimum use of these devices. There has been fear of the computer and resistance to change at all levels. Foremen and workers on the shop floor have fought the additional paperwork which computer scheduling requires, and at

---

[5] For example, the computer may make it possible to operate with lower inventories. But low inventories require that each manager adhere rigidly to his production schedule.

times they have sabotaged the instructions the computer gives them. Middle managers have been no more accepting, particularly those managers whose functions are downgraded or who are forced to conform their activities to the computer's rigid routine. At times open warfare occurs between computer staffs and line management. But all these problems should pass in time. At the moment, the chief function of the computer is to relieve management of its simple, routine problems.

THE IMPACT OF CHANGE ITSELF

It is almost trite to suggest that the future will see rapid changes in technologies and markets. Product life cycles will grow shorter, much equipment will become obsolete long before it is fully depreciated, technical knowledge and skills will constantly have to be relearned; both machinery and people may become obsolescent.

Perhaps more important than change itself is the fact that in many industries change is now institutionalized and even routinized. Though there are still surprise breakthroughs, technological advances are now deliberately created, planned, and even scheduled. How could it be otherwise when annual investments in R&D are coming to be almost as great as investments in plant and equipment?

However, the speed of change and the degree of its predictability will differ substantially among industries. For convenience, therefore, we may oversimplify the real world and divide industries into three categories: (1) those in which change is slow, (2) those in which change is rapid but predictable and therefore subject to control and scheduling, and finally (3) those in which change is fast but relatively unpredictable in nature.

The first category may include a large number of industries, but we will ignore it for the moment. The second category is more interesting, for here change will be routinized. Indeed, the automobile and ladies' garment industries have routinized change for more than fifty years (true, changes in these industries occur within narrow limits). Much more dramatic are the industries spawned by NASA and the defense programs. Here a technology has been created which makes it possible to create innovations on demand and largely on schedule. As long as the nature of change is predictable, fairly routine procedures can be adopted to handle it.[6] Often change is introduced in a predetermined sequence.

But an organization which produced changes on a routine, assem-

---

[6] To given an example, style changes in the ladies' garment industry are routine and roughly predictable; the introduction of synthetic yarns was not.

bly-line basis is not the same as an organization which never changes. Just as a production assembly line requires an effective scheduling function, so assembly-line change requires that there be close coordination between manufacturing, research and development, and sales.[7] Under these conditions good "lateral relations"—the ability to get along with other managers at one's own level—may be even more important than upwards and downwards relations. Just as the foreman of today has almost hourly interchange with maintenance and production scheduling, so the manufacturing manager in the fast-change organization of tomorrow will be in practically constant contact with his counterparts in R&D, sales, etc. In fact, a realistic organization chart might reflect this new state of affairs. It would deemphasize formal boss-subordinate relations and stress the lateral communications patterns required by the job.

As a consequence, the manufacturing manager's autonomy may decline. Indeed, he may become just another member of the team, and perhaps not the most important one.[8] Manufacturing and product engineering will have to work more closely; perhaps the difference between the two will decline.

The future may see the development of an even more radically different pattern of relations in the third category of companies: those with high change but low predictability. According to a number of studies, rigid structuring tends to break down whenever there is high uncertainty. Instead of change being handled through standard operating procedures, temporary ad hoc task groups are formed to deal with each major problem as it comes up. Such ad hoc groups normally cut across departmental lines and may even violate normal rules of rank. For example, two managers may both serve on two different task force committees. On Committee A, Man A may be chairman over Man B; the reverse may be true in Committee B. Under such circumstances where a manager's success depends largely on his ability to elicit the voluntary cooperation of his co-managers, formal authority or adherence to official company rules may not be of much help. Organizations of this sort have been called "open" or "spontaneous."

With both types of change, predictable and unpredictable, we see the development of "integrative functions," coordinating bodies whose job it is to make sure that the change process occurs as smoothly as possible. Such functions already exist in a number of companies, under

---

[7] Such coordination may be aided by computers, especially where there is "computer aided design," often referred to by the acronym CAM.

[8] Perhaps manufacturing's relative influence will decline, as opposed to R&D and sales, just as the percentage of the total company work force employed in manufacturing is also declining. Already a recent study of a presumably representative sample of companies suggests that within these companies marketing was believed to have more influence than manufacturing.

a variety of titles. With routine change integrators merely make sure that prescribed schedules are followed. When change is nonroutine, integration becomes far more difficult and the integrator is more of a psychiatrist than policeman. (Indeed the more sophisticated forms of organizational development, such as sensitivity training, seem to be more prevalent where change is unpredictable). Bennis and Slater offer the following prediction:

> Adoptive, problem-solving, temporary systems of diverse specialists, linked together by coordinating and task-evaluating executive specialists—this is the organizational form that will gradually replace bureaucracy as we know it.[9]

In my opinion this prediction will not apply to all industries, but for a select group of industries in which there is a high degree of unpredictable change it seems quite appropriate. In addition, it will be further developed in research and development than in manufacturing itself.

THE IMPACT OF NEW MANUFACTURING TECHNIQUES

One of the main lessons of recent research in the behavioral sciences is that what is the proper organizational structure for a given firm depends largely upon its technology. "Technology" is difficult to measure or categorize, but one of the most useful approaches in this area has been developed by Joan Woodward. Woodward thinks of technology as a continuum which can be divided into three main sectors:

1) *Unit or small batch production.* Typical operations may include a printing job shop, a factory making large, special-purpose equipment, or even one working on a space capsule. Here workers are rather highly skilled and many are real craftsmen. Many of the jobs are custom-made. The work is generally varied, organization tends to be relatively simple (though perhaps not in the space industry), and there is a strong planning or developmental group.
2) *Mass production or large batch.* The assembly line is typical of this sort of technology. Here the production worker's job tends to be simple and repetitive and scheduling is all important. Compared with other types of technology, there are a large number of workers reporting to each foremen.

---

[9] Warren G. Bennis and Philip G. Slater, *The Temporary Society* (New York: Harper, 1968), 74.

3) *Automated or process production.* Included here are highly automated operations in the chemical and public utility industries. Here most of the routine operations have been eliminated. The remaining workers are either skilled craftsmen or men whose primary function is to be available for an emergency (though they also are responsible for monitoring dials). With most of the blue-collar work force eliminated, the management-worker ratio is high.[10]

One hundred and fifty years ago, industry was characterized by unit or craft production. The period 1890–1930 was made notable by the development of mass production. Since 1930 we have been moving toward an age of automation. Undoubtedly this trend will accelerate and in manufacturing more and more routine jobs will be eliminated. (The picture in the service industries is less clear.) On the other hand, the unit-production sector may hold its own or even expand as more and more special purpose equipment is demanded.

What will be the impact of these changes on organizational structure? Mass production made possible a substantial improvement in our standard of living, but at the cost of making men into machine-tending robots. Automation seems to have reversed this process: there are fewer routine jobs, and those jobs which remain are more challenging. Roughly the same impact will occur if there is a new demand for unit-production. In either case the remaining blue-collar workers will be at least quasi-craftsmen.[11]

What is the likely effect of a relatively greater emphasis on unit production and automated processes? The research to date suggests the following:

1) Under both forms of technology the social gap between worker and supervisor tends to be less than it is under mass production. This is especially the case since many craftsmen know more about their jobs than do their supervisors.
2) Both forms of technology are characterized by a relatively small number of workers reporting to each first-line supervisor. Even if the overall number of blue-collar workers decreases, the number of first-line supervisors should increase.

Together these two factors mean that manufacturing management will more and more involve managing managers rather than managing

---

[10] Joan Woodward, *Industrial Organization: Theory and Practice* (London: Oxford University Press, 1965).

[11] This is as good a place as any to mention that some of the forecasts of the late 1950s have turned out to be, at least, premature. Automation may have slowed down the rate of growth of blue-collar jobs, but the blue-collar worker in manufacturing is far from obsolete.

workers while the differences between these two categories will decline.[12]

The factors discussed above will have impacts on two areas, functionalism-professionalism and decentralization.

FUNCTIONALISM-PROFESSIONALISM

It is reasonably clear that functional distinctions, largely based on professionalism, will grow in importance in the years to come. Not too long ago the majority of employees in most companies were in the line; they were engaged in the firm's primary functions, such as production in a factory or sales in a store. But the picture is changing rapidly; staff or functional groups—accounting, personnel, quality control, research and development—are growing in size and status.

In most large firms today, staff tends to deal not with line but with other staff departments. For example, a routine activity might start with the sales department securing a large order. Sales liaison passes it on to production scheduling, which in turn asks engineering for blueprints and specifications. Engineering then writes specifications on the basis of which production scheduling writes requisitions; with these requisitions in hand, purchasing places orders for components. A dozen different functional departments may be concerned before the "work flow" involves a single production worker or a single member of what is normally known as line management.

Normally interdepartmental "work flow" relations run smoothly, but even in the best run organizations there is considerable pulling and hauling among departments. Naturally each function seeks to advance its own point of view; design engineering, for example, looks for technical perfection, industrial engineering for manufacturing ease, and marketing for sales appeal. In addition to differences in point of view, there are status conflicts; each function feels that its importance is underrecognized by other functions and by top management.

To complicate matters further, there is evidence that many functional fields are turning to professionalism as a means of bolstering their own self-esteem, of raising their status, and of strengthening their position relative to other departments. Engineering and accounting have already achieved professional status; purchasing and, to a lesser extent, personnel, among others are working in that direction. Hopefully, once an activity is accepted as a profession other departments will be less likely to dispute its expert judgment. Further, as a profession it will be able to keep nonprofessionals from poaching on its preserves

---

[12] On the other hand, education, especially college degrees, may be creating an increasingly impenetrable barrier between nonsupervisory workers and management.

and will be able to resist orders from higher management which would require it to engage in what it considers to be unprofessional acts.

Consequently, functional loyalties develop which are separate from the overall organization. Each function has its own discipline of analysis (that of the accountant is very different from that of the engineer); though bargaining and human relations skills may be crucial in interdepartmental disputes, within the function analytical skills are most valuable.

Thus, the picture we get when we look at functional and professional departments is not that of a highly coordinated organization, tightly controlled by top management. We see rather a mass of competing functional groups, each seeking to influence company decisions in terms of its own interests, or at least, in terms of its perception of company interests.

All these problems are likely to be accentuated in the future. More and more functional fields will arise, each jealous of its territorial prerogatives. Consider, for example, the new field of "urban affairs" which has arisen in a number of companies as a result of the civil rights crisis. Furthermore, the new generation of "nonconformist" college graduates already shows less willingness than their elders to be merely loyal members of the team. Professionalism is particularly likely to flourish in the "spontaneous, temporary" systems which are characteristic of industries experiencing rapid and unpredictable change. In addition, functional staff departments often gain more power during periods of rapid change. In some cases, they are experts in introducing the change; in others their special services may be called upon to protect the organization from outside pressures. Regardless, staff men as the repositories of special knowledge are more likely to be called upon whenever conventional wisdom no longer suffices.

DECENTRALIZATION

During the 1940s and 1950s management writers tended to look upon decentralization as a panacea for every management ill. Enthusiasm among both academicians and practitioners has waned somewhat as both realize that the problem is more complicated than they once thought. What about the future? Will companies tend to become more centralized or more decentralized?

These are difficult questions, in part because there are no commonly agreed upon definitions of either term. At one time decentralization meant either some sort of geographical distribution of activities or some sort of formal delegation of authority. While it is now largely agreed that such definitions are superficial, it is difficult to progress beyond them. Decentralization may mean pushing decision making down to a lower level, but how does one measure what is a "decision"? Suppose management develops a thick book of standard operating procedures for subordinates to use. Is the subordinate who uses this book making decisions? Suppose the rules are "understood" rather than written? Clearly decentralization relates to the constraints within which the subordinate operates.

We have already examined the impact of computers. They make it easier for higher management both to make decisions and to check on the effectiveness of the decisions made by lower management. Thus, computers would seem to increase the opportunities for centralization.

On the other hand, as technology advances and changes occur with increasing rapidity, more and more decisions must be made. Even with the aid of the computer, top management will run the risk of being overloaded. Critical decisions, which under conditions of stability might be made by top management, will, under the press of circumstances, be made lower down, often on the basis of agreement among functional groups. To the extent this occurs the company will no longer be a highly integrated group closely controlled by top management; rather it will consist of a number of semi-autonomous functional departments which keep each other in line through a series of checks and balances. [13]

Subordinate expectations should also increase the pressure for decentralization. Subordinates will expect to be consulted more. Further, as we have stated earlier, they often know more about technical matters than do their supervisors.

Another factor leading to decentralization is the growth of conglomerates operating in widely differing industries. Though policies vary, the typical conglomerate head office staff is quite small. Top management limits its function to supervision by results and the maintenance of a management consulting group. Certainly the arguments for close central control are less persuasive here than in companies with tightly integrated technologies.

For some people decentralization means organization by product as opposed to organization by function (see Chapter 3). Among the advantages of product organization are: (1) easier communications about the product, (2) easier accountability and control (e.g., profit centers), (3) a lower point of decision making for some forms of decisions (not all), and (4) greater product identification on the part of personnel. Against these must be offset the advantages of functional organization, especially where: (1) economies of scale are present, (2) homogeneity of

---

[13] Top management's job then becomes that of designing a social system which, on the one hand, facilitates the harmonious disposition of such differences as are best resolved at lower levels, and, on the other hand, brings to higher management's attention those decisions which are appropriately its own.

values and outlook is needed, and (3) uniform policies are desirable regarding subjects such as quality control or labor relations.

Which way the organization of the future will go is far from clear. Product organization may simplify lateral relationships. It may also serve to counterbalance functionalism and professionalism. On the other hand, it may prevent the realization of important economies of scale in the use of both equipment and people. Further, it is predicated on the assumption that the present company product-mix will be fairly stable. Finally, the computer may shift the balance toward functional organization.

"Matrix" or "grid" organization represents an attempt to gain the advantages of both functional and product organization. Here each major subordinate has at least two bosses, one functional and one product, thus violating the principle of unity of command.[14] Matrix organization will be used most often in situations where there is rapid and uncertain change, coupled with a high degree of coordination. Under these circumstances "spontaneous cooperation" at the bottom level will be all important, since it will be difficult to impose interface relations from above. At best it will lead to an exceptionally high degree of creative teamwork which takes advantage of the self-motivation arising out of the challenge inherent in the job; at worst it will lead to anarchy and confusion. My opinion is that matrix organizations will prove useful only under fairly limited conditions.

SUMMARY

One thing seems reasonably clear: organizations in the future will be more varied in their structure than organizations have been in the past.

At one extreme we will have organizations which exist in stable, unchallenging environments with a relatively fixed, unchanging, easily understood technology. There will still be many such organizations in the years to come,[15] and there is little reason to expect that their structure will change in any significant degree, except to the extent that the computer will further routinize their operations.

At the other extreme will be the highly innovative, R&D-type industries which operate in situations with rapid and uncertain change.

---

[14] Actually, it may only formalize existing relationships. In most complex organizations, many individuals have more than one "boss." In a product organization, one boss is the line supervisor, the other is the staff man in charge of the individual's own specialty. In the functional organization, one boss is the functional chief, the other is the coordinator responsible for a given product (often called a "product manager").

[15] In fact, some of the most dynamic industries of today may become the stable industries of tomorrow. Railroad, automotive manufacture, and most recently chemicals, have all gone through this process.

Here we may have what has been called a "post-bureaucratic" organization, characterized by matrix structure and a large number of temporary, ad hoc task force teams. Here professional and group loyalties will be strong. The computer may be used extensively by certain groups for computational purposes, but it will not be useful or especially helpful in coordinating activities (unless there is a substantial breakthrough in heuristic programing).

Between these two extremes will come organizations which look superficially like many today, though there may be greater emphasis on lateral relations, and the distinctions between such present departments as manufacturing and engineering may become less sharp. Except where there are highly stable technologies and environments, the manufacturing managers of the future will have to develop a somewhat different mix of skills than at present. For example:

1) They will have to improve their handling of lateral relations.
2) They will have to deal with subordinates who may know more than their bosses do about their own work and who have learned to expect to participate.
3) In some circumstances, they will have to deal with highly unstructured relationships, such as temporary or matrix groups.
4) They will have to deal with situations in which relations with the government, customers, and the general public may be more sensitive and more important than mere economic or technical efficiency.
5) They will have to be prepared to relearn their jobs every few years as the world changes rapidly.

bibliography

Albers, Henry H. *Principles of Management: A Modern Approach.* 3rd ed. New York: John Wiley & Sons, 1969.

Allen, Louis A., "The Line-Staff Relationship," in Max D. Richards and William A. Nielander, eds., *Readings in Management,* 2nd ed. New Rochelle, N.Y.: South-Western, 1963.

Ammer, Dean S., "Materials Management as a Profit Center," *Harvard Business Review* (January–February, 1969), 73–75.

Argyris, Chris. *Personality and Organization.* New York: Harper, 1957.

Avots, Ivars, "Why Does Project Management Fail?" *California Management Review* (Fall, 1969).

Barnard, Chester I. *Functions of the Executive.* Cambridge: Harvard University Press, 1938.

_____. *Organization and Management.* Cambridge: Harvard University Press, 1952.

Beach, Dale S. *Personnel: The Management of People at Work.* New York: Macmillan, 1965.

Bennis, Warren G., "Organization Change—Operating in a Temporary Society," *Innovation* (May, 1969).

_____, and Phillip G. Slater. *The Temporary Society.* New York: Harper, 1968.

Bright, James R., ed., *Technological Forecasting for Industry and Government: Methods and Applications.* Englewood Cliffs, N.J.: Prentice-Hall, 1968.

Brillouin, Leon. *Science and Information Theory.* New York: Academic Press, 1956.

Cleland, David I., "Why Project Management?" *Business Horizons* (Winter, 1964), 83.

Dale, Ernest. *Planning and Developing the Company Organization Structure,* Research Report *Number 20.* New York: American Management Association, 1952.

Dalton, Melville. *Men Who Manage.* New York: John Wiley & Sons, 1959.

Daniel, D. Ronald, "Reorganizing for Results," *Harvard Business Review* (November–December, 1966).

Davis, Keith, "Group Behavior and the Organization Chart," *Advanced Management—Office Executive* (June, 1962).

Drucker, Peter F. *The Age of Discontinuity.* New York: Harper, 1969.

_____, "Management's New Role," *Harvard Business Review* (November–December, 1969).

_____. *The Practice of Management.* New York: Harper, 1954.

Eddington, Arthur. *Nature of the Physical World.* Ann Arbor: The University of Michigan Press, 1958.

Ewing, David W. *The Human Side of Planning.* New York: Macmillan, 1969.

Fayol, Henri. *General and Industrial Management.* Translated from the French by Constance Storrs. London: Pittman, 1949.

Fenn, Dan H., ed., *Management's Mission in a New Society.* New York: McGraw-Hill, 1956.

Ford, Robert N. *Motivation Through the Work Itself.* New York: American Management Association, 1969.

Foulkes, Fred K. *Creating More Meaningful Work.* New York: American Management Association, 1969.

241

Gaddis, Paul O., "The Project Manager," *Harvard Business Review* (May–June, 1959).

Gellerman, Saul W. *Management by Motivation*. New York: American Management Association, 1968.

———. *Motivation and Productivity*. New York: American Management Association, 1963.

Graicunas, V.A., "Relationship in Organization," *Papers on the Science of Administration*, edited by Luther Gulick and Leland Urwick. New York: Institute of Public Administration, Columbia University, 1937.

Greiner, Larry E., "Patterns of Organization Change," *Harvard Business Review* (May–June, 1967).

Gulick, Luther, and Leland Urwick, eds., *Papers on the Science of Administration*. New York: Institute of Public Administration, Columbia University, 1937.

Haire, Mason. *Psychology in Management*, 2nd ed. New York: McGraw-Hill, 1964.

Heckman, I. L., and S. G. Huneryager. *Human Relations in Management*. New Rochelle, N.Y.: South-Western, 1967.

Herman, Stanley M. *The People Specialists*. New York: Alfred A. Knopf, 1969.

Herzberg, Frederick. *Work and the Nature of Man*. Cleveland: World, 1966.

Howe, Raymond E., ed., *Introduction to Numerical Control in Manufacturing*. Dearborn, Mich.: Society of Manufacturing Engineers, 1969.

Jasinski, Frank J., "Adapting Organization to New Technology," *Harvard Business Review* (January–February, 1959).

Johnson, Richard A., Fremont E. Kast, and James E. Rosenzweig. *The Theory and Management of Systems*. New York: McGraw-Hill, 1967.

Katz, Daniel, and Robert L. Kahn. *The Social Psychology of Organizations*. New York: John Wiley & Sons, 1966.

Katz, E., *et al. Studies of Innovation and of Communication to the Public* (Studies in the Utilization of Behavior Science). Stanford, Calif.: Stanford University, 1962.

Koontz, Harold, and Cyril O'Donnell. *Principles of Management*, 4th ed. New York: McGraw-Hill, 1968.

Lawrence, Paul R., "How to Deal with Resistance to Change," *Harvard Business Review* (January–February, 1969).

Leavitt, Harold J. *Managerial Psychology*. Chicago: The University of Chicago Press, 1964.

———, and Thomas L. Whistler, "Management in the 1980's," *Harvard Business Review*, Vol. 36, No. 6 (November, 1958), 41–48.

Likert, Rensis. *The Human Organization: Its Management and Value*. New York: McGraw-Hill, 1967.

———. *New Patterns of Management*. New York: McGraw-Hill, 1961.

———, "A Motivational Approach to a Modified Theory of Organization and Management," in Mason Haire, ed., *Modern Organization Theory*. New York: John Wiley & Sons, 1959.

McGregor, Douglas. *The Human Side of Enterprise*. New York: McGraw-Hill, 1960.

McLarney, William J. *Management Training*, 4th ed. Homewood, Ill.: Richard D. Irwin, 1964.

McMurray, Robert. *Tested Techniques of Personnel Selection*. Chicago: Dartnell, 1966.

Maier, Norman R. R. *Appraisal Interview*. New York: John Wiley & Sons, 1958.

March, James G., and Herbert A. Simon. *Organizations*. New York: John Wiley & Sons, 1958.

Marting, Elizabeth. *AMA Book of Employment Forms*. New York: American Management Association, 1967.

Maynard, H. B., ed., *Handbook of Business Administration*. New York: McGraw-Hill, 1967.

Megginson, Leon C. *Personnel: A Behavioral Approach to Administration*. Homewood, Ill.: Richard D. Irwin, 1967.

Parsons, T. *Structure and Process in Modern Societies*. New York: Free Press, 1960.

Peterson, Russell W., "New Venture Management in a Large Company," *Harvard Business Review* (May–June, 1967).

Pfiffner, John M., and Frank P. Sherwood. *Administrative Organization*. Englewood Cliffs, N.J.: Prentice-Hall, 1960.

Pierce, J. R. *Symbols, Signals and Noise: The Nature and Process of Communication* (Harper Modern Science Series). New York: Harper, 1961.

Pond, John H. *Your Future in Personnel Work*. New York: Richards Rosen Press, 1962.

Reeves, Elton T. *Management Development for the Line Manager*. New York: American Management Association, 1967.

Roethlisberger, F. J., and W. J. Dickson. *Management and the Worker*. Cambridge: Harvard University Press, 1939.

Rosenstein, A. B., *et al. Engineering Communications.* Englewood Cliffs, N.J.: Prentice-Hall, 1964.
Scott, Brian W. *Long-Range Planning in American Industry.* New York: American Management Association, 1965.
Shannon, Claude E., and Warren Weaver. *The Mathematical Theory of Communication.* Urbana: University of Illinois Press, 1949.
Simon, Herbert A. *Administrative Behavior,* 2nd ed. New York: Macmillan, 1957.
———, "The Corporation: Will It Be Managed by Machine?" in *Management and the Corporation, 1985,* edited by Melvin Asher and George L. Bach. New York: McGraw-Hill, 1960.
Singer, T. E. R., ed., *Information and Communication Practice in Industry.* New York: Reinhold, 1958.
Smith, Alfred G., ed., *Communication and Culture: Readings in the Codes of Human Interaction.* New York: Holt, Rinehart and Winston, 1967.
Stevens, S. S., "Introduction: A Definition of Communication," *Journal of the Acoustical Society of America,* Vol. 22, No. 6 (1950).
Stieglitz, Harold, and C. David Wilkerson, compilers, *Corporate Organization Structures,* Studies in Personnel Policy *No. 210.* National Industrial Conference Board, 1968.
Taylor, Frederick W. *The Principles of Scientific Management.* New York: Harper, 1947.
Terry, George R. *Principles of Management,* 5th ed. Homewood, Ill.: Richard D. Irwin, 1968.
Thompson, James D. *Organizations in Action: Social Science Bases of Administrative Theory.* New York: McGraw-Hill, 1967.
Urwick, Lyndall F. *The Patterns of Management.* Minneapolis: University of Minnesota Press, 1956.
Vernon, Ivan R., ed., *Introduction to Manufacturing Management.* Dearborn, Mich.: Society of Manufacturing Engineers, 1969.
Whyte, William F. *Money and Motivation.* New York: Harper, 1955.
Wickesberg, A. K., and A. C. Cronin, "Management by Task Force," *Harvard Business Review* (November–December, 1962).
Wilson, James Q., "Innovation in Organization: Notes Toward a Theory," in James D. Thompson, ed., *Approaches to Organizational Design.* Pittsburgh, Pa.: University of Pittsburgh Press, 1966.
Woodward, Joan. *Industrial Organization: Theory and Practice.* London: Oxford University, 1965.

index